New Directions in Telecommunications Policy

Volume Two

Information Policy and Economic Policy

Edited by Paula R. Newberg

|||||||||||||||||||||||||||||||||||||||||||||||||||||||||||||||||||||||||||||||||||||||||||||||||||||||||||||||||||||||||||||||||||||||||||||||||||||||||||||||||||||

New Directions in
Telecommunications Policy

Duke Press Policy Studies

Duke University Press   Durham and London 1989

Printed in the United States of America on acid-free paper ∞
Library of Congress Cataloging-in-Publication Data
New directions in telecommunications policy.
Includes bibliographies and index.
Contents: v. 1. Regulatory policies, telephony and
mass media—v. 2. Information policy and economic policy.
1. Telecommunication policy—United States.
I. Newberg, Paula R., 1952–
HE7781.N49   1989   384'.068   89-1446
ISBN 0-8223-0916-5 (v. 1)
ISBN 0-8223-0941-6 (pbk. : v. 1)
ISBN 0-8223-0923-8 (v. 2)
ISBN 0-8223-0948-3 (pbk. : v. 2)

Contents

||||||||||||||||||||||||||||||||||||||||||||||||||||||||||||||||||||||||||||||||||||||||||||||||||||||||||||||||||||||||||||||||||||||||||||||||||||||||||||||||||||||||||||

Introduction

Paula R. Newberg

Technological innovation has always extended the boundaries of communications and the worlds among which we communicate. This is particularly true for telecommunications technologies. Calligraphy, printing presses, telegraphs, radios, and telephones have not only brought to individuals the capacity to transform their societies, but have allowed societies to further the reach of these technologies through exploration and discovery. More recently, rapid change and potential convergence in such technologies as fiber optics, computers, and satellites underscore not only the pace, depth, and reach of telecommunications technologies at the end of this century, but are also helping to define the capacities and possibilities for the next. As a form of invention, discourse, connection, and interaction, as microcosm and macrocosm, telecommunications has become a practical and metaphorical lens through which to view politics, economics, and society.

The essays included in this volume take as their focus transformations in telecommunications research and development, their effects on politics and the world economy, and their implications for policy. They inevitably raise issues similar to those in the first volume in this series on telecommunications policy, seeking to extend discussions of regulation and technological convergence to the more general arenas of political economy and political theory. While the policies considered here are primarily those of the United States, the essays assume implicitly that telecommunications forges new relationships among power, money, and people.

With the long march of technology has come the active involvement of private and public capital, values and policies. World history has taught us, however, that political goods and economic goods are not always coterminous or concurrent. The vocabulary of economic efficiency is not necessarily comprehensible in the language of social equity or political well-being; what is understandable to individuals is not necessarily meaningful to communities, and what is intelligible to economists often makes little sense to politicians. In the age of early industrialization, for example, the interests of newly urbanized labor did not comfortably fit those of feudal landlords or ward politicians; in the era of imperialism the concerns of investors could conflict not only with those of conquering armies and invaded cultures, but often with the public exchequer as well.

Today, we see these dichotomies written into public policy debates in telecommunications. Subsidizing rural America's telephones, once an imperative for an agricultural society, may now be one of its vestiges; economic inefficiencies, underscored by the changing demography of modern America, still conflict with political agendas built around complex perceptions of American identity. Large research and development budgets for national projects like space exploration and nuclear breeder reactors have, in visceral but inchoate ways, come to define this country's emotional future as much as pork barrel politics and are thus hard to evaluate objectively. Technologies do not develop in political vacuums. In each case major public policy decisions about regulation and expenditure, about public initiative and public gain, and about social aspiration and economic welfare are calculated on the basis of circumstances, facts, and interests. As always, they are mediated through theories, values, and ideas.

Today, comparable problems surround telecommunications policy as swiftly developing information technologies meet traditional communications media. Not only does broadcasting increasingly resemble telephony, but computing has brought the worlds of information and telecommunications remarkably close. The substance of communications—information—and the process by which it is transmitted—telecommunications—are part of the same conceptual and policy problem.

Moreover, public policy defines these political and economic interests and determines criteria and methods to reconcile inevitable conflicts. Civil and military regimes, or democratic and autocratic governments, for example, will appraise individual privacy protections differently. In a high technology age such assurances can affect the development of overseas finance through transborder data flows, private profits through software copyright, or individual rights through personal identity cards. The public policy metaphor of property rights, long a staple in American civil law, has entered the lexicon of telecommunications policy in ways which affect directly relationships among citizens and reigning concepts of the public interest. It also helps to organize government's sense of its ownership of public information. The policy questions such technology raises are often not new; they now exist in a new environment, however, which can determine their future compass.

International dimensions of these problems increase in proportion to their complexity and their intrinsic value to the societies they affect. What is private in one place is not necessarily private in another; protecting electronic data is an intricate business, and transborder protections are more elaborate still. Furthermore, using data can itself be socially and politically interventionary, both at home and abroad. An international financial services industry, made feasible by sophisticated telecommunications, can manipulate or disrupt national economies with startling speed and intensity. Owning information is a form of power, and governments traffic in such currency; new kinds of telecommunications can ease the exercise of information and at the same time bestow upon it an unfortunate opacity.

Constructing public policy in the new information age is difficult: the currents of politics and technology seem at once tightly woven and particularly changeable now, and establishing goals to fit the public interest is at best unclear. Devising public policy for the United States—an apparent international power with economic vulnerabilities—is therefore an insecure, though vitally important enterprise. The successes and failures of policy may partially determine the economic and political futures of this country and its partners.

It is not at all clear that the United States has pursued its own interests well in this new age. Daily reports about the international computer industry offer scant praise for American private initiative or public support for innovation—calling into question not only current competition but future competitiveness. The progress of international finance, dependent in part on harnessing new technologies, seems to have eluded American capital markets and industries—calling into question the nature of American industrial power and policies. Battling burgeoning deficits, American foreign economic policy has concentrated on short-term policies toward familiar friends and foes in Western Europe and Japan—calling into question long-term, mutual interests with the Third World.

At stake in public policy deliberations are not only specific policies, but the nature of American participation in international systems of commerce and political cooperation as well. Exporting public policy is a tricky business. The lessons of telephonic development, clear to economists schooled in one pragmatism, are not obvious to those educated to other values. The telecommunications infrastructure, especially interconnection, is crucial to international economic futures; policies undertaken now will help to determine how such connection comes about and the form it will take. The United States will have to resolve the relative merits of multilateral and bilateral policies, the value of promoting an integrated world economy or striking out independently, and the primacy of telecommunications in such choices. Judgments about the form of participation multilaterally will inevitably be transposed into decisions about telecommunications domestically; the reverse transposition is equally true.

If there is an underlying sense of urgency to these questions, it is because some decisions, if not irrevocable, will pave the way for developments which are harder to erase. The way the telecommunications infrastructure is laid in less developed countries, for example, will fix many of their economic and political capabilities for many decades, as it did in industrialized countries. Opportunities which exist now are unlikely to reappear in the same form later. How the United States chooses to handle uncertainty—in technological innovation, economic flexibility, and political control—will reveal a great deal about the nature of government in domestic communications and about America's future international role and powers.

INFORMATION POLICY

Privacy
Citizen Access
Copyright
Civil Remote Sensing

Data Wars: Privacy Protection in Federal Policy

||||||||||||||||||||||||||||||||||||||||||||||||||||||||||||||||||||||||||||||||||||||||||||||||||||||||||||||||||||||||||||||||||||||||||||||

James B. Rule

In 1966 federal officials and private users of government information had an historic inspiration. The federal government, they noted, possessed rich repositories of information on private citizens, ranging from census data to Internal Revenue Service (IRS) files to Social Security data. The trouble was that these data were dispersed; even where regulations permitted it, the costs of locating and assembling them were prohibitive. What was needed was a National Data Center to collate and centralize such information and make them quickly and economically available.

The Data Center, as then conceived, was to provide aggregate information to researchers, rather than data on identifiable individuals to administrative or enforcement agencies. Still, the idea tapped a sensitive nerve among elected officials concerned about their constituents' privacy. As Congressman Frank Horton stated, "Good computermen know that one of the most practical of our present safeguards of privacy is the fragmented nature of present information. It is scattered in little bits and pieces across the geography and years of our life. Retrieval is impractical and often impossible. A central data bank removes completely this safeguard."[1] The administration of President Lyndon Johnson got the message. Plans for the National Data Center, though originally backed by powerful interests within the executive branch, were shelved without legislation ever being submitted to Congress.

The brief controversy over the National Data Center idea might be taken to mark the beginning of federal controversies over what has come to be called "privacy protection." Ironically, the groundswell of suspicion of that project, and the diffident response of the Johnson administration, were little indication of the pattern of events to ensue.

Privacy protection debates show remarkable parallels to other policy controversies considered in these volumes. All turn on disputes over creation, maintenance, and use of various forms of information; all take on special intensity in the context of sale or appropriation of data against the will of those who consider it "their own." Such questions arise in policy disputes over automatic identification of callers' phone numbers in telephone communications; over copyright disputes concerning software and computer chip design; over licensing of radio and television stations; and in a host of other contexts. In the privacy issue these themes follow certain familiar lines. When may personal information be collected for filing and use by government and private organizations? When *must* such collection be done? Who may use the data, what decisions may be based on it, how are those decisions to be made, and with whom may the data be shared? When do those depicted in such data files have the right to shape the uses of "their" information, and what should the specifics of such rights be? Controversies on these themes have generated an extensive but ambiguous legacy of federal "privacy protection" principles, which now have their parallels both in the fifty states and abroad.

This essay reviews this legacy and assesses the possible directions that might follow from it. It concentrates on legislation and policy at the federal level in the United States, with passing comparisons to developments in other Western democracies. It does not treat the often vigorous and extensive efforts on these same issues in state, county, or local settings within the United States, though most of the approaches noted in federal controversies, and the dilemmas that they entail, have their equivalents in the states.

Certain other practices that might reasonably be considered to involve privacy issues are also not examined in detail here. These include individually targeted surveillance efforts, in government or corporate espionage, where information is collected in unique ways for specific investigatory purposes. While such cases obviously hold much interest, they raise somewhat different issues from the regular and routine creation of bureaucratically usable information of the sorts considered here. As it has turned out, the routine application of data-gathering and data-management has attracted most public and legislative attention.

"Privacy" is in fact a curious name for these issues. When we use the term in ordinary English, we usually refer to withholding certain forms of information, disclosure of which might be embarrassing or otherwise uncomfortable; maintaining privacy is to defend boundaries across which certain forms of personal information may not pass. Yet in privacy controversies of the sort considered here, the passage of personal data is often taken for granted. The record systems —computerized or otherwise—that have been at the center of these controversies have been created in the expectation, both by the organizations that create them and by the people to whom they refer, that the flow of such data is essential for specific purposes. The difficult political and ethical questions that they raise have to do not so much with the possibility of absolute concealment, but with questions of controlling the flow of personal information and the uses made of it.

Origins of the Issue

There can be no doubt that the American public perceives life in the United States as marked by increasing pressure on privacy. Public opinion polls show consistently rising concern over these issues since at least the 1970s. These anxious attitudes have ample basis in actual social practice. Consider the points in the life of a typical American where a particular relationship or transaction is shaped by the content of a written or computerized "record" on the person concerned. Early this century one might well have expected to go through life untouched by such encounters; the great "trunk lines" of personal information flow—in consumer credit, Social Security, income taxation, insurance, and banking—had yet to arise. In the late twentieth century, in contrast, an enormous variety of life junctures require recourse to one's "record" before they can be successfully completed. Not only income taxation, consumer credit and Social Security, but also access to insurance and medical care, treatment by law enforcement agencies, international travel, purchases made by credit and debit cards, and a wide variety of other life junctures are dominated by the content of one's "file."

How is one to account for these growing demands by organizations for personal information? For most people, one suspects, the origin of these trends is in the rise of computing. But this explanation is incorrect, at least in this simple form.

In fact, many key forms of personal record-keeping, now thoroughly computerized, were already well instated before the computer. Consumer credit records, now held and transmitted through sophisticated computerized systems, existed in the tens if not scores of millions before computerization. Social Security, income taxation, passport, insurance and a variety of other record systems served many of the same purposes under conventional technologies. Some of these systems, including welfare-state benefit systems abroad, go back as far the early decades of this century. Computing has undoubtedly streamlined the growth and impact of these systems, but it has hardly created them de novo.

For many organizations, both public and private, an essential "product" or output is some form of treatment of people. Such organizations use personal information to shape these treatments. This statement holds true for the widest variety of data-using organizations —from law enforcement systems to consumer credit, from schools and hospitals to tax collection bureaucracies. For all such bodies a key task is to administer precisely the "correct" action to each of what may be millions of individuals, in light of the full detail of relevant facts on each separate case. Thus a constant flow of decisions: for merchants and financial institutions, to deny or grant consumer credit—and if to grant, to what extent; for law enforcement agencies, to arrest, to monitor, or to ignore a particular individual —and if he or she is arrested, what sanctions to apply; for insurance firms, to deny insurance or to offer it—and if the latter, at what rates; for tax collection agencies, who is liable to pay—and how much. Such examples could extend endlessly. The contents of these actions may be welcome or unwelcome to the individual; they may be benign or coercive. But in all such cases the quest for discrimination in treatment requires development of, and attention to, written or computerized records.

Thus, it is easy to understand why large-scale systems of personal records compiled and used by organizations have attracted so much controversy. They matter enormously in what happens to individuals. They govern whether someone will be promoted or dismissed, accorded welfare payments or denied them, kept under surveillance or favored with benign neglect. We should hardly be surprised at the breadth and intensity of disputes that have grown up over the workings of these systems.

Three Dimensions of Debate

What does it mean to "protect privacy" from the abuses of large-scale personal record systems? What constitute reasonable legal and institutional strategies for supporting both individual rights and the abstract values, such as freedom of expression, affected by such systems? A variety of approaches have been entertained.

Institutional versus Self-Acting Measures

The United States is virtually unique among countries with significant privacy protection legislation in lacking a permanent national institution responsible for monitoring personal data systems and defending privacy interests in the workings of these systems. Such a body was envisaged in the legislation that was to become the Privacy Act of 1974. But strong opposition from the Ford administration resulted in its removal from the final version.

Canada and most Western European countries now have such boards. Their responsibilities vary by country, but in general they are charged with investigating and publicizing personal data systems and defending individuals in some way aggrieved by the systems.[2] In some countries the boards also license systems in the private sector. Typically the boards have little peremptory power to force keepers of data systems to change their practices, but they do have power to attract public attention and to recommend that other public agencies consider forceful action.

In the United States the Privacy Act of 1974, like most other privacy legislation, normally requires individual action by an interested party to set its provisions in motion. In the words of the Report of the Privacy Protection Study Commission, there is an effort to create an "assertable interest" on the part of individuals to act in their own behalf. Such powers of oversight over compliance with the Privacy Act as exist within the executive branch are lodged with the Office of Management and Budget.

Omnibus versus Piecemeal Measures

In the earliest debates over privacy policy, a number of commentators advocated what was termed "omnibus" legislation on the subject—

that is, laws and regulations applying similar restrictions or regulations to all forms of personal data. Thus, for example, individuals might enjoy some sort of blanket control over "their own" information, regardless of the kind of information involved. Some of the inspiration behind such efforts no doubt arose from "property" theories of privacy, to the effect that individuals ought to have the same kind of interest in "their" information that they do in copyright or in physical possessions.

Omnibus privacy legislation has never come close to enactment. But it bears reflection as a contrast to prevailing practice. If people had some absolute right of control over their data for commercial purposes, for example, then collection and sale of such information for mailing lists, market research, and the like would require permission of the individuals concerned. The result would undoubtedly be a more private world—one much different from the one we know.

Substantive versus Procedural Measures

The bulk of legislation and policy on personal data systems consists of what might be called procedural measures. These guide the flow of data, once it is collected, and set down ground rules for what the parties to the data-keeping relationship may and may not do.

Distinct from such principles are those that define what forms of information can or cannot be collected in the first place, or what kinds of information systems do or do not have the right to exist. One might call these substantive rules. European privacy protection boards enforce substantive restrictions when they consider whether to license personal data systems. American legislators created substantive barriers when they specified that sex and gender could not be used as bases for declining applications for consumer credit.

Politically, it has always appeared easier to create apparently equitable "rules of the game" to channel the workings of personal data systems than to engage head-on conflicts as to whether such systems should or should not exist. Yet this pattern leaves some important questions unanswered in the longer historical run.

Early Legislative History

Until the late 1960s the American public seems to have been largely unaware of the existence of the credit reporting industry. Credit reporting bureaus, then just beginning to computerize, devote themselves to collecting, storing, and selling data on "private" consumer creditworthiness. These data included—and still include—information on income, performance in paying past credit accounts, history of bankruptcies, litigation, liens and the like, along with address, family status, and similar data. The contents of such reports did, and do, have major influence on applications for credit and, sometimes, employment and other opportunities. But Americans in the late 1960s were shocked to find that the industry responsible for generating such reports was virtually free of legal obligations to ensure accuracy of records or to open credit records to the people depicted in them.

The Fair Credit Reporting Act of 1970 established such a legal framework. It authorized reporting for virtually all purposes for which firms had been accustomed to doing so—including credit, employment, insurance, licensing, and to any buyer who "otherwise has a legitimate business need for the information in connection with a business transaction involving the customer."[3] It authorized provision of data without subpoena from credit files to police and other investigators. It limited the age of information that can be reported in credit reports, though the limits (normally seven years) are beyond what most agencies would find it profitable to report.

Perhaps most importantly, the act requires that credit reporting agencies disclose to people the contents of their own records and to correct inaccuracies in such records when they are pointed out. Buyers of credit reports who decline applications as the result of such reports are required to refer the applicants to the bureau.

The Fair Credit Reporting Act is noteworthy both for the changes it dictates in record-keeping practice and in the limits it sets for itself. In the terms used above the thrust of the act is overwhelmingly procedural, rather than substantive. Its provisions make the information processes it addresses more open, less mysterious and more subject to influence by the persons concerned. To this extent it has undoubtedly smoothed the flow of credit transactions and avoided certain injustices and inconveniences, especially those stemming from mistaken identity.

At the same time virtually nothing in the law restricts access of the industry to its key sources of personal data, nor does it interfere with other entrenched practices that many would consider invasive of privacy. The Fair Credit Reporting Act creates "rules of the game" in which both institutions and individuals can pursue their interests, on the assumption that nothing must be allowed to interfere with the flow of data "needed" for the smooth processing of credit transactions.

The principles underlying the Fair Credit Reporting Act became the basis for key pronouncements and legislation in the years to follow. The year 1973 saw publication of *Records, Computers and Rights of Citizens* by the Department of Health, Education and Welfare (HEW); this influential document took stock of privacy controversies and proposed a core of principles for dealing with them.[4] As summarized by Priscilla Regan of the Office of Technology Assessment, these are as follows:

- —There must be no personal data record-keeping system whose very existence is secret.
- —There must be a way for an individual to find out what information about him or her is in a record and how it is used.
- —There must be a way for an individual to prevent information about him or her that was obtained for one purpose from being used for other purposes without his or her consent.
- —There must be a way for an individual to correct or amend a record of identifiable information about him or her.
- —Any organization creating, maintaining, using or disseminating records of identifiable personal data must assure the reliability of the data for their intended use and must take precautions to prevent misuse of the data.[5]

While an unexceptionable manifesto for privacy protection, these precepts were not intended to apply to all record systems, even in principle; records maintained for investigative or espionage purposes were exempted from consideration ab initio.[6]

The Privacy Act of 1974 took its inspiration directly from the principles enunciated in the HEW study. The act remains the most fundamental and far-reaching of federal privacy legislation. Passed at the height of impact of Watergate on American opinion, it clearly represented the effort of Congress to respond vigorously to public indignation at government data-gathering. The Privacy Act deals with record systems maintained by government institutions; it excludes the Central Intelligence Agency and most law enforcement bodies from most of its provisions.

With some exceptions the act requires that creation of new personal record systems be acknowledged in a Federal Register notice. It requires that federal agencies covered by the act maintain only such records as are "relevant and necessary to accomplish" their missions; they are to collect data "to the greatest extent practicable from the subject individual," and to inform persons of the authority on which information is demanded on them.

In a particularly significant provision the act limits disclosure from agency files to other agencies having "routine uses" of the record for purposes "compatible with the purposes for which it was collected" —and to law enforcement agencies. This provision has been subject to some remarkable interpretations over the ensuing years.

Finally, like the Fair Credit Reporting Act, the Privacy Act provides for access to files by their subjects and makes provision for subjects to dispute contents and make changes. Individuals dissatisfied with the content of their files are, as in the credit legislation, entitled to add a statement of their own to the files, to be disseminated with the files themselves.

Like the Fair Credit Reporting Act, then, the Privacy Act is far more procedural than substantive. The great emphasis is on opening up record keeping procedures and creating protections against inaccurate or incomplete information. The act recognizes no conflict between expansion of record-keeping and protection of individual privacy interests.

One exception is the "routine uses" provision. This provision presupposes that more comprehensive, more thoroughgoing, more efficient uses by government of information on individuals may not always be a good thing. Instead, it implies the wisdom of artificial barriers, such that information available to one government agency should not flow automatically elsewhere. The fact that data of one kind are made available for medicare transactions, for example, should not necessarily mean that these same data are to be used for tax collection purposes or security checks. Such assumptions turn out to be important in the elaboration of legislation and policy during the years since 1974.

In lieu of creating a permanent privacy protection agency within the federal government, the Privacy Act provided for creation of the Privacy Protection Study Commission (PPSC). This temporary body was to recommend further legislation extending the act to organizations in the private sector. The commission mounted a significant research effort into personal data practices in such diverse areas as direct mail, credit card companies, and insurance, including both many documentary searches and public hearings. Its ensuing report contained some 162 recommendations for further legislation.

Continuity with the principles underlying earlier official thinking and legislation is evident in these recommendations. The Privacy Commission authors state their guiding aims as follows:

  −to create a proper balance between what an individual is expected to divulge to a record-keeping organization and what he seeks in return (*to minimize intrusiveness*);
  −to open up record-keeping operations in ways that will minimize the extent to which recorded information about an individual is itself a source of unfairness in any decision about him made on the basis of it (*to maximize fairness*); and
  −to create and define obligations with respect to the uses and disclosures that will be made of recorded information about an individual (*to create legitimate, enforceable, expectations of confidentiality*).[7]

True to the tradition of which it is part, the Privacy Commission proposed few recommendations that would block major established record-keeping practices. Most of its recommendations aim at making existing procedures more accessible to the individuals concerned and more subject to due-process rules.

Here and there, however, commission recommendations did call into question the efficiency of record-using organizations as the unique value at stake in personal data management. For example, they recommend restrictions on access of investigative agencies to "personal papers" of private individuals held by third parties—for example, bank account records and credit files—access which is certainly efficient from the standpoint of the agencies involved. Similarly, they recommend against use of the polygraph by employers.[8] These recommendations are important, for they point to some serious issues not often acknowledged in writing and legislation on privacy protection: substantive issues of how much information should be collected and used, or of what organizational purposes are important enough to warrant such collection and use. Compared to the goals of making existing or prospective data systems more open to scrutiny and participation by those affected and more just, these substantive questions are considerably more nettlesome.

Privacy since the PPSC

The Privacy Commission offered an impressive agenda for legislation. Few of its recommendations, however, have been transformed into federal legislation. In retrospect 1974 represents the high water mark of political concern for privacy protection. By the time the commission presented its report in 1977, legislative interest had lost the intensity it had during the height of the Watergate era. The Carter administration made little headway on privacy issues during the late 1970s, and the Reagan administration has, for the most part, been downright antagonistic to privacy protection efforts and even to enforcement of the Privacy Act of 1974.

Perhaps the most damaging blow to the Privacy Act has been the interpretations applied to its intended restrictions on uses of personal information to purposes "compatible with the purposes for which it was collected." These restrictions aimed at imposing some artificial constraints on the unlimited "free flow" of personal data among government departments and agencies. Those who framed the act understood that data provided to one federal agency in one context could become the basis for actions unfavorable to the individual if mobilized by another agency in a different context—for example, use of IRS data by draft boards or use of criminal record information by federal employers. Hence the "purposes compatible" provisions.

These provisions have effectively been circumvented through an interpretation of the act that exempts "routine uses" of records; these provisions permit disclosure for purposes "compatible with the purpose for which the records were originally collected."[9] Yet, the interpretations placed on this language have construed "routine uses" so widely as to mean virtually any other use that a government agency might have for the record in question.

Thus the whole program of "computer matching" that has grown up since the Privacy Act has remained unchecked by the act. Computer matching is the technique by which information in one set of government files, or files available to government, are checked against others, in efforts to detect fraudulent or improper representations. For example, welfare records are checked against computerized bank records to detect unreported assets; lists of student loan defaulters are checked against those seeking tax refunds from the IRS. Techniques of this kind can greatly increase government enforcement powers, precisely because of the efficiency of combining resources of different data repositories created for purposes that are, at least in the minds of the individuals on whom data are used, quite distinct.

Clearly the intent of the Privacy Act was to curtail unlimited symbiosis among personal data systems. No less clearly, the constituency for exploiting such symbiosis has grown much stronger since 1974, often under the banner of attacking government waste. According to statistics compiled by the Office of Technology Assessment, a total of 127 computer matches were being carried out by federal agencies as of April 1985.[10]

Matching programs, and the fate of Privacy Act provisions intended to limit them, point to an enduring ambivalence among policymakers, and indeed among the American public. On the one hand, most people share a reflexive repugnance to the notion that people lose control altogether over "their" data whenever it is provided to a public or private organization; the interests of privacy, most would agree, are served by compartmentalizing information in such settings. On the other hand, the desire to maximize government efficiency is obvious. Many people wax indignant at the idea that those who take money improperly from government should receive payments from other government agencies, or indeed any other favorable government action.

These two instincts often lead to contradictory actions or policies. Within a few years of passage of the Privacy Act, the Congress also enacted a number of measures specifically authorizing use of data from IRS and Social Security files for purposes potentially unfriendly to the individual. Included here was legislation requiring the IRS and the Social Security Administration to provide information on the whereabouts of parents who had absconded on child support judgments to the child's remaining parent or guardian or to state agencies responsible for the child's support. This requirement obviously represented a significant breach in the confidentiality of these files. This breach was especially noteworthy in the case of Social Security, whose founding was attended by elaborate assurances that its files would be used only for Social Security purposes.[11] Such developments should remind us that the principles guiding creation of personal record systems cannot be assumed to be as enduring as the bureaucratic capabilities of the systems themselves.

Protection of "Personal Papers" and Communications

A particular strength of the report of the Privacy Protection Study Commission was its analysis of the status of "personal papers." The report noted the differing degrees of legal protection accorded to papers held in private persons' homes versus those held elsewhere. The Constitution created strong guarantees against unreasonable search and seizure of possessions held at home. But it could hardly have been expected to provide protections for the vast array of written and computerized files that are "personal" to private individuals, yet which are now held by financial institutions, credit agencies, mail order firms, computer mail systems, and other institutions.

Many such organizations have become targets of regular demands from investigative bodies seeking personal data held in files and transaction records. The investigative bodies involved here range from the IRS and the Federal Bureau of Investigation (FBI) through the entire array of federal, state, and local law enforcement agencies. Traditionally, banks, credit agencies, and other institutions developed a habit of satisfying demands from these bodies without question, and without alerting the individual concerned.

The Privacy Commission recommended against these relaxed practices.[12] The resulting Right to Financial Privacy Act (1978) was arguably the only national legislation to stem directly from commission recommendations.

The broad theme of the act is the creation of a requirement of notice to the individual before an investigative agency may gain access to personal papers of a financial nature. The act specifies a period of fourteen days in which subjects of records may challenge the rationale for the inquiry in question. The result sought here is clearly, in the words of the Privacy Commission Report, to create an "assertable interest" in protection of one's own files and to prevent such files from being scrutinized without the knowledge of the subject.

Disappointing to privacy advocates, however, are the exceptions to provisions of the act. It fully exempts domestic espionage operations and the Secret Service. In addition, the act permits investigative agencies to avoid advance notification to the individual by persuading a judge that giving notice may complicate investigative work. According to figures compiled under requirements of the act, this provision has been used rather sparingly: a total of forty-seven notices were served under it between 1979 and 1985, all of which were granted.[13]

Relatively little other federal legislation aimed at protecting private papers and communications has been passed in the years since the Privacy Commission's report. The Electronic Funds Transfer Act of 1978 establishes requirements that financial institutions notify customers about third-party access to files of electronic transactions. The Debt Collection Act of 1982 sets down comparable procedural rules for notice to individuals before information on debts to federal agencies can be disseminated to credit bureaus. The Cable Communications Privacy Act of 1984 requires that cable TV subscribers be notified of information held about them, the length of time it may be held, and the uses made of it; it also establishes some limitations on the purposes for which such data may be collected and disclosed.

Perhaps the most noteworthy privacy-related federal legislation during this period has been the Electronic Communications Privacy Act of 1986. This law protects messages communicated by new technologies such as electronic mail and teleconferencing. It gives these forms of communication the same protection accorded to telephone communications under the Communications Act of 1934, which forbids interception and disclosure of information transmitted by that medium. The immediate impulse for such legislation seems to have been concern by the telecommunications industry, rather than immediate grass-roots demand. Such judgments reflect an assessment that public fears about eavesdropping would interfere with marketing the new technologies.

On the other hand a grass-roots feeling seems to have had some role in legislation being considered in Congress in 1988 aimed at control of information on individuals' choices of books and video tapes from libraries and rental centers. Called the "Bork Bill" because of the publicity surrounding disclosure of video tape rental choices by the former Supreme Court nominee, this legislation is modeled after the Cable Act of 1984.

In the near future we can no doubt expect more legislative

skirmishes over the fate of personal information held in account files and other third-party locations. Some of these will result from public indignation at the release of what was thought to be "private" data. Others, like Reagan administration initiatives on bank reporting requirements, will stem from government attempts to claim more information from such files. In the latter case the administration has sought to broaden the information banks must report to the government concerning especially large transactions, particularly those effected in cash.

These efforts are apparently aimed at identifying drug traffickers, but they follow a broader pattern characteristic of official interest in "personal papers." As technological change makes it possible to move, condense, and analyze more information of all kinds, new opportunities constantly arise for using personal data that have always in some sense been "available." Thus if someone discovers a form of organizationally generated or organizationally held information that helps to predict AIDS or participation in terrorism or drug use, pressure to share those data will follow inevitably. Will selections from home shopping services prove to predict income tax evasion? Will the patterns of destinations of long-distance calls (quite apart from the content of such calls) prove to predict involvement in the illegal drug trade? We have no idea which of such connections will remain in the realm of fantasy and which will yield efficient bases for government action. Given the fertility of technological change and the ingenuity of officials in finding new uses for old data, moreover, we can be sure that innovation of this kind will continue to exert pressure on what had been thought of as "private" information.

Workplace Privacy

Technological change has also sparked controversy about what information employers should or should not collect on employees. Computer technology makes it possible to monitor and total each keystroke made by word processors or to determine which employees are spending what proportions of their time in various locations at a job site. Such developments have led many to claim that computerization is leading to a net degradation in the quality of working life and to call for legislative restrictions on computerization of work.

In fact, many computer-driven pressures on workplace privacy do

not arise from the conscious intent of those who design computerized work arrangements. Increased knowledge of what staff are doing
often arises as a kind of by-product of computerization for other purposes. Computerization of the flow of raw materials in manufacturing industries, for example, may lead to identification of machinists
who are generating what management considers excessive amounts
of scrap—or who are obtaining and sequestering expensive materials
to be resold for their own benefit. Computerization of loan accounts
in a bank may ultimately make it easy to compare the profitability of
broad categories of loans and the judgment of the various loan officers
responsible for such loans. A National Science Foundation sponsored
study now being carried out by Paul Attewell and this author suggests that computerization of firms tends broadly to make all sorts of
aspects of the workplace more "transparent" to management, so that
the contributions of individual employees are more easily assessed,
whether or not this was the original intention.

Other controversies over workplace monitoring have arisen not so
much as direct results of technological change as from ordinary political struggles over options enjoyed by employers and employees.
For example, legislation pending in 1988 seeks to limit use of poly-
graphs by private employers. Far-reaching versions of this bill would
prohibit use of the polygraph by private employers, with a short list
of exceptions. Similarly, newly intensified enthusiasm for employee
drug testing stems not from availability of new technologies for such
tests, but from desperation to fight drug use at virtually any cost.
Future sessions of Congress are apt to see attempts at legislation aimed
at regulating such demands on employees. Other practices likely to
spark demands for privacy-protection legislation include screening
to identify employees susceptible to work-related diseases and testing of prospective employees to predict attitudes toward labor
organizing.

Documentary Identification and Monitoring of Public Activities

Growth in the amount of personal identification and documentation
required in a typical American's life has been relentless. Every decade seems to add another item or two to the basic array that begins
with credit cards, Social Security card, and driver's license and now

extends to include bank identification cards for automatic tellers, cards for medical insurance and prescription benefits, and items identifying special medical conditions. Particularly striking is the growing impact of such items on the lives of those who carry them.

The proliferation of such personal documentation means that more and more of people's movements and activities are subject to monitoring by the organizations generating and using the documents. There need be nothing malevolent about this. Organizations of all kinds constantly adjust their treatment of individuals to fit the full detail of what is known about them—hence, the desire to absorb information at more and more points. Such patterns are no less true of the administration of medical insurance than of counterespionage.

But in either the benevolent or the coercive case—or at any number of points on the continuum they describe—questions arise as to how much documentation and monitoring is desirable or permissable. Is systematic monitoring of private citizens' movements and activities to be regarded as a "neutral" activity, such that no legitimate interest of the individual is damaged by being subjected to it? Or is there some fundamental right to be left alone by governments and other powerful organizations, such that monitoring leaves the individual properly aggrieved?

Complicating matters is the fact that modern monitoring systems are often relatively unobtrusive. The Department of the Treasury administers an extensive system, for example, that monitors travelers entering this country—TECS, or Treasury Enforcement Communications System. Immigrations officials seek to enter the name of every entering person in the TECS memory; from there all such names are available to about a dozen federal agencies. One bureaucratic element in the program is the FBI's National Crime Information Center listing of wanted and missing persons. Wanted persons can be arrested at the vulnerable moment at which they pass through government control at the nation's borders, regardless of whether the crime for which they are wanted is related to their travels.

Participants in TECS obviously feel that simply monitoring the movements of persons "of interest" to government agencies poses no ethical or political issue. One wonders how far this reasoning might be extended. West Germany (FRG) has been planning to make domestic identification documents machine readable, so that routine identity checks by police can register in a central computer.[14] Thus the ques-

tion arises as to when ordinary citizens should be expected to identify themselves electronically to government agencies in the course
of their movements within their own countries.

Indeed, some closely related controversies have already arisen in
connection with the National Crime Information Center (NCIC). This
computerized clearing house was created to make available to law
enforcement bodies in all parts of the country information on criminal records and wanted and missing persons. Proposals to establish
the NCIC in the first place sparked controversy over whether the system would unduly centralize law enforcement practice. Such anxie-
ties have been sharpened by plans to add to the NCIC features enabling participating bodies to track persons not wanted for arrest. Under
this system, participants in the NCIC would enter names of persons
whose movements were of interest to them. Participating agencies
would also enter into the system names of individuals encountered
in their day-to-day operations—for example, in checks of driver's
licenses or in names taken in reports on crimes. Thus, police in California seeking to extend their surveillance of a figure of interest to
them could enter the target's name and receive reports on his or her
presence wherever it was registered across the country. Individuals
could be electronically tracked from one jurisdiction to another without their knowledge.

Against such plans, many privacy advocates would argue that private citizens have a right to go about their affairs unmonitored, unless they are actually wanted for a crime. Defenders of the plans would
insist that computerization systems like TECS represent no fundamental change in the mission or the activities of the agencies involved.
Law enforcement agencies have always concerned themselves with
the movements of certain persons not immediately wanted for arrest:
if police forces or government agencies monitor the movements of
persons of interest to them by conventional means, what objection
can there be to streamlining and centralizing such capabilities? In
response privacy advocates would insist that quantitative changes in
the numbers of persons under surveillance and the scope of such
surveillance surely amount at some point to a qualitative difference.
The debates are typical of widespread themes in controversies over
treatment of personal information.

Similar themes arise in connection with "smart cards," a striking
new technology that combines characteristics of identification docu-

ments and individual computer files. Miniaturization of computer components now makes it possible to store and manipulate extensive data files within a card similar in size and appearance to a credit card. These "smart cards" could be imprinted with the bearer's picture, fingerprint, or any other identifying information that the issuing organization saw fit.

The resulting card would be authoritatively linked to the bearer, yet could contain the equivalent of many organizations' files of data about him or her. Many uses have been suggested for such cards. Most prominently, they could function as a substitute for cash. Credited electronically by a paying source for a certain amount of purchasing power, for example, they could be gradually debited by electronic transactions until totally depleted or replenished. Infusions of cash could take place without any personal contact, as by a visit to an automatic teller where money from one's bank account could be transferred to the card. For such consumer uses smart cards would possess a significant advantage over credit cards as presently used. With the latter large purchases typically require a check by telephone to the card-issuing organization to determine whether the transaction should be permitted. The smart card would contain its cash "inside" it, so to speak, so that the authorization step would not be necessary.

Financial institutions and retailers are giving close scrutiny to the potential of smart cards to substitute for cash and credit cards. Cash registers could be fitted as computer terminals to debit the cards directly, although this step would entail significant start-up costs. Another attractive application would be for payment of government benefits, including welfare and Social Security. Many government agencies now have reason to prefer crediting payments via smart cards to present methods of issuing checks, since not all recipients have bank accounts, and checks are readily lost and stolen. Smart cards, by contrast, could bear photos of those to whom they are issued, making it difficult for them to be used if stolen.

Still more intriguing, the uses of smart cards by benefit recipients could be controlled in ways not true of cash. Food stamps can be sold and cash benefits diverted to uses other than defraying household grocery bills as intended by welfare programs. The computerized information held in smart cards could conceivably specify that the purchasing power credited to them was valid only for certain categories of purchases. The fact that many supermarkets now organize their check-out procedures by computerized bar codes would facilitate such discriminations. Hence, use of smart cards could ensure greater accountability in the uses of welfare payments and less privacy for recipients of such payments.

These are prospects that have already come into practical consideration. Looking farther into the future, one can imagine a range of other uses for smart cards that would be certain to raise privacy issues in their own right. The cards, for example, could readily be programmed with copies of people's medical histories, credit files, past tax returns, security clearance status, criminal history, or any number of other forms of data that would matter for the individual's dealings with authoritative organizations. The gains in efficiency of making individuals and their records inseparable in this way would often be dramatic to the organizations concerned and, in some cases, to the individual as well.

Should these possibilities become realities, many controversies would follow. Who should have access to the information held in smart cards? Should the contents of the cards be regarded as "private papers" in the personal possession of the bearer or as files that remain the property of the organizations originating them? What agencies should have the right to enter data on the cards? What role should individuals have in determining what is entered on their cards and when those cards are to be used? Would the cards become de facto national identity cards, a kind of individually held public utility where every individual would be expected to keep the files deemed necessary by the key organizations with which he or she dealt?

These are not policy questions for the immediate future. But they bear consideration well in advance, for the efficiencies promised by compiling all this information on a single card make pressures to move in these directions highly probable.

Long-Term Trends

Any system of authoritatively collecting data on broad categories of the population is apt to become attractive for purposes other than those for which it was originally conceived. The Internal Revenue System, after much bureaucratic investment and long public habituation, has created the expectation that virtually every adult will file a tax return. In some cases data from such returns are now made available by the IRS to outside agencies to aid them in one enforcement activity or another. Even in the absence of such cooperation, the fact that tax returns are required of everyone makes it irresistible to many private organizations (for example, banks) to demand that individuals present their own returns in the course of various dealings that they may have with the institution. Effectively, the national income taxation system has become a kind of "public utility," producing highly relevant, authenticated personal data for use by a variety of other bodies.

The same kinds of pressures for sharing personal data can be expected wherever authoritative personal data are known to exist, particularly where the data in question cannot be altered by the individual concerned. Thus, should "smart cards" develop as expected, predictable controversies will ensue: Who must have a smart card? (All welfare recipients? All aliens? All taxpayers?) What data may agencies insist on imprinting on the cards? (History of traffic violations? Parole status? All criminal history? Credit rating? Indebtedness to the federal government? Tax bracket?) When may agencies obtain data from the cards that individuals do not wish to yield? Such questions would represent new manifestations of controversies over personal data that are already familiar in existing record systems.

Arguments in defense of the proliferation of personal data systems always cite efficiency. Whether an organization is constituted to provide credit, license drivers, repress crime, deliver welfare, or something else entirely, more information on the people targeted for these attentions almost always appears better than less, and technological and management innovations always seem to offer opportunities for more and more usable personal data.

Yet, the long-term trend in developing these systems is always to accumulate more organizational power in the hands of those who manage them. For such reasons privacy advocates argue, caution should prevail in the creation of such systems, regardless of the evident bona fides of those who propose them. Efficiency, whether as an attack on government waste, enhanced scope of operations, or heightened profitability, is a very difficult value for modern organizations to renounce. The virtues of collecting and using less personal information as a value in itself do not easily withstand contest with claims of efficiency, once the efficiencies are instated in real, working institutions. This is nowhere so dramatically visible as in the fate of the

Privacy Act of 1974; its strictures against unlimited sharing of personal data have been reinterpreted to mean virtually the opposite of what the legislation was intended to mean.

A Program for Privacy Protection

There are no natural limits to the propensity of organizations to infringe on the "informational space" available to individuals. Accordingly, the only way to defend privacy interests is to create "artificial" barriers to such infringements in the form of policy measures to restrict or reshape information flow. The following policy recommendations offer some possibilities for such reshaping.

Enforce the Privacy Act

The simplest and most direct step toward asserting strong privacy interests would be to enforce the Privacy Act of 1974, in both letter and spirit. Initiatives could come either from the Congress or the executive branch.

The president, for example, could direct the Office of Management and Budget to make serious efforts to enforce the act throughout the federal bureaucracy. This would mean, among other things, requiring more rigorous reporting from agency officials charged with monitoring compliance within their organizations.

Perhaps even more useful would be an Executive Order proclaiming a fundamentally conservative policy concerning establishment and maintenance of personal data systems. Such a policy would be predicated on the assumption that systems of this kind always pose potential risks and consequently require clear justification to create or maintain. Like potent industrial chemicals or powerful, battle-ready weapons systems, personal information should always be regarded as potentially harmful and treated with care. The burden of proof should rest on those who claim that creation of such systems is the only way of satisfying a legitimate administrative need; systems should be dismantled when such needs are no longer demonstrable.

A still more important step would be for the president to reverse the bizarre interpretations given to the "purposes compatible" language of the Privacy Act. Such a step alone would curtail countless data exchanges that have grown up in the last ten years—instances where personal information is used for purposes quite unrelated to those for which it is provided. In dealing with the federal government private citizens should be able to act on the presumption that information provided for one purpose will not be used for unrelated purposes, except in accordance with practices publicly specified in advance.

Some exceptions to absolute privacy are, of course, necessary and inevitable. Even the most ardent privacy advocates would probably grant the legitimacy of accessing certain normally confidential personal records where imminent risk to human life could be demonstrated, as in the use of Social Security records to trace workers discovered to have been exposed to serious risks of occupational disease. Most of the demands against personal data that have spurred privacy controversies in recent decades are nowhere near so dramatic.

In data systems like most of those discussed in this chapter, privacy interests are best served by creating a presumption like that intended in the Privacy Act: that data provided for one purpose will indeed be used only for that purpose and others compatible with it. Breaches in this presumption should be made only after full public debate and preferably after Congressional action. Such a strategy would countervail against the gradual erosion of privacy interests through often inconspicuous, incremental administrative decisions that has occurred in the United States since the late 1970s.

The Congress has mandated, for example, use of Social Security files as a means of tracking parents who abscond from child support obligations. Such a decision is a loss to privacy interests. But the loss at least occurred through the political process, where all concerned parties have the maximum chance to press their views.

Reestablishing and enforcing the presumption of confidentiality would block a host of troubling innovations that federal agencies have recently entertained. One example is the proposed use of the FBI's computerized NCIC files to track movements of persons of interest to various law enforcement jurisdictions but not wanted for arrest. Another application, considered but not yet realized, is the searching of computerized memos and correspondence of federal agencies to identify and locate persons "of interest" in various ways to authorities. Such "trolling" of vast masses of computerized data to obtain nuggets of information on persons whose names come up in quite different contexts is increasingly easy, given modern computing capabilities. It should be forbidden unless explicitly authorized by Congress, and Congress should be extremely reluctant to grant such authorization.

Establish Individual Rights in Sale of Private-sector Data

The goal of extending the logic of the Privacy Act to private sector organizations has largely gone unfulfilled. The Privacy Commission recommendations to this effect have not received much legislative attention, while new private sector demands for personal data continue unchecked. The most dramatic of these demands stem from growth in commercial use of personal account information. Such data can arise from a variety of different transaction files, including those associated with telephone calling records, direct mail transactions, home shopping services, credit card sales, banks and other financial institutions, political and charitable contributions, and many others. Such data convey pictures of personal consumption habits, finances, whereabouts, political and recreational preferences, and other potentially sensitive information. The sale and exchange of such computerized listings now represents a major industry, one whose activities exert pressure on privacy.

The strongest and most effective step Congress could take to protect privacy in these settings would be to create a property or copyright interest in such data. Private citizens, that is, should have rights over the commercial use of filed information about themselves akin to that enjoyed by celebrities over the commercial use of their public personae. Information in data files should not be sold or exchanged for value without permission of the individual; private individuals should be able to withhold, give away, or indeed sell rights to commercial use of their files. Here, too, exceptions should be mandated only by Congressional action.

Establishing direct personal control over commercial uses of personal data might seem a bold departure, but the logic of such action is eminently just. Private citizens presently have very little say about the highly profitable sale of data about themselves, data created by their own activities. It is hard to think why they should not share in the growing profits from sale of such data or have the option of declining to have such data disseminated at all. Some people would undoubtedly prefer to maintain an absolute blackout on certain forms of transaction records, including those relating to political preferences or cultural consumption. Others would be happy to have all such records receive the widest possible dissemination, perhaps in hopes of receiving further solicitations. Undoubtedly, one result of such legislation would be the growth of personal information "brokers," who could acquire rights that private persons wished to sell in their own data and sell them in turn to the users.

Interests involved in the appropriation and sale of such data would of course seek exemption from such legislation for their particular kinds of files. Only Congress should be able to make such exceptions, if, indeed, any should be made at all. Most predictably, retailers and the credit reporting industry would lobby for such exemptions, insisting that sale of credit reports is highly useful to retailers and that giving consumers the option of remaining anonymous would undermine the entire system.

The first claim is substantially true, the second more dubious. Consumers should retain the right of remaining outside the credit reporting system altogether, if they wish, while accepting the consequences that the absence of a credit record brings in a credit-oriented world. The industry, however, should be protected by provisions that forbid an individual's dictating which particular credit data should be compiled. In other words, if a consumer wishes to permit any credit information to be collected about himself or herself, the reporting agency should be able to draw from all sources available for any other credit report.

Without comprehensive legislation embracing all private sector sales of personal data, Congress will have to consider piecemeal measures addressed to particular settings. One controversial case concerns reporting on tenants and medical patients. Reports are based on listings designed to enable landlords and physicians to exclude those whose tenancy has dissatisfied previous landlords or patients who have in the past filed malpractice claims. To the extent that this reporting is permitted at all, the Congress would have to consider some sort of "ground rules" to govern activities of these firms, perhaps modeled after the Fair Credit Reporting Act.

Such rules would have to provide means for individuals to review their own records and contest questionable entries. Appeals procedures would have to be specified for unresolved disputes, along with procedural rules as to what facts could be reported and to whom. To be just any procedures so established would probably have to be complex and, most likely, cumbersome. By contrast, the comprehensive principle proposed above would be much simpler. By merely granting people the option to remain outside the system, their privacy rights would be preserved; the most cautious landlords and physicians could choose not to deal with persons lacking positive records.

Another form of private sector information requiring special attention are records reflecting cultural and intellectual consumption. The Congress has already begun to address this issue in legislation relating to video rentals (the "Bork Bill"). This legislation goes farther than that considered above by restricting disclosure of all kinds, not just sale of transaction logs. Similar restrictions should be enacted for other records reflecting cultural, political, sexual, or intellectual tastes, including book club selections and cable TV subscriptions. Under the copyright approach proposed above individuals would be able to decide whether their data were available for sale. Nonetheless, were such an approach adopted, Congress would still be wise to prohibit outright other forms of disclosure.

Prohibit Collection of Inferential Data on Employees

Controversies surrounding personal data uses in the workplace differ from those considered above, in that they mostly do not involve questions of transmission of personal data from one organization to another. Rather, these controversies arise from struggles over what forms of testing and monitoring of employees employers may legitimately carry out in their own interest.

Do employers have the right to claim any and all information that they might see fit to collect from employees? Recent polygraph legislation is predicated on the assumption that there must be limits to employers' actions. Few would dispute that some such limit must be specified. The question is where to draw the line between legitimate interests of employers and unacceptable invasion of privacy?

Privacy interests demand that employers only collect information from employees relating directly to their performance of job duties, in addition to information required for such nonevaluative purposes as tax withholding and fringe benefit administration. Legislation should proscribe data collection used to evaluate employees for promotion or continued employment where the relevance is indirect or speculative. Thus, recording the number of widgets that a production worker produces is not controversial, but developing medical profiles to screen out workers believed likely to submit workmen's compensation claims should not be acceptable. Nor should employers be permitted to collect data on the identities of those involved in or associated with labor organizing. None of these data describes directly how much or how well workers perform the duties for which they are hired.

Much the same distinction is required concerning drug testing. The striking invasion of privacy entailed in being obliged to yield bodily fluids for testing can only lower the threshold of tolerance for other privacy invasions. The considerable public acquiescence to such testing thus far is deeply disturbing. Mandatory testing in the workplace for drug use should be permitted only where employees give some prima facie indication of drug use and where such use is apt to endanger life or safety. Note that such principles would not prevent employers from disciplining or discharging those whose job performance is deficient. But the performance deficiency, not the supposed reasons for it, should be the basis for such action.

Curtail Government Appropriation of Private-Sector Data

Some of the sharpest privacy debates concern claims by government agencies on data generated and used within the private sector. Much of the Privacy Commission's work dealt with such issues. The commission gave particular attention to the ambiguous legal status of "private papers" held by third-party organizations, especially banks and other financial institutions. Its report forcefully showed how such papers lacked the protections accorded to private papers held in the home. Many commission recommendations aimed at creating legal protections for such papers held in third-party institutions. The goal, still unrealized, should be to accord such papers the same protection in third-party hands as private hands.

Therefore, court orders should be necessary before government agencies are permitted to inspect personal data from any private sector record system. Such systems include those maintained by credit card firms, airlines and travel agents, hotels and car rental firms, telephone companies, cable television firms, publishers and book clubs, and many others. Such data should not be, as they often are now, available for casual inquiry by local, state, and federal investigative bodies. Such agencies should be required to show that such information forms part of an investigation into specific wrongdoing before access is granted.

The Right to Financial Privacy Act of 1978, though flawed by certain exceptions, does point in this direction. Federal investigators must provide notice to individuals whose records they seek from financial institutions and give record subjects the right to appeal to the courts to block the investigation. Another kind of personal data that needs protection from arbitrary government access is that generated by computer communications networks. These networks make it possible for people who may never see one another to exchange ideas, gossip, advice, and other information, either by directing communications at named individuals or by "posting" messages on a computerized "bulletin board."

Government interest in these communications may arise either as part of a broader investigation of a particular participant or in response to what appears to be transmission of information of a criminal nature. In the latter case, for example, bulletin board participants have occasionally posted third-party credit card numbers or telephone numbers where child prostitutes may be located. What should be the prerogatives and limitations of government agencies in investigating such communications?

The interests of privacy protection require that individually "addressed" computer communications enjoy the same sanctity as letters passing through the post; they should be opened only on court order. Ideally, both postal and computer communications should be protected from manual or electronic "mail covers," or notation by investigative agencies of the origins and destinations of communications. A more complex question arises where contraband information is posted on a publicly accessible computer bulletin board. The best rule to apply here would make the individual responsible for such a posting subject to investigation where the communication bears an electronic "signature." Where the posting is anonymous, the keeper of the bulletin board should bear responsibility.

Create a Permanent Privacy Advocate

The United States is unique among Western democracies in having a tradition of privacy protection efforts, yet no permanent federal body whose sole mission is privacy protection. In Canada and Europe such boards have varying powers. Some are responsible for licensing personal data systems and thereby enforcing official codes of privacy policy. Some can intervene in the workings of such systems on behalf of individuals who feel themselves aggrieved in the treatment of their information. Elsewhere, board powers are restricted to bringing privacy issues before the public. Thus some privacy boards can delay institution of new data systems, government or private, while public hearings are held.

By contrast, American policy has relied on creation of what the Privacy Commission called "assertable interests," which individuals may invoke to press their own cases. Certainly the logic of this approach often works in practice: many Americans avail themselves of access opportunities to records held by consumer credit firms or federal government agencies. But many others, no doubt, are mystified or intimidated by the prospect of confronting large organizations in an adversary role, backed only by their own intellectual and financial resources. A permanent federal institution for privacy advocacy could provide a counterweight to such imbalance. But it could accomplish even more: it could raise public debate over that most crucial and difficult issue, whether specific data practices should exist in the first place.

An effective privacy board could be composed of equal numbers of members appointed by the president and by Congress, to serve for fixed terms, supported by a small staff. This board need not exercise any licensing power but should have ample access to government and private data systems. It should be able to advocate the interests of aggrieved individuals against both public and private data systems, to create public forums and subpoena testimony, and to block changes in practice until privacy issues had been aired.

Such a board would substantially raise the level of public debate, both quantitatively and qualitatively. Had such a board existed, it would have been far more difficult for administration forces to ascribe disabling interpretations to the Privacy Act "compatible purposes" provision. The recommendations of the Privacy Commission would have been less likely to remain in the legislative limbo to which they have been consigned. Systems like TECS and the NCIC would not have grown as they have, largely unscathed by privacy considerations.

Such a body could unquestionably address an urgent need to politicize privacy issues, so that the choices involved are made in the fullest public awareness of what is at stake. The greatest losses to privacy typically occur under the cloak of bureaucratic "business as usual." Thus the public suddenly finds itself confronting systems like TECS, billed simply as a way of doing more of what federal agencies had been attempting all along.

Thoughtful citizens will always have diverse reactions to the public choices posed by privacy-relevant practices. There is simply no reason to assume that full consideration of such practices in advance will result in easy or unanimous directions for policy—if anything, quite the contrary. Such decisions, however, should not be made by default. Privacy advocates can ask for no more than the opportunity to place their case before the public. Creation of a permanent privacy-protection institution would assure that chance.

The Values of Privacy

The evolution of privacy debates forces us to consider fundamental values; ironically, these debates have often failed to articulate the essential public "goods" and "bads" at stake.

Many public pronouncements on privacy suggest a simplistic conclusion: the only reasonable objections to the growth and working of personal data systems have to do with their accuracy, fairness, and due process guarantees, and with their efficiency in accomplishing what organizations intend for them to accomplish. This view is deeply flawed. At some point personal data management simply becomes too sweeping and too intrusive in itself, regardless of how strong the procedural guarantees shaping its functioning. No one would want to live in a world where *all* personal information were held in file and shared for use by all interested organizations, even by all organizations that used such data for ostensibly "acceptable" purposes. We simply find some forms of monitoring excessive, even when undertaken in a "good cause." The problem is the difficulty in specifying the point of unacceptability.

Consider the systems discussed above for monitoring the movements of persons entering this country. Some Americans may object to such monitoring, since it applies primarily to persons not guilty of any crime or other infraction. Others find the system uncontroversial, arguing that no harm is done to those whose movements are thus recorded, and perhaps adding that immigrations officials have always had the right to note who enters and leaves the country.

What if such a system were extended to internal monitoring? Imagine that everyone crossing a state boundary within the United States had his or her name and the time and place of the crossing noted for the benefit of potentially interested government agencies. Would such monitoring of previously private activity seem excessive? If not, what if technologies were available to note crossings of county, municipal, or electoral precinct boundaries or simply crossing the street?

One can readily imagine how information generated in such monitoring could enhance the efficiency of many organizations, including law enforcement agencies, the Internal Revenue Service, or public welfare systems. At some point of frequency and intensity, however, monitoring simply becomes excessive, no matter how discreet, how fair, or how efficient. One reason is that it would rob us of the experience of privacy that most people cherish; another is that a system powerful enough to perform this sort of surveillance is too powerful for comfort—too potentially destructive, should it be used for abusive purposes.

A first line of attack by privacy advocates against new or existing personal data systems has often been that the systems do not accomplish what they are supposed to accomplish or do not do so efficiently. Thus, early critics of consumer credit reporting scored easy points by noting that credit reports often contained erroneous information that, in the absence of scrutiny by the individual concern, spread destructive effects for long periods without check. Similar in spirit are objections to computer matching programs on grounds of their cost effectiveness. Many of these programs, it is alleged, do not recover enough monies to warrant the investments made in them.

Such charges have often been accurate enough; in the longer run, though, they tend to backfire on those who make them. The response of system proponents has often been determination to ''reform'' the systems in question. Indeed, much privacy protection law and policy can be seen as just such a step. Responding to criticism that systems are inefficient and ridden with erroneous data, aggressive managers set to work to make them fairer, more open, and more effective. The result, in the long-run, is more—and more thoroughgoing—institutional record keeping. Critics, having objected on grounds that the systems are inefficient or unfair, can hardly object when they are made to work more effectively.

In debates over "privacy protection," as so often elsewhere, ordinary language provides instruments too blunt for the task at hand. Thus we often speak of protecting privacy as though there were some a priori distinction between personal information that is of inherent public interest and that which is fundamentally and immutably private. In fact, such distinctions are forever reshaped by social practice. Information that people once thought profoundly private—the biochemical properties of their bodily fluids, for example, or the details of their domestic finances or their political beliefs—are now of fundamental interest to various agencies. As such interest becomes the basis for more and more efficient bureaucratic practices, the realm of what was considered private is steadily reduced.

There are no "natural limits" to the areas of social life or private personality that might become subject to monitoring via record systems of the sort discussed in this chapter. Technological change and management ingenuity promise to keep turning up new, more efficient uses for personal data. Urgent public outcries for the control of threatening social conditions, from AIDS to international terrorism, help spur further innovation in monitoring and control of human behavior.

The only limits to unending extension of such monitoring are ones created by deliberate human decision. Only by deciding, through the fullest public debate, when systems of personal information management are too intrusive or too potentially overwhelming can intelligent limits be placed on their growth. The history of these controversies is scarcely rich in such decisions to limit the proliferation of potentially useful data systems. But if we hope to do more justice to the logic of privacy protection and to its original inspiration, we cannot avoid considering the hard questions that might lead to setting such limits.

The Right to Know:
Public Access to Electronic Information

||||||||||||||||||||||||||||||||||||||||||||||||||||||||||||||||||||||||||||||||||||||||||||||||||||||||||||||||||||||||||||||||||||||||||||||||||||||||||||||||||||||||||||||||||||||||||

Jerry J. Berman

The "public's right-to-know" about the business of government is a fundamental principle of our democratic government and open society. In the present era of computerized government information, this right will only be ensured if public law and policy guarantee and expand citizen access to electronic public information.[1]

Over the past two decades the federal government has systematically exploited computer and communications technology to conduct its business more effectively, efficiently, and economically. In the process federal agencies have converted public information from paper documents and data files into electronic database systems. Federal agencies routinely manipulate this computer data to fulfill agency missions from determining the taxes owed by citizens to calculating eligibility for Social Security benefits. A growing number of agencies require businesses and corporations to provide data collected for regulatory purposes in electronic formats and in turn the government fulfills its information disclosure responsibilities by disseminating electronic public information through government, commercial, and nonprofit interactive computer and communications networks.

This fundamental transformation of public information and public decisionmaking into computerized data processes has occurred without serious public policy attention being paid to how it may affect the public's right to know. Moreover, there has been no public policy debate or concerted effort initiated to resolve electronic information policy issues with citizen access rights as a core concern.

This debate is of critical importance today. As federal officials tout the potential emergence of wholly "paperless" agencies by the year 2000, the laws and policies that spell out citizen access rights to government information in the age of electronic government are woefully out of date. The Freedom of Information Act, the principal federal information access statute, was enacted prior to full-scale government computerization and was crafted to resolve citizen access rights to published information or to printouts from computerized files. The Paperwork Reduction Act of 1980 was designed to streamline federal information resource management in part through increased government computerization. The act offers little guidance on how federal information management goals should be achieved in relation to public access rights to electronic information.

When these statutes were enacted, it was valid to assume that government policy did not have to consider such a right of access. The ability to own and use powerful computers capable of receiving, storing, and manipulating government electronic data was beyond the economic and technical reach of most of the constituencies that seek and use government information to conduct their business or monitor government decisionmaking. In the last several years, however, advanced computing power has been brought within the reach of most citizens and organizations who use government data. Today, small businesses, public interest groups, the press, and other users of government information do not have to rely solely on published public information or printouts of computerized government data. They possess the technical potential for receiving and analyzing electronic public information.

If this potential is to be realized, the constituencies that principally rely on published government information first need to understand their stake in achieving effective access to electronic public information. Public policy supporting citizen access rights to electronic information will not be instituted until constituencies committed to the public access rights actively work to formulate and implement such a policy.

A principal purpose of this essay is to describe through concrete examples how citizen access to computerized government data can be a powerful tool for monitoring government and private sector decisionmaking which affect important public interests. The Environmental Protection Agency's effort to implement a congressionally mandated database to disseminate information on toxic chemical emissions into the environment will provide a vivid case in point.

The case for new electronic information policy also involves public awareness of how traditional access to published government information, as well as computerized public data, may be compromised if public rights to electronic information are not instituted. As this essay documents, outmoded government information law and policies are creating new forms of government secrecy in the computer age and inequities between different constituencies in terms of their ability to afford, access, and use electronic public information.

To establish why expanding public access to electronic public information through on-line databases and other information technology mediums should be a public policy goal is only the first step. Significant legal, policy, and practical issues need to be addressed and resolved by the Congress and the executive branch before effective access will be realized. This essay attempts to identify some of the critical electronic information access issues and sets out a number of policy initiatives and proposals for addressing them. It also recommends policy initiatives to achieve the ultimate goal—an "electronic" Freedom of Information Act.

Electronic Government

The federal government is ushering in the era of electronic government by developing electronic information collection, processing, and dissemination systems. Federal government expenditures for information technology and electronic data systems are increasing at a significant rate. In 1982 the federal government spent $9.2 billion for information technology. Recent estimates indicate that expenditures for electronic data systems have now reached over $15 billion annually.[2]

As the government transforms public information into electronic formats and databases, this information is then made available to the public by government and commercial information providers. By one estimate there are over 440 government databases disseminating electronic information to the public today. The Commerce and Labor departments provide on-line databases of significant business and labor statistics and reports. The Census Bureau makes statistical data and reports available over its CENDATA system. The Commerce Department's National Technical Information System (NTIS) distributes tapes and diskettes of scientific research reports and statistics. The National Library of Medicine, a government agency which markets information in many ways similar to a commercial firm, offers a number of on-line technical information databases through its MEDLARS electronic dissemination system.[3]

Commercial information industry providers such as DIALOG, MEAD Data, and BRS are principal disseminators of electronic public information.[4] As government data increasingly resides in electronic mediums, these firms actively seek out and obtain government computerized data, add "value enhancements" to make the data more useful and "user-friendly," and sell it to commercial subscribers. They also serve as "gateways" for public systems by offering their subscribers many of the government databases available directly from federal agencies.

The development of these public electronic databases greatly enhances the ability of those who access these government and commercial systems to monitor government activity and regulatory affairs. They permit users to access time-sensitive data, search through document databases to seek out and rapidly find relevant information, and work with data subsets to perform complicated statistical and data analysis.[5]

If the federal government's development of electronic public information systems were guided by an overall policy to enhance public access, one would expect to find evidence of government-wide programs to implement electronic data systems to serve a cross-section of public constituencies. For example, one might find major electronic projects underway not only to disseminate information about business, scientific, and business regulatory affairs but also electronic data relating to government programs and decisionmaking in areas such as environmental protection, law enforcement, and occupational health and safety. In developing these databases, policymakers would be wrestling with issues of pricing to ensure that interested constituencies could afford to use these information systems. They would also be exploring necessary system requirements to make these databases readily accessible to computer users who are not proficient in computer skills.

Instead, the major federal agency electronic collection and dissemination systems under development are concentrated in the business and regulatory area. Significant federal expenditures are targeted for the development of electronic systems such as the Patent Office's Automated Trademark System, the Federal Maritime Commission's electronic tariff filing system, the Department of Transportation's International Tariff Filings, and the Security and Exchange Commission's (SEC) Electronic Data Gathering System (EDGAR). For example the EDGAR system, which will handle over 6 million pages of security filings per year, making the SEC potentially the first "paperless" agency of the future, will cost $50 million over the next five years.

While the development of these systems will serve important governmental interests, the principal government policy objective has been to improve the efficiency and cost effectiveness of its regulatory operations. Commercial markets already exist for this information vital to business and regulated industries. Such potential in turn has spurred members of the growing information industry to develop partnerships with government to design and build major systems and to structure them to develop commercial markets for this data.[6]

The government's preoccupation with cost savings over public access considerations is illustrated by its efforts to establish an Automated Trademark Office. Even though the rates charged for electronic databases are a major factor in determining who may be in a position to afford to use them, the Patent and Trademark Office tried to minimize the government's cost to develop an Automated Trademark system in a way which would make it expensive for potential users. The Patent and Trademark Office attempted to satisfy its internal needs for electronic trademark data by entering an agreement with a private information contractor under which the Trademark Office would use the system at no cost; in exchange, the private contractor would have the exclusive right to sell electronic trademark data under non-competitive conditions. This "bartering" arrangement, which had the potential for creating a private information monopoly over electronic trademark data, was successfully opposed by a members of Congress, user groups, and other information vendors.[7]

In contrast, the SEC's EDGAR system has been designed to meet government needs for electronic data but to broaden public access to EDGAR data through a diversity of information sources and competitive pricing. EDGAR, the product of give-and-take between SEC officials, the Congress, and information industry representatives, is viewed as a possible model for future electronic information systems.[8]

As structured, the SEC will expend appropriated funds to establish the basic EDGAR system. All "value-added enhancements," such as sophisticated search capabilities and menus which make the system user-friendly, will be developed by the contractor who markets the

EDGAR data commercially. However, to prevent the development of a private information monopoly and create a "level playing field" among competitors, the statute governing EDGAR mandates that other information vendors may purchase the EDGAR data at the marginal cost of reproduction, add-value enhancements; they can also market the data. It is anticipated that competitive pricing will make the system affordable to many potential users.[9]

The EDGAR system constitutes an important step in the development of electronic information policy because it avoids creating an information monopoly and ensures a diversity of EDGAR data sources. However, it does not resolve critical issues about how to design and implement electronic information systems to ensure broad public access to electronic information.

While the public at large may be uninterested in security filings and studying "10-B forms," public interest groups, investigative reporters, and academic researchers may well want access to this information. While competition among vendors may bring the cost of the EDGAR database systems within the reach of the general public, there is no guarantee that it will. If it does not, the government will have developed in effect a sophisticated information system which disseminates the most useful version of public information only to the affluent.

The EDGAR system's provision for general public access to the database demonstrates this point. Commercial users "dial-up," "download," and manipulate EDGAR data. Public users who may not be able to afford these services may use public terminals—but they are available only at SEC headquarters in Washington, D.C., and at its New York and Chicago regional offices.[10] Moreover, the system will be a basic version of EDGAR which permits reading files and searching through the database but will have none of the "value-added" enhancements, such as analysis capability which likely will be available through the commercial systems.

This system may provide adequate public access for security data. However, it will not be sufficient for meeting public access needs for the electronic dissemination of data of importance to wider public constituencies. For example, EDGAR's public access requirements would not provide sufficient public access to electronic data disseminated by agencies such as the Food and Drug Administration or the Environmental Protection Agency.[11]

The larger issue is whether electronic data systems will only be developed when the system is cost-effective because a ready commercial market exists for the information. If this is to be the case, it is difficult to foresee circumstances under which government will develop major systems on its own initiative dealing with health, education, and welfare—areas of vital public importance but where the profitability of electronic data dissemination is uncertain. In such circumstances public access and use may have to be underwritten by "fee waivers" or reduced fees similar to those available under the Freedom of Information Act.[12]

In fact, a few government agencies are making efforts to provide citizens with inexpensive on-line databases of public information and reports. These include agencies which have a statutory obligation to disseminate information to the public such as the Census Bureau, the Department of Agriculture, and the Department of Education.[13] Some agencies will undertake computer searches for citizens who lack computer skills or provide training to use their databases. Nonetheless, these systems are not the principal recipients of federal electronic information expenditures or the focus of information policy managers. The government is doing little to inform citizens about these programs or to make them readily accessible. It does not even provide a printed or computerized listing of available government databases. Thus, a computer user may be surprised to learn that some government databases may be directly available from an agency at half the price of accessing these same databases through a commercial network.[14]

The federal government will not develop government-wide electronic information systems for broad public information by itself. The public will have to demand access rights to electronic government information and address the legal barriers and public policy assumptions which today limit their ability to share in the benefits of the emerging electronic government.[15]

Legal and Policy Barriers

American citizens have broad statutory rights to the access of published government information but no clear right to electronic public information. The Freedom of Information Act, the principal statute establishing citizen rights to public information, was enacted in 1966 and significantly amended in 1974. While the legislation was considered when the government was in the process of computerizing its internal operations, it was not contemplated that the computer revolution would soon give citizens the capability to access and use computerized public information. Thus, the provisions of the act are crafted exclusively in terms of citizen access to published data. While the legislative history of the 1974 amendments deal with government computerization, the drafters did so only to make it clear that the act required federal agencies to conduct reasonable searches of their computerized databases and produce "printouts" of public records subject to disclosure under the act.[16]

The 1980 Paperwork Reduction Act guides government computerization. The act, designed to minimize the federal paperwork burden on citizens and "minimize the cost to the Federal Government of collecting, maintaining, using, and disseminating information" encourages federal agencies to use advanced computer and communications technology to accomplish these missions.[17] In its statement of purposes the act does not mention using this technology to enhance public access to information in the computer age. The aim of federal information technology management is to "ensure that automatic data processing and telecommunications technologies are acquired and used by the Federal Government in a manner which improves service delivery and program management, increases productivity, reduces waste and fraud, and whenever practicable and appropriate, reduces the information processing burden for the Federal Government."[18] Under the act the authority to develop and implement "uniform and consistent information management policies" is vested in the Office of Management and Budget's Office of Information and Regulatory Affairs (OIRA). In December 1985 OIRA published its final version of OMB Circular A-130, "The Management of Federal Information Resources," which sets out current federal information policy assumptions, procedures, and guidelines.[19]

As a statement of federal government management policy on electronic collection and dissemination, Circular A-130 adheres to the mandate of the Paperwork Reduction Act. It recognizes the value of the public's right to know by stating that "knowledge of their government" is essential for citizens and a means for ensuring "the accountability of government," and states that "the free flow of information from the government to its citizens and vice versa is essential to a democratic society." But the federal information management policy set forth in Circular A-130 assumes that the public's right to know is satisfied by access to published information.[20]

Circular A-130 defines access to information as the function of providing citizens, "upon their request," government information which they are entitled to under law. In managing federal information resources, Circular A-130 states that this "right to access government information must be protected."[21] However, the Freedom of Information Act does not establish a clear public right of access to electronic data. While judicial interpretations of the FOIA have held that computer data may be subject to the act, the courts have ruled that the government is not obliged to provide citizens with the electronic version of public information. If the information is available in published and electronic format, the government may choose which to provide in fulfilling its FOIA responsibility to respond to citizen requests for public record information.[22] Only one federal statute—Title III of the 1986 Superfund Law—explicitly requires the federal government to make electronic public information available to the public on-line and through other electronic information technology.[23]

The public policy implications of Circular A-130 are significant, since OMB's information resource management policy objectives include the active encouragement of federal agencies to develop electronic database collection and dissemination systems for their internal purposes and for disseminating information to the public. However, under this circular the justification for developing electronic information systems is to achieve government efficiency and cost savings rather than to expand the public's right to know:

> Over time, changes in laws, economic conditions, or information technology can result in changes in public demand, public purpose, or dissemination costs; for example, an agency's shift to electronic filing of reports, perhaps carried out primarily in order to improve internal information management, might generate a public demand for electronic dissemination that could be satisfied at minimal cost to the government and also improve the performance of the agency's information access function.[24]

To achieve cost savings and efficiencies A-130 requires federal agencies to place "maximum feasible reliance on the private sector for . . . dissemination of [information] products and services." Before agencies embark on developing electronic information systems, they also are required to examine private sector services to avoid possible duplication.[25]

While the requirement that federal agencies rely on the private sector for the development of information products and services has been criticized by some as detrimental, in and of itself, to public information rights, this is not the principal policy barrier to advancing public information access rights.[26] The private sector information industry may in fact develop or offer more economical and useful information products and services than the government develops on its own. Rather, the fundamental barrier to public access to electronic information is A-130's requirement that "where the information is already substantially available in printed form, agencies may consider dissemination in electronic form to be a service of special benefit the costs of which should be recovered through user charges."[27]

This, in effect, articulates a public policy which permits the development of electronic information dissemination systems structured to obstruct public access. To minimize the cost to the government of electronic information systems, costs are passed to the end-users. While this can create price barriers, government policy assumes that access rights are not infringed or affected because "the information is already substantially available in printed form."

Under Circular A-130 the only circumstances under which a government agency is obliged to make electronic data readily accessible to the public through fee waivers and reduced charges is when an agency has "a positive obligation to place a government [information] product in the hands of certain specific groups or members of the public and also determines that user charges will constitute a significant barrier to discharging this obligation, the agency may have grounds for reducing or eliminating its user charges for the product or service, or for exempting some recipients from the charge."[28] Since there are no general statutory requirements for federal agencies to disseminate electronic information to citizens when a printed version is available, the policy is inoperative.

In addition, Circular A-130 assumes that depository libraries serve as an information "safety net" for the citizenry: "The depository libraries provide a kind of information safety net to the public, an existing institutional mechanism that guarantees a minimum level of availability of government information to all members of the public.

Providing *publications* to the depository libraries program complies with the law and costs executive agencies virtually nothing."[29] However, in the context of present federal policy the "safety net" is shredded from the outset. The definition of "publication" in A-130 does not include electronic data tapes, diskettes, or other electronically formatted information products. In effect, federal agencies are merely required to supply paper documents to the depository libraries.

Government Secrecy in the Computer Age

The failure to establish or clarify citizen access rights to computerized data has a negative impact on the public's right to know. Public policy barriers can deny many citizens effective access to public information which the government affirmatively makes available through electronic databases. The uncertainty of citizen rights to computerized data also acts as a legal impediment to citizen access to both published and computerized versions of government information and transactional data which federal agencies do not want to make public or only consider making public under specific circumstances.

Transactional data concern the ways government "transacts" its affairs—from dispensing welfare to meeting its legal mandate to collect taxes or clean the environment. It is the kind of information sought under the Freedom of Information Act and is critical to protect open government and ensure government accountability. However, because the disclosure of this data often subjects the government to public criticism, agencies often attempt to resist citizen efforts to make it public by claiming that it is "exempt" from disclosure under the FOIA.[30]

Thus, the government uses computerization and the uncertain status of citizen access rights under the FOIA as a means to keep information secret, both in published and computerized form. A "technology of freedom" threatens to become a "technology of secrecy."[31]

Traditional Access Rights and Computer Secrecy

The federal government uses the fact that transactional information is stored in databases which require new programming or complex computer queries to extract it as a roadblock to access. Some sensitive transactional data is no longer readily accessible from agency "records" subject to disclosure under the FOIA.

The potential for a new form of secrecy in the computer age was broached as early as 1974. In "The Technology of Secrecy" Alan Westin observed that in computerizing its operations, the government was not concerned about the impact of computerization on public access to information. He determined that while computerization was making it no more difficult, and sometimes easier, for agencies to meet citizen demands for information under FOIA, these public access results were "essentially by-products of the primary goals of improving data services to clients and management. Improving the production of information to other parties, such as the press or public interest groups investigating government operations, was not a goal of computerization. Several of the agency replies stated this explicitly."[32]

Westin suggested that unless government made public access a goal of computerization by insuring that computers were programmed to extract information valuable to citizens, it was possible that citizens would not achieve the benefits of computerized information processing but instead would encounter new forms of government secrecy. To illustrate the positive case for access to computerized information, Westin used an example of data that would have been "difficult if not impossible to get from the previous manual file."

> When the Nader Congress project was under way in 1972, the researchers wanted to find out what stocks were owned by each Congressman and candidate for Congress in 1972. But Mr. Plesser noted, "We would have had to go through 10,000 files to get the names." However, the Nader group learned that the SEC had a name-access program for this ownership file, and asked to have a list compiled of each Congressman and candidate for Congress in 1972. . . . [T]he Nader group persuaded the SEC to supply the list, and it aided the Nader Congress research greatly.[33]

Westin also illustrated the possible negative implications for public access were government computers not programmed to respond to specific citizen requests for information:

> [T]he Nader associates [Plesser and Harrison Wellford] cited several examples where files had been computerized, but the absence

of a software program to produce the desired information prevented them from obtaining the data they needed. . . . [One] example involved meat-inspection reports and pesticide data. The Center for Responsive Law won the right to inspect these at the Agriculture Department. Some of these data were computerized, but when the Center wanted information on a statewide basis, it was told that it would require costly reprogramming which, Mr. Wellford observed, was "beyond our ability to pay."[34]

As Westin emphasized:

The Nader group experience underscores the fact that more information of the kind sought by public interest groups is potentially available in the computerized files than had been provided in manual records. But where the agency has not provided software programming to extract what these groups want, it is not yet clear under interpretations of the Freedom of Information Act whether a demand can be made that such expensive reprogramming, often interfering with vital computer services, can be required of the government.[35]

If citizens could not demand access to computerized data as a matter of right, or if government did not make it a public policy objective to develop computer systems to enhance citizen access to information, Westin feared that advancing computerization of government operations might continue to be "a case of lost opportunities and . . . potentially great danger" to the public's right to know.[36]

When Congress amended the Freedom of Information Act in 1974, the final statute did not require the government to program its computers to ensure that public information would always be available. Although such legislation was proposed by Senator Lee Metcalf (D.-Mont.), it was not included in the final amendments to the act.[37] While the legislative discussion made it clear that agencies would have to search through computers for "records" subject to disclosure, neither the act nor the legislative history dealt with citizen access rights to transactional information which reside in a pool of computer data rather than the computer equivalent of a manual record file and which would require new software programming or complex computer manipulations to make it available in ways responsive to citizen requests.

Westin's concerns have even greater resonance today.[38] Citizens concerned about health, safety, and other public matters have discovered that the computer can become a "black hole" for contested public information.

Recently, Public Citizen filed an FOIA lawsuit against the Occupational Safety and Health Administration (OSHA) to challenge its withholding of public information on grounds that it would require reprogramming to access it. Public Citizen describes several instances in which citizens have sought records from regional offices of the OSHA relating to such matters as inspection data on companies within a certain geographic region only to be informed that the documents no longer existed in published form or, if they do, are more readily retrieved from OSHA's central computers operated by OSHA's Office of Management and Budget Data Systems (OMBDS).[39]

OMBDS took the position that to access the information would require it to "reprogram" its computers. Federal agencies interpret "reprogramming" to mean the "creation" of a new record and aver that the creation of new records is not required under FOIA; OMBDS has told these requesters that they must "pay the computer programming costs which often run into hundreds and even thousands of dollars."[40] If the document existed in published form, it would not be a new record, and the requester would be entitled to a fee waiver. Public Citizen is litigating the issue of whether or not this reprogramming is a reasonable search within the meaning of FOIA and thus required to be conducted without cost to the requester.

OSHA acknowledges that "[w]here information is sought by occupational hazard or subject matter investigation . . . information cannot always be produced with existing agency programs." The public policy question that must be resolved is whether OSHA, or any other government agency, can "turn its computer system into a black hole for information that would otherwise be accessible under the FOIA."[41]

Officials at the Department of Energy have denied the existence of public information on similar grounds. The National Security Archive learned that the Department of Energy (DOE) maintains reports on microfiche and requires recipients to "agree to limit access . . . only to those persons and organizations authorized to receive them." The archive filed a FOIA request for the list on the grounds that this was public information subject to the Freedom of Information Act. DOE responded that "there is no list that covers the items."[42]

When the National Security Archive pressed its case, it transpired that the "limited access list" could be produced, but not without reprogramming DOE computers to retrieve it. On appeal the Department of Energy's Office of Hearings and Appeals held in favor of the National Security Archive and ordered the list produced on the grounds that the reprogramming was a reasonable search under FOIA.[43] Nevertheless, the troubling issue is the initial "no record" response to the archive's request. Unless computer programming issues are resolved by the courts or by law, this can become a common agency response to requests for information under the FOIA in the computer era and signals the emergence of a new form of government secrecy.

Government Secrecy and Electronic Data

In an era of personal computers and complex search software programs, new computer age investigators and government "watchdogs" are requesting access to electronic public data from the government to monitor and investigate government decisionmaking. For example, Susan Long, director of the Center for Tax Studies at the University of Syracuse and David Burnham, an investigative reporter, are seeking to establish an institution to gather important government transactional electronic data to study government operations and to make both their analyses and the data available to other reporters, researchers, and citizens interested in government decisionmaking.[44] Without an established legal right of access to computerized public information, such efforts may be compromised. Government, resistant to citizen probes of the inner workings of government, has fought diligently to block citizen access to computerized information.[45]

Litigation has been necessary to win access under the FOIA to computerized "transactional information" from the IRS. In 1979 an important case provided access to the IRS computer program which determines who will be audited.[46] Using the computer tapes for analytical purposes, the Center for Tax Studies has demonstrated that the mathematical formula which the IRS uses to select returns for audit does a poor job. In another study computer analysis showed that citizens in one part of the country are more likely to be audited than in another.[47]

The government, however, won a Ninth Circuit Court decision denying access to computer data concerning other tax information. The decision was based in part on the government's contention that the request for the data without personal identifiers to protect citizen privacy required reformulating the information and therefore required the "creation" of a new agency record which is not required to be disclosed under the FOIA.[48] Assuming that privacy rights could be protected, the only logical reason (cost notwithstanding) that the government fought the case is its fear of what citizens might learn from this data.

The federal government's recognition of the power of computers to delve into public records and its concomitant fear of public access to sensitive information is best exemplified by recent restrictive efforts in the name of national security and other federal interests. In September 1984 President Reagan issued a secret National Security Decision Directive (NSDD 145) that gave the Department of Defense (DOD) government-wide responsibility to protect telecommunications and computer security.[49] In 1985 a DOD official testified that the genesis of NSDD 145 was the recognition that "virtually every aspect of government and private information is readily available to our adversaries—unfriendly governments and international terrorist organizations are finding easy pickings in the flood of unprotected telecommunications and automated data processing information afloat in this country."[50] In an interview with the *Washington Post* the same official expressed other worries: "I'm very concerned about what people are doing—and not just the Soviets. If that means putting a monitor on Nexis-type systems, then I'm for it. The question is how do you do it technically without unnecessary interference."[51]

Pursuant to NSDD 145, the government issued a National Telecommunications and Information Systems Security Policy, defining "unclassified sensitive information" broadly to include

> information the disclosure, loss, misuse of which could adversely affect national security or other Federal Governmental interests. National security interests are those unclassified matters that relate to the national defense or the foreign relations of the U.S. Government. Other government interests are those related, but not limited to the wide range of government or government-derived economic, human, financial, industrial, agricultural, technological, and law enforcement information, as well as the privacy or

confidentiality of personal or commercial proprietary information provided to the U.S. Government by its citizens.[52]

At the same time, DOD officials announced that in order to limit foreigners and citizens from using computers in ways which might adversely affect federal interests, they were not only considering monitoring who uses government and commercial computer systems but

> limiting the availability of on-line data in government databases; placing selective limits on who may access government databases; refusing to release or sell . . . [some] . . . data in electronic form; licensing government database information subject to restrictions on access or further dissemination; contracting with private database companies to provide database services subject to restrictions on access or further dissemination; . . . [and] . . . reclassifying data already disseminated to private data vendors.[53]

Congress and a broad public interest and information industry coalition roundly condemned NSDD 145 and DOD's plans as a threat to the free flow of information. As a consequence, the policy directive defining unclassified sensitive information was rescinded and legislation was passed to restrict DOD's authority to set computer security policy for unclassified data systems.[54] The government also retreated from implementing the proposals to limit access to computer data.

Nevertheless, the government might again claim authority to impose such access restrictions. For example, it might take sensitive technical database tapes off the shelf of the National Technical Information Center or use licensing schemes to restrict public use of computerized data—exercising what amounts to de facto copyright controls over public information.[55] It could base such actions on case law which suggests that electronic data is exempt from the FOIA or that the public is not entitled to data in electronic form if a hard copy is available. In fact, the Department of Commerce attempts to limit through contractual arrangements the sale of database services to companies likely to transfer the information to any foreign third party and the National Library of Medicine offers public information databases to the public under licensing restrictions similar to those used for copyrighted materials.[56]

Democratizing Access to Electronic
Public Information

The ultimate case for establishing a legal right of access to electronic data is to enhance the public's right to know. Since most citizens have not used on-line government databases, they need concrete examples to show why acquiring rights of access to electronic public information is a matter of what Alexis de Tocqueville termed "self interest rightly understood."[57] The best illustration can be found in new regulations which mandate, as a matter of law, that the Environmental Protection Agency (EPA) must make significant transactional information on toxic chemical emissions into the environment available to all citizens by electronic means. The statute's provisions, the process EPA is following to deal with information providers and potential users of the database, and the way in which significant policy issues are being identified and resolved are important precedents for developing federal information policy in the era of electronic government. These developments are also potential guideposts for future efforts to establish rights of access to electronic public information.

The TRI Database

In 1986 Congress passed the Superfund Amendments and Reauthorization Act (SARA).[58] Congress was determined to strengthen the power of states, localities, and citizen organizations to force government and industry to clean toxic waste dumps and prevent future disasters. As part of SARA, Congress passed Title III, the "Emergency Planning and Community Right to Know Act of 1986."[59] Title III establishes statewide and local community emergency planning agencies and includes a number of important industrial information reporting and disclosure requirements to provide both government and citizens with information about toxic chemicals in the environment. Over 30,000 industries are required to file reports on their storage and use of over 300 toxic substances. They must state how much and in what manner these toxic substances are emitted into the environment on an annual basis.[60]

The act includes the first federal statute requiring a federal agency to collect significant public data and to disseminate it to citizens by electronic means. The EPA administrator is required to "establish and maintain in a computer database a national toxic chemical inventory based on data submitted to the Administrator under this section. The Administrator shall make these data accessible by computer telecommunications and other means to any person on a cost reimbursable basis."[61]

While other federal databases are "accessible" to the public on a "cost reimbursable basis," the SARA Conference Report makes clear that Congress intends EPA to develop the national toxic chemical database (now referred to as the Toxic Release Inventory or TRI Database) principally to accomplish Title III's "community right to know" objectives rather than goals of economy and efficiency. The SARA Conference Report states that while the administrator may charge "user fees" for accessing the database, they must not be "prohibitive." More important, like the Freedom of Information Act, the Congress encourages EPA to establish a "reduced or fee waiver" policy for certain requests which are "in the public interest." To protect traditional access rights the Conference Report states that "other means" includes "responding to reasonable requests for printouts of data for those who do not use or choose not to use computers."[62]

In an interview in *Chemical Times and Trends* Charles Elkins, director of the EPA Office of Toxic Substances and the official in charge of implementing the TRI Database, describes TRI in these terms:

> The program is quite revolutionary when you think about it. We have never had . . . (this) . . . kind of information, even here at EPA. As it is said, "information is power," and these data will give citizens more power over toxics in their environment. . . . Specifically, we are looking for the ability for people to sit at their computer terminals, dial up this database from anywhere in the country, and be able to not only look at each individual emission report, but actually analyze the data. So they could ask questions like: "How many tons of carcinogens are released in the air in my community?" Or "how does company X compare to the companies in its standard industrial code?"[63]

As Elkins observes, the TRI Database has the potential to alter traditional power relationships between government and citizens. In the past citizens had to rely on EPA analyses of environmental problems and issues. Title III "really turns this process upside down": "EPA collects the data, puts it up on the computer and people analyze it any way they want to. There will be no EPA press release or 'editorial' from EPA. That's the way the statute was written, and our assistance to the community in understanding the data will have to be supplementary to this primary task."[64] Citizens will now be able act independently of EPA by using the TRI Database: a newspaper reporter could access the computer, issue queries about a company in a particular location, sort the data in a number of ways, and create unique reports for a story. Under the headline "Local Plant Dumps Toxic Chemicals in Crystal River" the following hypothetical story could appear:

> The ABC Manufacturing Co. in downtown River City dumped more than 200 tons of toxic chemicals, including several cancer-causing substances, into the Crystal River last year according to reports made public yesterday by the U.S. Environmental Protection Agency. The river is the major source of drinking water for River City and most of surrounding Utopia County. The reports also show that ABC, a leading producer of chrome-plated industrial widgets, released nearly 50 tons of toxics into the River City's air in 1987, and sent another 300 tons of potentially poisonous material to the Utopia waste-treatment plant for disposal. Last year, the plant reported to EPA that it stores more than 1,000 tons of hazardous substances within a few blocks of River City High School. On three different occasions over the past six months, plant accidents have released clouds of hazardous and toxic chemicals into the surrounding neighborhoods.[65]

While citizens could report independently on "Crystal River," chemical companies and other industrial firms could produce computer reports to prove that they are obeying the law.[66]

If the TRI Database works as described by EPA, it has enormous precedential value for charting the future course of the public's right to know in the electronic age. If it empowers citizens concerned about toxic waste, a public demand may develop to replicate the TRI Database to disseminate other important environmental data. The public might also demand similar databases at other agencies.

Public Access Policy Issues

Before any of these demands for electronic public information can be met, significant policy issues must be resolved. As EPA's effort to develop the TRI database demonstrates, demanding access to electronic public information is only the first step toward making computer data readily and easily available to citizens.

EPA's Office of Toxic Substances has been working to resolve a number of significant information technology policy and technical issues posed by the TRI Database. Without precedent in federal law or practice, EPA must determine how to satisfy the congressional mandate requiring that the TRI database "shall . . . [be] accessible by computer telecommunications . . . to any person on a cost reimbursable basis." EPA must develop a cost-effective system which is accessible to citizens at rates which are not "prohibitive." This includes determining whether government or the private sector should develop the TRI Database to meet goals of economy, efficiency, and public access.

From the outset EPA's Office of Toxic Substances actively sought to involve interested parties in its deliberations. It conducted a user requirements survey, issued a public report on its plans and recommendations, and held a public hearing to solicit comments on its development options.[67] EPA regularly consulted with environmental organizations, the Chemical Manufacturers Association, and other potential users of the TRI Database to resolve conflicts and refine its system design. As a House Government Operations Committee Report on electronic dissemination systems points out, such a process maximizes the possibility that an electronic information system will serve both the needs of government and potential users.[68]

If citizens want electronic data systems to serve their needs, they must actively take part in the agency planning process. Since the enactment of Title III, a coalition of environmental groups has been meeting regularly with EPA to express their views about EPA's plans.[69] Taking a lesson from the information industry, environmentalists have brought in their own technical assistance group, the Public Interest Computer Association, to understand EPA's system specifications and to ensure that the final system will better serve user needs.[70]

On 4 March 1988 EPA issued a "Public Report for Options to Make the Toxic Release Inventory (TRI) Database Accessible to the Public." The Public Report sets out EPA's interpretation of the system requirements necessary to meet Title III's mandate that the TRI Database must be "accessible . . . to any person." It outlines the process EPA followed to explore both government and private sector options for developing the TRI Database, and it sets out the factors incorporated in EPA decisions.

The Public Report states that EPA explored the feasibility of meeting system or user requirements at three levels of service: "System requirements were considered in three tiers, i.e. Tiers A, B, and C, where Tier A requirements represent the minimum requirements mandated by legislation and/or specified by EPA, and Tier B and C requirements represent optional enhanced characteristics which are desirable for the TRI public database to enhance data utility and analysis and display characteristics."[71] In common parlance these levels of service may be described as basic, enhanced, and user-friendly. At Tier A the system would be "accessible," have "aggregation capabilities," and include "search and retrieval" software and minimum "user support." At Tier B users would have in addition "statistical analysis software" and access to "complementary files" for doing more complex analyses. At Tier C the system would have "menu driven screens," "mapping capabilities," and "crosslinks to EPA databases."[72]

After establishing system requirements, EPA determined the most efficient and cost-effective way to develop the TRI Database. After determining that existing systems were too expensive or inappropriate for the TRI Database, the EPA explored four options.

The EPA considered contracting with the private sector by placing a notice of system requirements in Commerce Business Daily and entered into discussions with two commercial information providers. It also explored system development through Purdue University, a nonprofit institution, and considered establishing its own electronic clearinghouse. Finally, it examined the possibility of setting up the system through an interagency agreement with the National Library of Medicine (NLM). Throughout, EPA considered cost to the government, cost to the user, the risk of delays or problems in contracting and implementation, and conformance to system requirements.[73]

The Public Report recommends establishing an intergovernmental agency relationship with the National Library of Medicine. Initially, NLM will provide service essentially at the basic level; at the same time, EPA will make the database tape available through the Commerce Department's National Technical Information Service (NTIS) to "encourage" the private sector to develop alternative TRI database systems.[74]

EPA chose NLM because, compared to other system options, it permits "enhanced" service to users at the outset, despite funding constraints. Unlike the EPA clearinghouse or private vendor options, NLM will provide users of the initial system with access to "complementary files" of "health and environmental effects data" and more user training and support. Given the complexity of this new technology, EPA's commitment to develop an enhanced or user-friendly database is critical.

Resolving System Requirements Issues

The Public Report does not provide sufficient detail to permit informed public judgment about its accessibility. Although EPA is proceeding with an interagency agreement with the National Library of Medicine to implement the TRI Database, neither the Public Report nor EPA's preliminary EPA/NLM interagency agreement contains sufficient information or system design specificity for the public to determine whether EPA's recommendations are cost-justified or reasonable.[75] Neither the public nor EPA is in a position to judge whether the NLM system will meet either public needs or EPA's expectations.

For the general public the fundamental issue is whether the TRI Database will function in the manner described by EPA. Will an environmentalist, local government official, or newspaper reporter be able to "dial up" the National Library of Medicine and query the database in the way described by the director of the Office of Toxic Substances? The generality of EPA's Public Report makes it difficult to determine the soundness of EPA's recommendations.

In fact, Tier A may be useless for most citizens. At this level of service citizens may "access" data but only with search and retrieval software based on Boolean logic and without menu driven screens, cross links to other data files, or much user support. As EPA concedes in its draft interagency agreement "It is recognized by both the EPA and the NLM that two levels of users (novice and sophisticated) will want to access the TRI database. While the current user training services and search guides offer excellent assistance to searchers comfortable with searching online systems, additional training which addresses the novice or new searcher will need to be developed."[76]

Yet EPA's justification for limiting the system within budgetary constraints is not clearly supported by its cost estimates. According to the Public Report's summary of costs, the National Library of Medicine option at Tier A is estimated to cost $437,686 for the first year. At Tier C the cost would be $742,686, a difference of only $305,000. Averaged over a five-year period, the cost difference between Tier A and a user-friendly system is estimated to be only $85,000 per year.[77] In fact, developing a user-friendly system at the outset may even prove less costly because it will increase system use by making it more accessible to the public.[78] Given a congressional appropriation of $10 million to implement Title III—with only a fraction necessary to make the computer system accessible—EPA's justification for funding only Tier A service appears unreasonable.

In enacting the "Community Right to Know Act," which includes the requirement to establish the TRI Database, Congress wanted local governments, planning groups, community leaders, and environmentalists to know about toxic dangers in their communities without having to rely on EPA reports.[79] The database, as the head of the Office of Toxic Substances stated, is intended to make citizens less dependent on EPA's published reports and analyses. Unless citizens can use the database, they will continue to be dependent on EPA for data.

EPA has also indicated that "value-added" enhancements to the TRI Database are necessary to resolve its own concerns. Its officials worry that citizens may misinterpret the data by translating information about toxic "emissions" into the atmosphere directly into an indication of "exposure" levels. To help citizens understand the data analytic software must be added to the database.[80]

The failure to establish detailed system requirements not only places the public at a disadvantage in understanding the TRI Database. EPA has also failed to give NLM sufficient information for it to know what software to purchase or what programming needs to be done. If the TRI Database does not work as EPA contemplates, EPA's failure to specify system requirements may make it impossible to hold NLM accountable.

EPA is exploring further enhancements to clarify system requirements. This includes specifications covering such matters as how TRI data will be maintained, how user accounts will be administered, software design, query or menu screens, help screens, gateways to other databases, and training and technical support functions. Policy matters such as "fee waiver" standards will also need to be addressed.[81]

The development of the TRI Database has important implications for evolving public policy on government electronic information systems. EPA has demonstrated that public access rights can be achieved without sacrificing other important public policy objectives. In particular it is possible to build a public access system while giving the private information industry an opportunity to develop the system and insuring that the government does not gain monopoly control over electronic data.

Public Access Systems and the Private Sector

Under OMB Circular A-130 government agencies are required to place "maximum feasible reliance" on the private sector in developing government electronic dissemination systems to avoid duplication and to ensure that systems are developed in the most cost-effective manner. It is important to keep the government from developing databases which the private sector may establish more efficiently and effectively.

Another goal of federal information management policy is to ensure a diversity of information sources: the growth of the private sector information industry is important for the economy and a diversity of information sources is essential to ensure the free flow of information.[82] Unfair government competition may stifle the private sector and create government monopolies over information. Some contend that this policy objective can be accomplished in most circumstances by limiting the government to developing "basic" electronic databases and leaving all "value-added" services to the private sector.[83]

Fully consistent with Circular A-130, EPA gave the private sector information industry an opportunity to state their interest in developing the TRI Database by placing a notice of the system and EPA's requirements in Commerce Business Daily.[84] While two commercial firms came forward, neither was particularly enthusiastic about the TRI Database. As the Public Report suggests, their cost estimates were very tentative and higher than those projected by the National Library of Medicine and Purdue University. In fact, there is good reason to believe that the commercial firms did not believe there was sufficient government funding or potential market demand to get involved.[85]

However, the position that a diversity of information sources can only be assured if the government is limited to providing "basic" service needs to be reexamined in light of the TRI Database. Assuming that users of the TRI Database or similar government systems need a "value added" or user-friendly system, how can this be accomplished except by government initiative if the private sector does not want to compete or sees no commercial advantage in a particular database?

Since the absence of a commercial market may apply to many potential public databases relating to matters of health, safety, and welfare, the government should be able to develop these databases with "value-added" services without having to wait for a market to develop. Nor should the government have to establish that there is no likelihood that the private sector may be interested before proceeding to establish important electronic databases of government information. Following the EPA example, the government should only have to give private sector information providers an opportunity to develop the system and then resolve the diversity of sources issue by making the basic database available for private development.

The public interest is best served by this arrangement. If EPA produces a database that does not work well, there is the potential for private development of the TRI Database. In fact, other sources of TRI data should be encouraged. When sensitive data is involved, such as toxic chemical information, the government may attempt to clamp down on public access to the information. For example, the government could claim more information should be unavailable because of the need to protect trade secret information. If this occurs, the more who have a stake in the information, the better the chances are for protecting the public's rights.

Government as Electronic Publisher

While the government should be able to develop "value-added" systems, the EPA experience challenges the assumption that the government should become the principal provider of electronic public information. Although EPA chose another government agency to develop the TRI Database, it did so after rejecting the possibility of establishing its own electronic clearinghouse. In some cases relying on the government to develop a system may not resolve public access needs. According to the Public Report, creating an EPA electronic clearinghouse would have been very costly for the government and for users.

It also posed the greatest potential for delay and would prove to be the least user-friendly. A principal reason for such problems was EPA inexperience in disseminating electronic information to the public: "The EPA Clearinghouse is at a major disadvantage in regard to user support services, because support infrastructures for public database access do not currently exist within the Agency and will have to be established for this option."[86]

Never having provided citizen access to its data systems, EPA would have had to contract with commercial firms for hardware, software, and to establish a user support structure. This option would be most costly and might delay the implementation of the TRI Database: "Contract vehicles exist for most of the hardware/software proposed for the EPA Clearinghouse. However, acquisition of equipment, preparation of the facility, and development of a support group will be time consuming and has the potential to delay . . . [implementation]."[87]

If EPA built the initial Tier A basic system, as a consequence of its internal systems design, the agency would not be able to provide easy access to complementary files. Because other relevant EPA files such as the National Pollutant Discharge Elimination System (NPDES) and files on "permits, air releases, etc." are not networked within EPA, extensive costs would have to be incurred to enhance the system: "It also will require costly and extensive software development to provide access to complementary health and environmental effects files and to crosslink to other EPA files."[88]

With the clearinghouse ruled out and the commercial bids too high, EPA chose the National Library of Medicine because NLM "has had several years of experience providing user support, training, and marketing for a user community of primary health care professionals" and because it would cost less for users and provide them with ready access to complementary files.[89]

Policy Recommendations

Over the last two decades the federal government has transformed public information from paper documents and data files into electronic database systems. Government information is now being disseminated to the public through government and commercial electronic dissemination systems. Yet no serious public policy debate has taken place, and no concerted effort to resolve electronic information policy issues with citizen access rights as a core concern has been undertaken.

It is vitally important to initiate this policy debate. As citizens ply the government for information, they encounter new access roadblocks resulting from the failure to design and program government computer systems to access information. Citizens have no clear legal right to the electronic version of public data. At the same time many citizens can neither afford nor have the skills to use electronic public information disseminated by the government.

Public demand for access to electronic government information is likely to increase significantly as the "PC revolution" continues. Already, increasing numbers of citizens and organizations are using computers to communicate, analyze, and disseminate information.[90] New electronic systems such as *Reference Point* will soon make it easy for groups which have only begun to use computers to communicate and disseminate information to the public through electronic means.[91] Public access to databases will soon be facilitated when the telephone system becomes a "gateway" for electronic information services.[92] As these developments expand the capability to use databases, more citizens will want to access electronic public information.

It is therefore necessary to initiate a public inquiry and debate on access to electronic information.[93] Congress needs to explore the impact on the public's right to know of the federal government's own creation and use of electronic public information for internal governmental processes, as well as the public access implications of government electronic collection and dissemination of information. The Subcommittee on Information of the House Government Operations Committee has held initial hearings on the issue and plans to explore it further.[94] The Senate Judiciary Subcommittee on Technology and Law is another appropriate forum. Both subcommittees have jurisdiction over the Freedom of Information Act.

This policy debate should focus on both near- and long-term policies to establish public rights of access to electronic public information. A series of legislative initiatives need to be considered by both the Congress and executive branch.

Congress should establish a right of access to electronic information under the Freedom of Information Act. In doing so Congress will have to resolve a number of complex issues, including the definition of an agency record, reasonable search requirements, fee waiver policy, and the distinction between providing information and analyzing it. It must also ensure that access rights are consistent with other FOIA goals, such as protecting citizen privacy. As Congress works on these issues, some initial policy initiatives may be taken.

First, Congress could require by law that if funds are authorized or appropriated for any new internal government database system which contains public information, the system must be programmed to ensure that the information is accessible pursuant to the FOIA. All agencies who plan to upgrade an existing database containing public information with appropriated monies shall be required to expend funds to reprogram the database to make public information accessible. For systems developed or upgraded pursuant to this requirement, the government shall thereafter be required to reprogram the system at government expense to satisfy a request for information subject to the FOIA.

Second, Congress can establish a requirement that information which must be published or made available for copying under the FOIA without awaiting a request, such as agency missions, regulations, and decisions should be "accessible to any person by computer telecommunications on a cost-reimbursable basis" similar to the requirement for the EPA Toxic Release Inventory Database.[95] Third, Congress can amend the FOIA to provide that requesters under the FOIA may access *either* the printed or electronic version of information which must be disclosed under the act.

As the federal government develops electronic collection and dissemination systems, it must consider more than goals of economy and efficiency. Electronic dissemination systems must also serve to ensure and enhance public access to information.

Public access requirements may vary depending on the nature of the particular information system. For example, providing public terminals may be sufficient for the EDGAR system dealing with security filings but wholly inadequate for EPA's Toxic Release Inventory Database. One possible solution is legislation to amend the Paperwork Reduction Act or enactment of specific legislation that would change information management resource policy: first, by requiring that federal agencies consider "adequate provision for public access" as one of the factors that must be weighed in developing information system plans in addition to factors such as avoiding duplication or looking to the private sector to develop information services and products;

second, by requiring federal agencies to actively involve potential commercial and nonprofit institutions in commenting on agency information system plans both through notice in the Federal Register but also by actively seeking their participation in agency planning deliberations as EPA has done with respect to the TRI Database; third, by establishing system requirements that mandate contractors to submit plans for providing access to noncommercial users such as educational institutions, depository libraries, and other nonprofits at reduced rates. Public access requirements for specific database systems would be established through the give-and-take between federal officials, information providers, potential users, and the Congress.

In addition, enhancing citizen access to electronic public information can be accomplished by considering other initiatives. The federal government should be required to establish an electronic and hardcopy index of all public databases which describe their contents, how they may be accessed, what they cost, and what user supports are available. It should be updated annually. The electronic index should be available through the Government Printing Office, the Depository Library Program, and NTIS. The government should also be encouraged to establish government-wide open network architecture requirements and standard formats to make databases more easily accessible to citizens. In addition, efforts should be made to develop "electronic pilot projects" through the Depository Library Program. The Joint Committee on Printing, the library associations, and the information industry need to explore "new partnerships."[96] Finally, legislation can be crafted to achieve public access goals by establishing electronic databases to disseminate data on matters of health, safety, welfare, education, and other matters of public importance based on the EPA TRI Database model.

At the end of these scenarios is an "Electronic Freedom of Information Act." Citizens might then be able to dial the federal FOIA database with an index of agencies and subjects, choose an agency and receive a computer "gateway" to the agency's FOIA database. With a user-friendly menu and screen prompts a citizen should be able to access files already mandated to be made public pursuant to the FOIA. A citizen might also make an electronic request for other public information and "files" electronically maintained by an agency. Within a statutorily specified time the agency should then respond to the request by electronic mail to inform the requester that the request is granted and asks whether the requester wants the information delivered electronically or in hardcopy form by regular mail or fax. The citizen responds via electronic bulletin board that he or she wants the information electronically and enters a credit card number to have an account charged for the FOIA search and reproduction fees. The information is transmitted to the requester's computer. The citizens might also use the Electronic FOIA at public libraries and through commercial and nonprofit organizations which have used the electronic FOIA to make special collections of information on national security issues, on children's rights, or on FCC or FDA regulatory matters, or which have incorporated "value added" enhancements which permit basic information to be analyzed and compared in more complex ways.

The electronic information revolution has already inspired new legislative possibilities. As the chairman of the House Government Operations Subcommittee on Information recently stated,

[T]he new technology is putting considerable pressure on the laws that were passed to regulate Government information policy when information only existed on paper or other hard copy formats. There may soon be a need to recognize the consequences of the new technology. For example, there may be a need to pass an Electronic Freedom of Information Act in order to make certain that the benefits of broad disclosure of Government information are not lost as Government information becomes electronic.[97]

Copyright Law and Policy

Paul Goldstein

The federal government's principal role in communications policy is to foster channels of communication. The great bulk of information that occupies these channels, ranging from private telephone conversations to the exchange of business information, requires no government intervention to support its production. However, some of this information will not be produced, or will not be produced in adequate quantities, unless government provides direct subsidies or creates private property rights—specifically copyright—in the information. This essay examines the public policy issues that are likely to surround copyright law over the near and long term.

Several forms of intellectual property protection secure investments in producing information: patent and trade secret protection for technological information, trademark and unfair competition for marketing information, and copyright protection for literary, artistic, and musical works. Of these several forms of intellectual property, copyright most directly affects the information that travels the standard communication channels. Broadcast and nonbroadcast channels alike are filled with copyrighted entertainment, educational, and public affairs programming. Business and educational communications networks daily transmit copyrighted data and databases.

This essay depicts the balance that copyright law strikes between the need to give authors and their publishers sufficient inducements to produce and disseminate original literary, artistic, and musical works and the need to allow others to draw on these works for their own creative endeavors. It then examines the economics of copyright. This essay then addresses four central issues that are likely to dominate copyright policymaking over the next several decades: (1) the forms of information that copyright properly should protect—is it, for example, appropriate for copyright to protect technological subject matter such as computer programs, or is this subject matter better protected under patent law or under a sui generis scheme of protection? (2) whether and when new uses of copyright subject matter should come within copyright control—for example, should the law prohibit private photocopying or off the air videotaping of copyrighted work? (3) how the rights of United States copyright holders can and should be enforced in other countries; (4) the rights creative individuals should have in an increasingly depersonalized information environment.

Congress contemplated several aspects of these four issues in the lengthy deliberations that led to passage of the 1976 Copyright Act. In passing the act Congress resolved some aspects of these issues and deferred resolution of others. New questions have emerged in the decade since the act came into effect. Over the course of this decade the perception has grown that the pace and complexity of new technologies affecting the production and distribution of copyrighted works have outstripped Congress' ability to stay ahead of the technological curve. This essay describes the institutions and processes that policymakers have employed in seeking to adjust copyright to emerging technologies and indicates future possibilities for developing more effective processes and institutions for policymaking.

The Copyright Balance

Copyright law strikes a balance between the incentives that authors and publishers need to produce original works and the freedom that they and others need to draw on earlier copyrighted works. To give authors and publishers greater property rights than they need to produce the desired quantity and quality of literary, musical, and artistic works would impose costs on users without any countervailing benefits to society. To give fewer property rights than are needed to support this investment would grant users freer access but to works that in number and quality are less than socially desirable.

The United States Constitution reflects copyright law's balancing role by granting Congress the power to secure "for limited times to authors ... the exclusive right to their ... writings," in order "to promote the progress of science."[1] According to James Madison, copyright is a case in which the "public good fully coincides ... with the claims of individuals."[2] The United States Supreme Court has observed that "[t]he limited scope of the copyright holder's statutory monopoly, like the limited copyright duration required by the Constitution, reflects a balance of competing claims upon the public interest: Creative work is to be encouraged and rewarded, but private motivation must ultimately serve the cause of promoting broad public availability of literature, music and the other arts."[3]

The utilitarian balance of social benefit underlies virtually every aspect of United States copyright law. It should also form the touchstone for legislative decision on emerging copyright issues. Policymakers should recognize, however, that the wisdom of the copyright balance is by no means exclusive and that other values must sometimes be weighed in shaping copyright legislation. For example, a decision to extend copyright liability to home videotaping of copyrighted works may also affect the pricing of video recorders and videotapes and, consequently, incentives to invest in innovation in this hardware and software.

The Economics of Copyright

Unlike other consumer goods, information is intangible. Once information is disclosed, it can be used by anyone who gains access to it. As a consequence, the producer of information will often be unable to appropriate the value of its information. Unable to capture the value of its investment, a firm will either not invest, or will underinvest, in producing information.[4]

An information producer can partially overcome the problem of inappropriability by sequestering its information rather than publishing it, by encrypting the information or obtaining contractual undertakings of payment and nondisclosure from those to whom it discloses the information. Such measures may be effective for certain kinds of information, such as trade secrets, whose value can be substantially captured within the firm or from a small group of licensees. But self-help measures will not work for other kinds of information such as novels, musical compositions, and motion pictures, whose value lies in their widespread public use.

The fact that information is intangible also means that information is indivisible. Specifically, an unlimited number of users can consume a work without depleting the information in that work. One person's use of the information in a work will not diminish the ability of anyone else to use the information. Once information has been produced, its use by a prospective consumer may confer a benefit on the consumer without any corresponding cost to other consumers. The indivisibility of information implies that the marginal cost of access to information is zero. If the producer charges for access to the information, some consumers will not obtain access to the information, leaving them worse off.[5]

The fact that the value of information is largely inappropriable means that, absent government intervention, firms will underinvest in producing information. The fact that information is indivisible means that governmental intervention in ways that lead to a charge for access will produce a welfare loss. "Put succinctly, the dilemma is that without a legal monopoly not enough information will be produced but with the legal monopoly, too little of the information will be used."[6] Virtually every legislative debate on copyright over the past two hundred years, and virtually every legislative debate on copyright that is likely to occur in the foreseeable future, can be reduced to competing views on how best to resolve the problems of appropriability and indivisibility in copyright.

The problem of appropriability breaks down into two questions. First, to what extent will the failure to protect information against certain uses dissuade firms from producing that information? For example, while the Copyright Act proscribes the unauthorized theatrical performance of motion pictures, the act imposes no liability on the unauthorized rental of motion picture videocassettes once copies of the cassettes have been sold by the copyright owner. Does this lead to the underproduction of serious motion pictures aimed at audiences that avoid movie theaters in favor of watching rented videocassettes at home? Second, if legal protection is given, to what extent will transaction costs preclude negotiated licenses, thus impairing market signals about the appropriate direction of investment? For example, in determining whether to give a right against home videotaping of copyrighted programs off the air, the second question asks whether the cost of negotiating licenses with home viewers will be insurmountably high, depriving producers of information about those programs that home viewers most want to record.

The problem of indivisibility raises a third question. Assuming that producers would invest in producing the desired number of works without protection, should they receive protection nonetheless? If motion picture producers would still produce an "adequate" number of films without a right against home videotaping, indivisibility might argue for placing home videotaping outside the boundaries of copyright. Specifically, since the rationale for allowing producers to charge for access to information is that firms would not otherwise invest in producing information, it can be argued that information should be priced at zero in situations where firms already possess adequate incentives to produce it.

It can also be argued, however, that information producers should receive the full value of their product and should receive the sums that all users in the aggregate would be willing to pay for access to the copyrighted work. Given a choice between entitling Margaret Mitchell and her publisher to the minimum amount they would have required to write and publish Gone With The Wind—say $100,000—and entitling them to the hundreds of millions of dollars the public has been willing to pay for access to the story in all of its forms, this view would choose the higher figure. More generally, this view holds that, subject to the inability of producers perfectly to price discriminate, producers should be allowed to capture the full value of their works to all who use them.

The Direct Subsidy Alternative

One solution to the problems of appropriability and indivisibility is for government to give direct subsidies to creators and publishers to support the production and dissemination of literary, artistic, and musical works. Subsidy would relieve creators and publishers of the need to capture their investment through the price mechanism and would give consumers unlimited access to these works at no cost. Government subsidies to research and development and to the creative and performing arts are examples of the government's perception that consumers should have access to information at no cost. The subsidy solution is far from perfect. Absent a mechanism for gauging consumer demand, government may overinvest or underinvest in the production of information. Apart from the problem of obtaining the correct level of investment, there is no assurance that government will direct investment toward the information that consumers most desire. Government subsidies to the production of information, particularly literary and artistic information and information bearing on public affairs, may also jeopardize interests in free speech and press.

What Types of Information Should Copyright Protect?

The decision whether to grant intellectual property rights to a particular form of subject matter will affect the level and direction of investment in that subject matter. For example, both copyright and patent law have historically denied protection to the products of basic research—fundamental ideas, discoveries, and principles of nature —on the ground that private control of this subject matter, even where tempered by the price mechanism, will improperly curb research and development by competitors. In a world without subsidies this means that firms will invest in basic research only at a level at which they can recapture their investment through secrecy measures, through lead time in the marketplace, or as a consequence of firm scale and industry structure.[7] In a world without subsidies this also means that firms will direct their investment toward those kinds of ideas, discoveries, and principles that can most readily be subjected to secrecy, lead time, scale, or monopoly. In short, they will invest in those things from which the resulting benefits can be most easily appropriated. Recognizing these limits, and recognizing the deficiencies of intellectual property protection, Congress has generally supported basic research through direct subsidies.

The decision to protect subject matter through one intellectual property system rather than another also has implications for the level and direction of investment. A decision to protect information through trade secret law will lead to investment in subject matter that most easily conforms to trade secret law's requirements of secrecy and competitive advantage. Copyright law, to take another example, expressly excludes protection—and thus offers no incentive to investment—in any idea, procedure, process, system, or method of operation. However, this subject matter can often be protected, and thus the object of investment, under patent and trade secret law.

Although intellectual property protection presupposes that consumer demand will to some significant extent affect the direction of investment, the extent to which investment responds to consumer demand will depend upon the degree to which an intellectual property system succeeds in capturing all valuable uses of the protected subject matter. For example, patent law, with its robust array of rights to make, use, or sell protected subject matter, may more closely respond to consumer demand than copyright law with its several exemptions and compulsory licenses.

In situations where the alternatives of government inaction, government subsidy, and existing forms of intellectual property are deficient, it will sometimes be appropriate to enact a new, hybrid intellectual property system tailored to the distinctive features of the subject matter in issue and to the private and public interests at stake. Subject matter requirements and the scope of exclusive rights can in a hybrid system be carefully tailored to attract not only the appropriate level and direction of private investment, but also to assure that the existence of private property rights do not hamper further competitive investment in producing advances on the protected subject matter. Hybrid intellectual property systems are not costless, however. Apart from the expenditure of effort required to write on a clean slate, the uncertainty created by any new legal system implies both private and social costs.

In choosing between alternative approaches for attracting investment to new forms of subject matter, Congress should address four sets of questions. First, does society desire innovation in a particular form of subject matter? What level and kind of innovation does society want? To what extent is society willing to pay for this innovation, either through direct subsidy—and higher tax levies—or intellectual property—and higher prices?

Second, how much investment will be required to produce the desired level of innovation? Will government intervention be required to attract the investment needed to produce the desired level of innovation? If so, does direct subsidy offer the most efficient, and politically palatable, vehicle for investment? To what extent will investment in innovation benefit from industry structure? Will any existing system of intellectual property attract the necessary level of investment to the innovation? Will a hybrid intellectual property system attract the necessary level of investment more effectively?

Third, apart from whether government intervention is required to attract the necessary level of investment, will government intervention be required to assure the appropriate direction of investment? If government intervention is required, can direct subsidy programs be structured to respond to patterns of consumer demand? If intellectual property rights must be limited by compulsory licenses because of the problem of transaction costs, can license payments for the prohibited uses be expected to provide correct signals of consumer preference?

Fourth, what effect will the selection of one mechanism over another have on other innovative activities? For example, where subsidies unattended by intellectual property protection are employed, the resulting innovation will usually be available for other producers to use in developing their own works. By contrast, since intellectual property protection typically implies a positive price for access to the innovated subject matter, it usually creates a cost barrier to further innovation in the field. Do existing intellectual property systems correctly balance the incentives needed for investment by one firm against the deterrents to investment faced by succeeding firms? Can a hybrid intellectual property system be designed to strike the correct balance?

Two sets of constraints surround these questions. First, an economic system that favors private choice over public choice implicitly establishes a hierarchy of preferred mechanisms for attracting investment to innovation: an unregulated marketplace comes first, followed by government intervention in the form of private intellectual property rights, followed by direct subsidy. In equipoise between nonintervention and intervention through intellectual property, nonintervention will prevail. In equipoise between intellectual property and direct subsidy, the intellectual property solution will be preferred. As a practical and political matter this means that, once it is determined that government intervention is required, intellectual property will be the preferred solution unless its opponents can show that it is less attractive than the direct subsidy alternative.

Second, the nature of the empirical questions being asked, and the practical difficulties of providing answers, suggest that in the usual case intellectual property will be the preferred solution. Empirically, it will rarely be difficult for advocates of government intervention to show that some intervention is needed to obtain correct levels of investment. But, because the competing considerations are so intricate, it will often be impracticable to demonstrate empirically that subsidy is preferable to intellectual property. In factual equipoise intellectual property will therefore be the preferred choice. Three institutional considerations abet this preference for intellectual property: the committee system in Congress, the absence of an organized lobby for subsidies in this area, and Congress' relative inability to pursue detailed empirical inquiries.

Three Case Studies

Congress has not always considered the questions listed above in reaching decisions on whether and how to protect new forms of subject matter. For example, in authoritatively admitting computer programs into the subject matter of copyright in 1980, neither Congress nor the National Commission on New Technological Uses of Copyrighted Works, on whose recommendations it relied, systematically inquired into the full range of these questions.[8] Congress did, however, weigh some of these considerations in expressly rejecting copyright protection for semiconductor chip designs and choosing instead hybrid intellectual property protection in the form of the Semiconductor Chip Protection Act of 1984.[9] A brief comparison of these two legislative approaches will underline the importance of asking these questions early in the decisionmaking process. This comparison will in turn illustrate how these questions should be asked when Congress addresses the next new form of subject matter that is likely to arise on the legislative agenda—works that are created mechanically rather than through direct human intervention.

Computer Programs

The United States Copyright Office has accepted computer programs for registration as literary works since 1964.[10] Acceptance of computer programs for registration says more about copyright law's catholicity than it does about copyright law's ability to strike the correct balance between incentives and deterrents to originators and their competitors in producing computer programs. Congress and the courts have long refused to withhold copyright protection on the basis of the quality or content of a work.[11] Copyright law has protected books of nonsensical code words and business and telephone directories alongside the most elevated works of literature. Computer programs, whether written in source code or object code manifestations, easily fit within this broad conception of protectible literary works under both the 1909 and 1976 Copyright Acts.[12]

The fact that the Copyright Office already considered computer programs to be copyrightable doubtless led CONTU to recommend, and Congress to accept, that computer programs should continue to be protected by copyright. But historical accident and inertia are hardly a prescription for sound public policy. To be sure, computer programs do fit within the traditionally broad definitional confines of literary works, but the fit is far from perfect. The limited protection that copyright law has historically given to functional works is not calculated to attract investment to more than small incremental advances in software.[13] Ironically, recent judicial decisions have departed from the traditional, limited scope of protection given to functional works and have given these functional works more protection than they deserve, consequently hindering competitive efforts.[14]

The Copyright Act's life plus fifty-year term of protection far exceeds the useful life of the usual computer program. Discounting this term to its present value offers firms little additional incentive to investment *ex ante*. But the term does create considerable opportunity for *ex post* abuse by copyright owners. Because copyright is far easier to obtain and enforce than any other form of intellectual property, it enables copyright owners of computer programs to stifle competition by obtaining preliminary injunctive relief against competing works on the basis of monopoly grants that have not been subjected to systematic administrative scrutiny.

Had Congress chosen to write on a clean slate, and to enact a hybrid software statute, the act would doubtless have looked more like the patent law than the copyright law. Patent law's premise is that by setting the standards and level of protection high, inventors and firms will be inclined to invest in—because they are rewarded for investing in—only substantial technological improvements. Copyright law's premise is that by keeping the standards and level of protection low, authors and publishers will direct their efforts—and be free to direct their efforts—toward expressively different works.[15]

Semiconductor Chips

Congress took a more refined approach to the question of protection for semiconductor mask works—the designs of the intricate stencils that are used in manufacturing semiconductor chips. The Semiconductor Chip Protection Act of 1984 is a hybrid form of intellectual property protection. The act adopts some elements of the Copyright Act: it conditions protection on the work's fixation in a tangible medium, requires the work to be both original and expressive, and grants exclusive rights and remedies against reproduction, importation, distribution, and contributory infringement. But the Semiconductor Chip Act also imposes a higher standard of protection than the Copyright Act, requiring a protected work to be creative as well as original and expressive. The act's ten-year term of protection is far shorter than the copyright term, and its array of exclusive rights is more closely circumscribed than those prescribed by the Copyright Act.

The Semiconductor Chip Act's most significant departure from copyright tradition is the broad "reverse engineering" defense that it carves out from its exclusive rights. The defense astutely balances the need for incentives to investment in chip designs against deterrents to continued research and development in mask works. The most instructive aspect of this departure is the empirical premise on which Congress rested it. Congress enacted the defense largely in response to "testimony of industry representative [sic] that it is an established industry practice to . . . make photo-reproductions of the mask work in order to analyze the existing chip so as to design a second chip with the same electrical and physical performance characteristics as the existing chip (so-called 'form, fit and function' compatibility), and that this practice fosters fair competition and provides a frequently needed 'second source' for chip products."[16]

One reason that Congress took a hybrid approach to semiconductor chip mask works may have been the perception that neither patent law nor copyright law offered even barely adequate incentives for investment in chip design. The House Report on the act observed that patent law can protect basic electronic circuitry, but that the layout and design efforts involved in producing semiconductor chips will rarely rise to the Patent Act's required level of invention.[17] The House Report also observed that while the Copyright Office had registered drawings of chip layouts and masks, the Copyright Act effectively limited protection for these works to their unauthorized duplication in finished, commercially useful articles.[18]

Mechanically Created Works

Current developments indicate that automation will in the future play an important role in creating literary, musical, and artistic works. Computer programs can write other computer programs. Computers play an important role in colorizing motion pictures and may in the future substantially displace human effort. Digital sampling techniques can create entire musical compositions from shards of sound. Automation promises increasingly to displace human efforts as these technologies become more sophisticated and as pressures mount to economize on labor-intensive creative endeavors.

The day when automation will completely displace human effort in the creative enterprise is far off; indeed, it may never arrive. While computers may not completely displace human effort, they may —indeed they may already—displace economically, artistically, and legally significant elements once created by humans.

The question whether, and what form of, government intervention is needed to stimulate investment in the automation of creative endeavor can be framed in the same terms as public policy questions about investment in innovation generally. Does society desire such works? The cost savings and consequent reduction in the price of creative products suggests that at some level it does. Is government intervention needed to assure investment in these works? Although the answer is by no means clear, it seems likely that some form of intervention is needed. In light of the general preference for intellectual property over direct subsidy, intellectual property represents the more likely course for government intervention. The most pertinent question, therefore, is what form intellectual property protection should take and what the subject matter of that protection should be.

The choice for protectible subject matter is between the programs that are designed to produce creative works and the creative works themselves. CONTU concluded that copyright protection should attach only to the final creative work, relying on the assumption that computers and computer programs merely facilitate the individual artist's creation of the final work.[19] This conclusion is problematic for at least two reasons. First, once the program for producing a certain kind of work is created, little investment, apart from the cost of electricity, will be needed to produce the works themselves. Second, because of the virtually limitless numbers of works that can be created at low cost through automation, copyright in these works could severely hamper competitive activity.

Protection for the programs that create electronically produced works seems preferable to protection for the works themselves. Unlike the final creative works, which can be produced at low cost, the programs that create these works will probably require substantial investment. Indeed, the required investment may be so high that copyright, with its low level of protection, may not be the appropriate form of protection. Further, to give copyright to the programs that generate these works will, as the CONTU Final Report recognized, typically require those who disseminate the works to obtain licenses from the copyright owner of the underlying program. A hybrid intellectual property system could avoid this result, and the attendant high transaction costs, by carving out an exemption or compulsory license for certain of these uses.

The history of copyright protection for computer software and of hybrid protection for semiconductor chips suggests that, unless Congress is specially prodded to deal with the issue on its own terms, it will decline to give hybrid protection and will instead rely on a copyright solution. Like computer programs, works produced through automated techniques will doubtless fall within the catholic embrace of copyright law. Unlike semiconductor chip designs, the question of protection for this subject matter appears likely to attract no natural constituency opposed to copyright protection. Trade unions—whose writer, director, and musician members face a loss of jobs from automation—have an interest in opposing any legislation that encourages automation. But it is not clear that trade unions will choose copyright rather than collective bargaining agreements as the forum for attacking the problem.

What Uses of Copyrighted Subject Matter Should Come within Copyright Control?

From the time of the first Copyright Act copyright law has allowed consumers to make many uses of copyrighted works without compensating the copyright owner. Using a map borrowed from a friend or reading a book borrowed from a public library is of value to the user but gives no returns to the copyright owner beyond the revenues received from the initial sale of the borrowed copy. Until the mid-twentieth century the volume of these uncompensated uses was affected only by growth in the population. But the volume of these uncompensated uses has increased dramatically with the advent of new technologies for inexpensively reproducing and disseminating copyrighted works: home audiotaping and videotaping; library, educational, and industrial photocopying; and computer access and downloading from copyrighted databases. Apart from growth in absolute scale, these new uses threaten to shift the primary economic locus for the use of copyrighted works from compensated uses to uncompensated ones.

The shift in use of copyrighted works from compensated to uncompensated uses has important implications for the level and direction of investment in copyrighted works. Firms will invest no more in the production of works than they can expect to recoup from users. Yet, as the number of consumers who must pay for a work shrinks—as has happened with interlibrary "loans" of photocopied works replacing individual or library subscriptions—so may the ability to capture total revenues at earlier levels. To some extent consumer surplus among the remaining users (large research libraries, for example) may support higher prices. But some consumers will choose not to pay the higher price, thus reducing the consumer base further. Equally important, as the consumer base shrinks, signals of ultimate consumer preference inevitably weaken.

The principal hurdle to collecting revenues from decentralized uses of copyrighted works is the problem of transaction costs. The expense of negotiating a license and collecting payment will often exceed the value of the use. Congress has responded to the problem of transaction costs in three ways. First, in situations where the social value of a particular use is greater than the value of alternative uses to the copyright owner, but transaction costs will prevent the user and owner from negotiating a license, Congress has carved out several exemptions from liability. Second, Congress has prescribed compulsory licenses in four situations, enabling payments to flow from consumers to producers without the need to incur transaction costs. Finally, in circumstances where institutional or technical devices can reduce transaction costs to below the value of the decentralized use, Congress has prescribed exclusive rights against the decentralized use.

Exemptions

The 1976 Copyright Act carves out several exemptions from its exclusive rights to reproduce, distribute, perform, display, and prepare derivative works based upon copyrighted works.[20] Section 108's exemptions from the reproduction right typify the operation of exemptions generally. Section 108, particularly subsections 108(d) and (g) which exempt photocopying of journal articles in specified circumstances, strikes a balance between maintaining the appropriate level and direction of investment in these works and sustaining research activities against the dislocation and delays that would occur if researchers had to obtain a license each time they sought to make a photocopy of a journal article for research purposes.

Section 108 allows a "library or archives, or any of its employees acting within the scope of their employment, to reproduce no more than one copy or phonorecord of a work, or to distribute such copy or phonorecord" under prescribed conditions. Section 108(d) extends the exemption to copies made for library patrons and section 108(g) expressly permits "the isolated and unrelated reproduction or distribution of a single copy or phonorecord of the same material on separate occasions." This exemption does not extend to situations in which the library "engages in the systematic reproduction or distribution of single or multiple copies or phonorecords of [the] material." But a library or archives may participate in "interlibrary arrangements that do not have, as their purpose or effect, that the library or archives receiving such copies or phonorecords does so in such aggregate quantities as to substitute for a subscription to or purchase of such work."

Section 108 has not been completely successful. Considerable doubt exists over the meaning of the terms "systematic reproduction" and "substitute for a subscription or purchase." Producers and users disagree over the extent, if any, to which section 107's fair use provisions augment section 108's exemption. Even if Congress or the courts resolve both these doubts in favor of journal publishers, section 108 seems likely to lead to underinvestment in works, such as medical, technical, and scientific journals, that particularly lend themselves to photocopying rather than to perusal of purchased copies. Federal subsidies to the publication of articles in these journals already substantially displace private decisions on both the level and direction of investment in journal articles. As section 108 narrows the market for subscription purchases and correspondingly increases the market for uncompensated photocopying, this displacement will increase.

Compulsory Licenses

The 1976 Copyright Act imposes five compulsory licenses on its otherwise exclusive rights. Sections 111 and 119 specify the conditions and fees under which cable television operators and satellite carriers, respectively, may transmit copyrighted programming without the consent of the copyright owner. Sections 115 and 116 prescribe the conditions and fees for re-recording musical compositions or performing them on jukeboxes without consent. Section 118 prescribes compulsory licensing of certain works, under certain conditions, in the context of public broadcasting. Chapter 8 of the 1976 act creates a Copyright Royalty Tribunal to oversee the administration of these provisions and to review and adjust the compulsory license fees.

The problem of transaction costs may in certain cases justify the imposition of a compulsory license. But consensus politics, not market economics, animated Congress' decision to enact these compulsory licenses. Faced with a welter of contending industry, user, and regulatory interests, Congress sought a compromise lying somewhere between exclusive rights and no rights at all. The history of section 111 reflects these politics and illuminates the compulsory licensing mechanism in copyright generally.

Section 111. The earliest cable television systems consisted of prominently placed antennae connected by coaxial cable to the homes of subscribers in the surrounding area. The purpose of these early facilities was to provide television signals to locales that had been physically cut off from television. Under the prevailing business arrangements in the broadcast industry, everyone stood to gain from this new service. Television stations and networks obtain their revenues from advertisers and as a rule advertisers will pay more as the size of the audience delivered by a station increases. The interests of copyright owners generally coincided with the interests of the television stations and networks that they licensed to carry their programs. As broadcast markets and advertising revenues increased, so did the prices at which broadcasters bid for copyrighted programs.

As cable outgrew its early role of expanding television markets and increasing broadcasters' revenues, broadcasters and copyright proprietors began to perceive the threats posed by the new medium. By the 1960's cable systems were importing the broadcast signals of distant independent stations into markets that were already served by independent stations and the three networks. Cable thus began to compete with local broadcasters, capturing portions of the local broadcast market with programs received at no cost. In some communities cable systems improved the quality of local signals already being received. Cable systems also originated their own programming.

The Federal Communications Commission (FCC) at first responded erratically to complaints from broadcasters and from the copyright owners who supplied them with programming. But in 1972 the FCC settled on the regulatory approach that later formed the basis for section 111's compulsory license provisions.[21] The basic approach of the FCC regulations was embodied in the division between "must carry" signals—essentially local signals—that a cable system was required to carry and "may carry" signals that the system could, but was not required to, carry. The precise number of signals assigned to a cable system in each category was determined by a calculus of technical and economic factors. The regulations further limited distant signal carriage through exclusivity rules under which a system could not import a program if a local station was carrying the same program at the same time. These distant signal quotas and syndicated exclusivity rules were intended to substitute for copyright license restrictions.

Because the fortunes of copyright owners are in part tied to the fortunes of broadcasters, the FCC's compromise between broadcasters and cable operators was also a compromise between copyright owners and cable operators. Section 111 takes the logic of this compromise as its starting point by providing that, subject to prescribed conditions, "secondary transmissions to the public by a cable system of a primary transmission made by a broadcast station licensed by the Federal Communications Commission or by an appropriate governmental authority of Canada or Mexico" will be subject to compulsory licensing "where the carriage of the signals comprising the secondary transmission is permissible under the rules, regulations, or authorizations of the Federal Communications Commission."[22] In short, retransmission of "must carry" and "may carry" signals came within the statute's compulsory license.

Section 111(d)(1) requires a cable television system whose retransmissions of broadcast signals are subject to the section's compulsory license to deposit with the Register of Copyrights a semiannual statement of account and payment reflecting its royalty obligation. As a general rule, the cable system's royalty obligation will consist of the sum of a series of prescribed percentages—essentially based on the number of distant broadcast signals carried by the cable system—of the system's gross receipts from subscribers for the basic service of providing secondary transmissions of primary broadcast transmissions during the six-month period. Section 111(d)(3) directs the Copyright Royalty Tribunal to distribute these license fees among copyright owners "who claim that their works were the subject of secondary transmissions by the cable system during the relevant semiannual period."

The history of section 111 reveals a defect that characterizes other compulsory license systems as well. The system took on a life of its own apart from the economic realities that gave birth to it. The economic and regulatory environment of cable television has changed dramatically in the years since Congress passed the 1976 Copyright Act. The FCC's repeal of its distant signal carriage and syndicated exclusivity rules—a prospect that Congress had anticipated in section 801(b) of the Copyright Act—led to a substantial increase in the royalty rates that cable systems are required to pay under the compulsory license.[23] The commission's repeal of its "anti-leapfrogging" rules—under which a cable operator that wished to import distant signals had to take those that originated closest to the operator's market—led to the growth of superstations, local broadcast stations whose signals are retransmitted nationwide under the compulsory license.[24] The judicial determination that the commission's "must-carry" rules violate the first amendment undercut an important premise of section 111.[25]

Defects of Compulsory Licenses. The failing of copyright compulsory licenses of the sort embodied in section 111 and the four other compulsory license provisions of the 1976 act is that they contradict the historical premise that the copyright system should leave the valuation of works to private decision. Producers usually proportion their investment to the value of expected returns. Compulsory licensing undercuts this investment mechanism by placing an artificial ceiling on the amount that can be recouped in the marketplace. Since no work will attract investment in excess of the aggregate returns under the prescribed ceilings, compulsory licenses may reduce the range of differentiation among works produced.

On the other hand, even under a regime of exclusive rights, copyright does not encourage a wide range of product differentiation. Also, the statutory compulsory licenses do permit some differentiation in returns. In the case of recorded musical compositions, and less directly in the case of jukeboxes, cable television, and educational broadcasting, aggregate license fees are tied to frequency of use, thus giving the copyright owner some economic incentive to gamble on the investment required to create a popular work. Further, the act's five compulsory licenses limit only some rights in some works. No work under the 1976 act is completely circumscribed by a compulsory license. Because dramatic, literary, and pictorial works enjoy a wide array of exclusive rights, compulsory licensing for their transmission by cable and educational broadcast will in all probability not substantially affect investment in these works.

Exclusive Rights

Exemptions and compulsory licenses represent the exception rather than the rule in the United States copyright system which generally relies on private bargains under exclusive rights to reward investment in producing literary, artistic, and musical works. A regime of exclusive rights will obviously work in situations, such as the licensing of motion picture rights to a popular novel, in which the value of the transaction substantially exceeds the costs of negotiating and concluding the license. But a regime of exclusive rights can also be maintained in the face of potentially high transaction costs if institutional or technological mechanisms can reduce transaction costs to a point at which private transactions become feasible. ASCAP and BMI, the principal music performing rights collecting societies, offer prominent examples of such an institutional mechanism, while a computer-based system for monitoring, negotiating, and billing for photocopying uses offers an example of a technological mechanism for reducing transaction costs.

ASCAP and BMI: The Collecting Society Approach. The cost of negotiating individual licenses for performances of musical compositions in every restaurant, nightclub, concert hall, and ballroom in the nation would be prohibitively expensive. By 1914 writers and publishers of musical compositions concluded that, if they were to enjoy the full economic value of their performance rights, they would have to organize into a single collecting society that could, for a flat fee, offer users the right to perform any work in the society's repertory. The society would collect these fees from users and distribute them among society members. The efforts of these writers and publishers, spurred by the popular composer Victor Herbert, led to the formation of the American Society of Composers, Authors, and Publishers, an unincorporated membership association. ASCAP's eventual success invited competition, primarily from Broadcast Music, Inc., a nonprofit corporation organized in 1939 by members of the radio broadcasting industry. Between them ASCAP and BMI license the nondramatic performance rights to virtually all domestic copyrighted musical compositions.

ASCAP's and BMI's methods of operation are roughly similar. Any composer, author, or publisher who meets standards specified by the organization may become a member of ASCAP or an affiliate of BMI. The member or affiliate then transfers to ASCAP or BMI the nonexclusive right to license the nondramatic performance of the member's or affiliate's copyrighted works. The two organizations generally license these performance rights through a blanket license entitling the licensee to perform any composition in the organization's repertory any number of times over a prescribed period, ordinarily for a flat fee or a percentage of the licensee's gross revenues. Licenses to television and radio broadcasters generate the largest proportion of ASCAP's and BMI's revenues.

After deducting overhead expenses, the two organizations apportion the license revenues among their members or affiliates under a distribution schedule that accounts for both the general character and standing of the member's or affiliate's works and the average number of times the works of each were performed over the relevant accounting period as determined through a sampling procedure. ASCAP and BMI also police the unauthorized performance of their members' and affiliates' works, obtaining license agreements from copyright infringers and pursuing legal remedies against infringers that refuse to take a license.

Antitrust consent decrees, entered into with the United States government, substantially shape the operations of both ASCAP and BMI. Under the ASCAP consent decree, for example, ASCAP can obtain only nonexclusive rights from its members and cannot interfere with the right of any member to issue a nonexclusive license to any user who wishes to deal with the member directly. Further, ASCAP must offer any broadcaster a choice between a blanket license for all programming over a specified period and a blanket license for only specified programs and must set its fees for these two licenses at rates that offer users a genuine economic choice between the two forms of license. In the event ASCAP and a prospective licensee are unable to agree on a reasonable fee the prospective licensee may apply to the District Court for the Southern District of New York for determination of a "reasonable fee."[26] Private antitrust actions have also dogged the operations of ASCAP and BMI.[27]

Technological Devices. Computer storage and retrieval technologies offer an important prospect for eliminating the transaction costs of negotiating and collecting payments under copyright licenses while enabling market prices with a degree of perfection that is unattainable either through compulsory licensing or through collecting societies such as ASCAP and BMI. But technological advances may also exacerbate the problem of appropriability. Computerized access to data bases may, for example, facilitate private copying and distribution of copyrighted materials to a degree that dwarfs present uncompensated uses. Indeed, unless adequately monitored, new information technologies can virtually eliminate all prospects for controlling a work's use.

The problem of obtaining licenses for photocopying individual journal articles offers an example of how computer-based technology can reduce transaction costs. Existing database technology could substantially reduce these transaction costs once all articles published in participating journals, as well as abstracts to the articles, are included in a readily accessible database. The copyright owner of the journal or the article would attach to each of its database contributions a flag indicating to the prospective user the proprietor's election of either of two positions: its willingness to license uses at a specified rate with the rate per unit of information indicated or its willingness to haggle over price on an ad hoc basis. If the first position is taken and the price is acceptable, then the prospective user will use the information and be charged accordingly, with the system itself administering billing and crediting. If the price is unacceptable, the prospective user will presumably forego use of the identified material and seek less costly alternatives. In either case there need be no contact between proprietor and user, no search or bargaining, at any point.

If the second position is taken, the problem of transaction costs remains. But these costs will be lower than those that presently obtain. The prospective user will be provided with ready information as to the proprietor's whereabouts and its willingness to bargain — information that the user presently bears the cost of discovering. At the same time, the present transaction costs to the copyright owner, the costs of bargaining, will be unchanged. The first consequence puts the prospective user in a better position than she presently occupies; the second brings the two, owner and user, into a relationship more nearly approaching parity and probably would exert some pressure on the proprietor to choose the first mechanism over the second.

Strategies for Regulating Decentralized Uses of Copyrighted Works

When faced with the question whether to proscribe a new use of a copyrighted work or to subject the use to a compulsory license or to an exemption, Congress today tends to choose a compulsory license or exemption. The choice is understandable. Congress is concerned that, because of the problem of transaction costs, imposing full liability on a new use of a copyrighted work will effectively prevent the use and thus thwart an emerging industry. Advocates of an exclusive right can rarely offer palpable evidence to counter this concern. At best they will argue that, in theory, the failure to establish exclusive rights will lead to a decline in the production of works subject to the compulsory license or exemption.

The congressional premise that an exemption or compulsory license is needed to resolve the problem of transactions costs will often be a self-fulfilling prophecy. Once an exemption or compulsory license is given, users and producers have no incentive to form institutional arrangements to reduce transaction costs. The imposition of an exemption or compulsory license will also remove any incentive to invest in technological innovations for reducing transaction costs. Had the question of copyright liability for performances of musical compositions first arisen today rather than a century ago, it is likely that Congress would have resolved the transaction cost problem by prescribing a compulsory license for these uses. As a result neither ASCAP nor BMI would have come into being.

Any time a question arises about imposing full liability on new uses of a copyrighted work, Congress should start from the premise that an exclusive right is appropriate and should place the burden on those who oppose the exclusive right to show why transaction costs will prevent licenses from being negotiated and why technological or institutional innovations could not resolve the problem of transaction costs. Congress might in these situations also adopt certain meliorative steps to assure that transaction cost-reducing mechanisms will emerge and operate effectively. For example, Congress could adopt the exclusive right on a prospective basis, providing that the right will come into force only after a specified period from the date of enactment. This would give the interested parties the opportunity to implement the needed transaction cost-reducing mechanism. Further, and particularly in the case of collecting societies, Congress should consider altering antitrust rules that impede efficient operations.

International Enforcement

Of all the questions on the nation's intellectual property agenda, none is more important than the role the United States will play in the international copyright community in the coming decades. The United States long stayed outside the international copyright community. During its first century, as a developing country and net importer of copyrighted works, this isolationist position served the nation's economic interests. In the twentieth century, when the United States, as a net exporter of copyrighted works, first joined the international copyright community through a multilateral copyright treaty, it did so on its own terms—by joining the minimalist Universal Copyright Convention rather than the more rigorous Berne Convention.

Current concerns about the nation's trade imbalance generally, and the recognition that uncompensated uses of United States copyrighted works abroad contribute significantly to this imbalance, have increased pressures for the United States to adhere to the Berne Convention and for the government to pursue the implementation of intellectual property rights as part of the current GATT round. These concerns, together with the present disarray in the international copyright community, have also led the United States to enter into bilateral arrangements with offending countries.

The long isolation of the United States from the international copyright community, taken together with the current pressures for aggressive enforcement activities abroad, is likely to raise three policy questions between now and the end of the century. To what extent, and how, should United States domestic law be reconciled with the laws of the nation's prospective partners in Berne and in the GATT? How can effective enforcement mechanisms be designed to enable United States nationals to capture the value of their works against uses abroad? How will differences between developed and developing countries best be resolved within the new international framework?

Accommodating United States Law to Laws of Other Nations

The United States' adherence to the Berne Convention raises the question—already addressed in both houses of Congress—of the extent to which adherence requires the United States to conform its laws to the rules of the convention as exemplified by the laws of member states.[28] The problem of nonconformity should not be overstated. Ostensible departures in United States law from the norms of Berne and Berne member nations may not in fact or in practice constitute departures at all. For example, although United States law does not expressly extend protection to architectural works, the 1976 Copyright Act gives sufficient protection within the general framework of its protection of artistic works to qualify the United States for membership in Berne.[29]

It will be more important to assess how evolving Berne standards will require changes in United States law. The reason is not that noncompliance will require our exclusion from Berne. As a practical matter that seems unlikely. It is more likely that Berne standards will eventually become GATT standards, with the result that noncompliance may put the United States in violation of the GATT and subject to its sanctions.

Enforcement

Adherence to the Berne Convention does not of itself assure United States nationals that their copyrights will be effectively enforced in other Berne countries. Berne membership requires only that a country adopt a copyright law that conforms to the Berne standards and imposes no requirements respecting the operational details of enforcement. Nor does inclusion of intellectual property within the GATT agenda assure more than indirect pressures for compliance. Local rules on access to courts and limitations on civil and criminal relief, as well as different attitudes and priorities for criminal enforcement, may significantly undercut enforcement efforts by United States nationals without violating either Berne or GATT. This suggests that self-help and a closer study of local cultural and political institutions may represent the most important preliminary step to effective enforcement.

Nonindustrialized Countries

The division between nonindustrialized countries that want exemptions or compulsory licenses for certain uses of imported copyrighted works, and industrialized countries that see such exemptions and compulsory licenses as a significant drain on revenues, represents an important issue for international copyright policy. The most important methodology for the United States and other industrialized countries to adopt is one that will enable a principled line to be drawn between those uses that should be exempted or subject to compulsory licenses and those that should not. Care should also be taken to distinguish between those uses whose effects are confined to the nonindustrialized country's domestic market and those uses that, through export of copies, will compete in other markets.

In part the methodology for determining exemptions and compulsory licenses abroad can follow the methodology employed domestically, exempting or subjecting to compulsory licenses those uses that cannot be licensed because of the problem of transaction costs. But the methodology should also be capable of separating, on principle, those uses that are peculiarly essential to a foreign nation's development from those that are not. Exemptions or compulsory licenses for the former uses should be more acceptable than exemptions and compulsory licenses for the latter uses. For example, this methodology might permit compulsory license for translations of educational textbooks for certain purposes, but not for piracy of tradebooks, motion pictures, and audiotapes. Further, a line should be drawn between those uses that are likely to enhance a nation's development and those that are likely to result in the export of unauthorized works in direct competition with United States exports.

The Rights and Role of the Creative Artist

The emergence of artists' and authors' rights movements over the past decade reflects a deep-seated concern that technological advances in the publishing and communications industries have displaced creative individuals from their pivotal role in the production of art, literature, and music and have separated artists from the products of their creative efforts. Agitation for, and enactment of, moral rights statutes in several states,[30] the recent introduction of the Kennedy Bill, S.1619, to protect the rights of fine artists, the quest to redefine the Copyright Act's "work for hire" provisions, and the mobilization of authors' groups advocating a public lending right all indicate a trend that is likely to accelerate rather than abate in the coming years. Two issues —the adoption of moral rights and of a public lending right—are paradigmatic.

Moral Right

The European doctrine of moral rights consists variously of the author's right to the integrity of her work, the right to be identified as the work's author, the right to withhold publication, and the right to withdraw her work from publication. Of these four elements the right of integrity and the right of paternity are paramount and are expressly required of member states in the Berne Convention. The concept of moral rights was born in Europe and flows logically from the natural law view of author's rights followed in civil law countries. The civil law tradition stands in sharp philosophical contrast to the instrumentalist, common law tradition of the United States which takes economic incentives rather than the natural rights as its linchpin. As a consequence, efforts in the United States to protect authors' rights apart from economic incentives have been interstitial and have only approximated the European doctrine of moral right.

Efforts to create an integrated doctrine of moral right in the United States that more fully approximates the European doctrine may be accelerated by United States adherence to the Berne Convention. Apart from opposition by industry groups, any such movement is likely to encounter two doctrinal hurdles. First, copyright in the United States is the province of the federal government, while protection of reputational interests has traditionally been the province of state governments. To implement an integrated moral right at the federal level may disrupt longstanding allocations of authority in the federal system. Any such effects must be carefully weighed before moral rights are adopted at the federal level.

Second, any steps to make the moral right inalienable, as it purports to be in some civil law countries, would contradict the strong tradition of free alienability of property interests in the United States. To be sure, certain reputational rights are completely or partially inalienable under the United States legal system. But, unlike moral rights, none of these reputational rights forms the basis for important industries. Thus waivers and transfers of these rights are not needed for firms to function effectively. Any step toward inalienability should be preceded by an examination of those foreign legal systems that purport to make moral rights inalienable with an eye to determining how industries in those countries manage to operate under a regime of inalienability.

Public Lending Right

Under United States copyright law, once an author or publisher parts with title to copies of a work, he loses copyright control over the resale or lending of the work.[31] Authors and authors' groups in the United States have over the past several years sought the enactment of a public lending right under which the author would receive compensation in the form of a royalty each time his book is borrowed from a library. In one form or another a public lending right now exists in many European countries. Although the public lending right movement is presently quiescent in the United States, it may emerge again within the next several years.

Enactment of a public lending right might seem to be an appropriate mechanism for improving the level and direction of investment in literary works by capturing a greater proportion of the value of a work and providing authors and their publishers with better signals about the relative value of their works to consumers. Enactment of a public lending right for these purposes might seem particularly appropriate if modern data retrieval and monitoring technology, when taken together with sophisticated sampling techniques of the sort employed by ASCAP, can reduce the transaction costs of monitoring and allocating payments for these newly regulated uses of copyrighted works.

Despite the immediate appeal of a public lending right, any move toward its adoption should first address four questions. First, how can the public lending right be accommodated to the great tradition of free public libraries in the United States? Second, to what extent will the public lending right be an author's right, and to what extent will it be a publisher's right? For example, can an author waive or convey her right to public lending right royalties in favor of her publisher? Third, are royalties to be distributed according to use—which would follow the market model—or according to a subsidy scheme, under which royalties from more successful works would subsidize less successful works? Finally, is the public lending right to be made a part of copyright, and thus subject to the duty of national treatment as provided for by both the Universal Copyright Convention and the Berne Convention, or should it be treated as separate from copyright, thus enabling countries to compensate nationals but not foreigners?

The Structure of Decisionmaking

Leading congressional figures in copyright policymaking have recently and repeatedly painted a bleak picture of Congress' ability to resolve issues arising at the intersection between copyright and the new technologies in a manner that is at once timely and well-informed. The principal problem has been to identify and resolve these problems before the technologies that underlie them become so entrenched that principled resolution becomes impracticable. For example, by the time the question of liability for home videotaping of copyrighted works reached the congressional agenda, the issue had already spent several years in the federal courts.[32] By the time of its final judicial resolution a vast number of American homes possessed videotape recorders, making it impracticable for Congress to impose an exclusive right against home videotaping—a solution that might have been possible had the question been presented to Congress five or ten years earlier when relatively few homes had VCRs.

The central issues raised by congressional response to the new technologies are institutional: To what extent should Congress await judicial resolution of an uncertain area before acting on its own? What institutions can and should Congress rely upon to identify specific issues and determine their relative magnitude and to gather and analyze information bearing on the issues?

Judicial and Legislative Institutions

In recent years several of the most important questions involving the scope of statutory rights have been resolved judicially, long before Congress acted to clarify the scope of the rights in issue. The question of cable television liability for retransmitting copyrighted signals came before the United States Supreme Court twice before Congress acted on the matter.[33] The questions of liability for library photocopying and home videotaping of copyrighted works were each before the Court once before Congress addressed these questions.[34] Because Congress is better able than courts to resolve broad-ranging questions of copyright policy, Congress should adopt and implement a methodology for identifying and addressing systemic copyright issues rather than wait for the judicial system to grind slowly to an eventual and usually incomplete resolution.

Although courts are institutionally well-equipped to decide interstitial statutory questions and to apply the language of the Copyright Act to novel fact situations, they are less well-equipped than Congress to decide systemic policy questions. The rules of evidence limit the information that courts can weigh, principles of stare decisis limit the ambit of decisions, and rules on statutory remedies closely confine courts' relative ability to shape practical resolutions.

Two other factors, which bear with particular force in copyright cases, indicate Congress' relative superiority in resolving systemic issues. First, the posture in which copyright cases arise inevitably exerts a subtle bias against dispassionate analysis of the investment effects of a decision. Because the plaintiff's copyrighted work is before the court, a natural tendency exists for the court to conclude that a decision denying liability will not reduce investment, since the work before it was created under conditions in which liability was not clear. Second, as indicated by the issue of liability for home videotaping, by the time a final judicial decision has been reached industrial realities may preclude a legislative decision imposing liability.

Legislative Institutions for Oversight and Analysis

Congress has traditionally relied on both ongoing and ad hoc institutions to identify and analyze new copyright issues. The congressional subcommittee hearing process and Copyright Office studies are the two most prominent examples of reliance on ongoing institutions. The work of the National Commission on New Technological Uses of Copyrighted Works and the Office of Technology Assessment's project, Intellectual Property Rights in an Age of Electronics and Information, are examples of ad hoc institutional efforts.[35]

The advantages of relying on ongoing institutions such as congressional subcommittees and staff and the United States Copyright Office is that their sustained exposure to copyright issues gives them both an expertise about the copyright system and a sense for the relative significance and positions of the affected interest groups. The possible disadvantage of relying on these institutions is that they may tend toward insularity and may apply the same perspectives to new problems that they applied to the old.

By contrast, ad hoc institutions are able to bring fresh perspectives and methodologies to new issues, unencumbered by traditional views. Unfortunately, they sometimes lack the necessary expertise about the governing legal system. This is particularly disabling in the context of copyright policymaking because copyright law, far more than other areas of law, is complex and burdened by layers of history and nuance. The brief duration of these ad hoc institutions sometimes deprives their staff of the time needed to acquire the expertise required for truly helpful proposals.

The relative advantages and disadvantages of ongoing and ad hoc institutions suggest that the best institutional approach to identifying and proposing resolutions to emerging copyright issues is to combine what is best in ongoing institutions with what is best in ad hoc institutions. Specifically, the most effective and efficient approach would be for Congress to delegate the oversight and analysis responsibilities to the appropriate subcommittees and to the Copyright Office and, at the same time—and particularly in the case of the Copyright Office—to provide budgetary support for hearings and analyses and the employment of outside consultants of the type retained by ad hoc institutions.

Civil Remote Sensing: New Technologies and National Security Policy

Peter D. Zimmerman

On 26 April 1986 the nuclear power reactor at Chernobyl in the Ukraine exploded, making uninhabitable an area sixty kilometers across. Radiation was spewed into the stratosphere, later to descend across all of Europe from Sweden—where the alarm was first sounded—to Italy. The Soviet government refused to permit foreign journalists to visit the site of the disaster, perhaps in part because of the danger and perhaps because of a desire to minimize the dimensions of the event.

The French-Swedish-Belgian SPOT 1 observation satellite was launched in February 1986 and had formally entered service only days before the Chernobyl catastrophe. A fortuitous confluence of launch date and orbital parameters placed SPOT 1 in position to image the burning reactor within hours; an equally great coincidence made it possible for the American LANDSAT 5 satellite to see the reactor on 28 April 1986. Journalists in the United States were quick to notice the opportunity; the first pictures of the nuclear accident to appear in the international press were taken by commercial "spy" satellites. Space-based reporting proved its value on the first try. But space-based journalism is only one use for the wonderful technique of remote sensing—the gathering of information about the earth from satellites in orbit above.[1]

Observation of the earth from space is an intrinsically international operation. Satellites, by their nature, must pass over most of the territory of the earth; remote sensing satellites cannot be designed to cover only the territory of a single nation since their orbits must move as far north and as far south as the maximum (north or south) latitude of the area they are intended to observe. At present remote sensing is unregulated on an international basis; it is more rigorously controlled by the policies of the individual governments operating satellites or with the capability to launch them in the future.

The technology required to build and launch observation satellites is now widespread around the world, and an apparent race to launch such satellites seems to be on. Nations engage in this activity perhaps as much for the sake of prestige as for the sake of being competitive. Nevertheless, a great deal of prestige does accrue to the nation operating the best such satellites because the images from them have caught the public's attention (because the images are beautiful and because the better images can be understood in principle by most people, unlike the data from other kinds of scientific satellites). The lack of an international regime regulating civil observation satellites has led to the rapid development of an industry which specializes in supplying, for example, militarily interesting information to nations which would not otherwise have the ability to gather information deep within the territory of their opponents.[2]

The international community is probably powerless to eliminate such uses entirely. Indeed, offering targeting services for sale to all might be viewed as simply redressing a balance which had formerly tipped too far in the direction of the United States and the Soviet Union and their clients and allies. From the American point of view this means that the United States must regain the lead in civil remote sensing so as to regain any influence lost because of competition.

The first remote sensing satellites were used to take very low resolution pictures of the earth for the purpose of seeing clouds and improving weather forecasting. Tiros 1 was launched by NASA on 1 April 1960 and went into an orbit 720 kilometers high, from which it and its successors transmitted meteorological data from around the world.[3] More important, perhaps, than the fact of the acquisition of the pictures was American generosity in sharing them with all nations, thus setting a course which led to the "open sky, open access" policy followed by LANDSAT and SPOT.

The Tiros project should be contrasted with another set of American remote sensing experiments carried out at about the same time —the Discoverer series of satellites, launched (as was Tiros) by converted Thor ballistic missiles with specially designed or modified upper stages.[4] Discoverer was meant to demonstrate American abilities to recover payloads launched into orbit; the first successful mission came on the thirteenth try—10 August 1960.[5] The Air Force claimed that Discoverer 13 did not carry cameras into space, a claim not asserted for the next satellite in the series, Discoverer 14, launched and recovered the following week.

If any Discoverer satellites did carry cameras,[6] to this date none of their pictures has been publicly acknowledged and released. Nevertheless, it is widely believed that the first Discoverer and SAMOS satellite flights did carry cameras and that their photographs led the Kennedy administration to conclude that the Soviet Union had only deployed fourteen intercontinental ballistic missiles. Reconnaissance satellite pictures thus put an end to the "missile gap," which played a prominent role in the 1960 presidential election.

To this day intelligence satellites provide information not obtainable in any other way. They are the "National Technical Means" used to verify the SALT and ABM arms control treaties. President Lyndon Johnson is reported to have justified the entire space program because it permitted him to know exactly how many missiles the Soviet Union had built.

Since few pictures known to have been taken by spy satellites have ever been made public, we cannot know how sharp they are or how small an object can be reliably detected by military imagery from space. The two pictures given to *Jane's Defence Weekly* by former U.S. Naval Intelligence analyst Samuel L. Morison are good, indeed.[7] Whether they are average, excellent, or mediocre examples of military satellite art is unknown, but objects just a few centimeters across can be relatively easily seen in those two pictures. It is apparent that the major problems involved with returning high quality pictures to earth from space have been solved, somewhere, by someone. Indeed, they may well have been solved in at least three countries: the United States, the Soviet Union, and the People's Republic of China.[8]

From the point of view of telecommunications and science policy, however, the development of military remote sensing represents a dead end, its products and techniques closed off from the rest of society except for their unique contributions to national security and international stability. The role of civilian remote sensing, in contrast, offers opportunities and challenges unexpected and unpredicted by most analysts as recently as the day before the Chernobyl explosion.

The Current State of the Business and the Art

Each of the existing civilian remote sensing satellites operates in a unique manner, returning pictures with significantly different characteristics. To understand these characteristics it is useful to regard the term "resolution," which usually describes the smallest physical objects which can be seen by a satellite's camera, as in fact being two-dimensional. The first dimension, spatial resolution, tells us the size of the smallest objects which can be detected in a picture.[9] SPOT 1's twin cameras provide the best spatial resolution commercially available in the West with a resolution of ten meters by ten meters in black and white (about the size of half a tennis court) and twenty meters by twenty meters (about half the size of an American football field) in false color. Soyuzkarta, the marketing arm of the Soviet remote sensing program, quotes a six meter resolution for the KFA-1000, and this appears to be borne out in careful studies of first-generation imagery obtained from the Soviet Union (six meters is a bit bigger than an average living room). The pixels provided by LANDSATs 4 and 5 are thirty meters on a side (the size of a baseball diamond). All other systems presently providing pictures commercially are inferior in their spatial resolution.

The second dimension is the spectrum of light, the "colors," reflected from the target being studied. Our eyes, by definition, see the visible spectrum ranging from deep purple to deep red. We are blind to the longer-wavelength infrared light which forms a large part of the sun's energy and which is strongly reflected by many compounds found in nature and made by man.

For example, plants, as we see them, appear green because they reflect green, and absorb red, light. Healthy plants, however, reflect even more strongly in the near infrared (the region of wavelengths just longer than we can see), and at still longer wavelengths, than they do in the green. To properly sensitive instruments grass is red, or at least infrared.

Instruments which can detect even longer wavelengths of "light" in the "thermal" infrared band see the heat radiated from warm objects. This technique was used by American researchers to study the temperature of the reactor cooling pond at Chernobyl after the explosion and fire.

The present generation of civilian remote sensing satellites, pictures from which are reasonably available, was launched by five different countries. At least initially, each was operated either by a national government or by a quasi-governmental body.

The Earth Observation Satellite Corporation (EOSAT)

The American LANDSAT satellites are now owned by the EOSAT Corporation, a joint project of General Electric and General Motors (originally a venture of Hughes Aircraft and RCA when the LANDSAT Privatization Act of 1984 took effect). The LANDSAT series of satellites was originally launched by NASA and operated by the Department of Commerce until the system was sold off during the Reagan administration. The first LANDSATs carried the eighty meter resolution Multispectral Scanner (MSS); even that very low resolution instrument was considered by some in the U.S. intelligence community and the Defense Department to have posed a threat to military operations and national security.

EOSAT's flagships, the LANDSAT 4 and 5 satellites, each carry Thematic Mapper cameras which provide imagery with a thirty meter ground resolution (at nadir) in seven spectral bands. Three of these are visible blue, green, and red (bands 1, 2, and 3); three more are in the short wavelength to mid wavelength infrared region (bands 4, 5, and 7); and the seventh (paradoxically called Band 6) is in the thermal infrared region. Band 6 has a resolution of about 120 meters, in contrast to the better image quality obtainable in the other channels. However, Band 6 can be used to determine absolute temperatures remotely and to measure very small temperature differences. Its most famous application was when it was used to determine that the surviving Chernobyl power reactors had been turned off.

EOSAT is currently defining the instruments to be carried on LANDSAT 6, for which it has received a U.S. government subsidy.

Satellite Pour L'Observation de la Terre (SPOT)

The SPOT 1 satellite was launched by the French space agency, CNES, and is owned and operated by that agency. The operation of the satellite and the sale of its images are handled by SPOT Image, S.A. (SISA) in France, its subsidiary SPOT Image Corporation (SICORP) in Reston,

Virginia, and by other licensees around the world. Most of the stock in SISA is held by the French government through various agencies including CNES (39 percent); the Swedish and Belgian governments own 6 percent and 4 percent shares, respectively. Some French aero-space corporations, including the Matra Group, also have less than 20 percent financial interest in the SPOT organization.[10]

The first SPOT satellite provides ground resolutions of ten meters (at nadir) in a single channel described as "panchromatic" and covering roughly the entire visible spectrum in a single block using each of its two High Resolution Visible (HRV) cameras. SPOT 1 also carries "Extended Spectrum," or XS, sensors in the HRV instruments. The XS sensors provide twenty meter resolution at nadir. Each camera can be pointed up to about 28° away from the nadir. This increases the area which can be covered on each orbit and also permits stereoscopic pictures to be taken over a period of time.

V/O Soyuzkarta, the Soviet Entry

Since August of 1987 the Soviet trading company, V/O Soyuzkarta, has marketed a limited selection of images. Soyuzkarta in its product literature advertises pictures with a claimed resolution of roughly six meters taken with its KFA-1000 cameras, but also offers to sell imagery of lower spatial resolution and greater spectral coverage taken with other cameras. Soyuzkarta is owned by the Soviet government, which operates the remote sensing program.

It is relatively difficult to purchase imagery from Soyuzkarta, as I have learned by experience. Furthermore, Soyuzkarta has informed me that they do not sell imagery of the Soviet Union or of the "Socialist Community."[11] Given the problems of dealing with it, it is difficult to be sure whether, despite its glossy promotional literature, Soyuzkarta is truly in the commercial remote sensing business.

Others

The Indian remote sensing satellite IRS-1 was launched on 17 March 1988 by a Soviet booster rocket. IRS-1 is operated by the Indian Space Agency and is intended by the Indian government to provide a low-cost remote sensing service to developing nations. As such, it operates with a significant government subsidy. IRS-1 is supposed to have a low resolution, wide angle camera providing seventy-two meter resolution and a higher resolution instrument which has a thirty-six meter resolution over one quarter the area of the wide-look system. The satellite transmits imagery in the blue, green, red, and near infrared bands, roughly corresponding to bands 1 through 4 of LANDSAT.

The Japanese space agency launched its Marine Observation Satellite, MOS-1, in 1987.

Comparing the Instruments

LANDSAT has the widest spectral coverage of any remote sensing satellite. It covers seven wavelength bands ranging from the blue, green, and red of the visible spectrum down through three relatively near infrared bands which permit the identification of vegetation, some chemicals, and several types of minerals and band in the thermal infrared. Perceptive uses of the LANDSAT infrared capabilities enabled at least two different groups of investigators to identify a roughly thirty kilometer radius area around the Chernobyl explosion in which virtually all of the conifer forest had been killed or severely damaged by radiation. This was information not available in any way to Westerners in the Soviet Union and probably not even apparent to a scientist able to walk through the area.

The greater the number of "color" bands to which a satellite's cameras are sensitive, and the greater the sharpness with which each "color" can be distinguished, the more useful the instrument is in detecting and identifying chemicals, heat emission, and chemical changes. To some extent, however, one must pay a technical price for the ability to see in color, and particularly to see in the extended color regions necessary for effective "multispectral" analysis. Instruments which can see in many bands tend not to be able to see small objects or fine detail in larger ones with great clarity. The black and white spy satellite pictures revealed by S. L. Morison are spectacular in their sharpness, compared to any available on the civilian market but did not reveal any ability to discriminate colors.

The LANDSAT satellites return pictures to the earth electronically, either by direct radio transmission to ground stations or indirectly through the TDRSS (Tracking and Data Relay Satellite System) network which covers only part of the globe. Areas not served by either a ground station or by the partially complete TDRSS network cannot be imaged by the LANDSAT satellites.

SPOT's images are either transmitted directly to ground stations around the world or stored for transmission to the ground stations at Kiruna, Sweden, or at CNES headquarters in Toulouse, France. Pictures can be obtained of areas not served by ground stations by use of the on-board tape recorder which can store up to twenty minutes of pictures at a time. The SPOT organization has repeatedly stated that their satellites operate under a policy of "open skies, open access," meaning that they will photograph any point on the globe and sell the picture to any and all customers. The tape recorder on board the satellite gives the CNES operating personnel the power to enforce that policy, if necessary, against the wishes of the operators of the network of ground stations.

Unlike the LANDSAT and SPOT systems, the Soviet satellites take pictures on photographic film which must be physically returned to the earth and recovered. Because the pictures are stored on photographic film, the KFA-1000 camera can be used to image any point over which the satellite flies.

There is no fundamental reason why the resolving power, spatial and spectral, of civilian remote sensing satellites should not continue to improve. The technical problems of achieving very sharp black and white pictures have already been solved, even if the solutions themselves have not been made freely available. It is worth noting that SPOT 1, if operated at 416 km altitude, instead of its 832 km altitude, would automatically have a five meter resolution, but would only be able to capture images thirty km on each side instead of the sixty km achievable at its present altitude. If the 832 km altitude were retained, the addition of a simple "teleconverter" to the optical system, weighing perhaps 200 grams, would raise the resolution, once again, to five meters at the cost of a certain amount of low-light sensitivity and, of course, coverage area. Because SPOT is in a "sun synchronous" orbit, it always takes pictures at about 10:30 A.M., local solar time. Consequently, low-light sensitivity is not a primary issue.

The principal barriers to higher resolution are three: the cost of the hardware, the need for a market for the imagery, and the perceived political consequences of improved pictures.

Political Policy Questions

Until the Reagan administration announced its new space policy early in 1988, the United States had in effect at least a formal bar to the licensing of U.S.-owned and operated satellites with resolutions better than ten meters.[12] The 1988 policy encourages American entrepreneurs to provide pictures at least as good as those available elsewhere, but still requires U.S.-licensed systems to operate to further the U.S. national security and to be consistent with U.S. foreign policy. These requirements, taken from the LANDSAT Commercialization Act,[13] are deliberately vague and provide little guidance to the prospective American operator as to which pictures will be encouraged and which will be suppressed under threat of the loss of the necessary license to operate.

Despite the intent of the U.S. government to encourage American entrepreneurs to build a remote sensing industry second to none, none of the nominally commercial remote sensing satellite systems presently in operation is profitable if the accounting methods require the amortization of the development and launch costs of the satellites themselves. It does appear, however, that the SPOT operation generates enough revenues to at least cover operating costs in the United States. Remote sensing, at present, cannot appeal to firms concerned about the quarterly bottom line; it requires a time period denominated in years if not decades. Nevertheless, at least five civil remote sensing systems are in existence with more planned or contemplated. Each of these receives a government subsidy of greater or lesser visibility.

SPOT is primarily owned by governments—and its satellite is wholly so. V/O Soyuzkarta is state-owned like all large Soviet enterprises. The Indian and Japanese systems are owned and operated by their national governments as well. Only EOSAT, the operator of the American LANDSAT system is wholly privately owned; even EOSAT is subsidized at present, although that subsidy has been unreliable.

When the EOSAT consortium agreed to take over and operate the LANDSAT system, the U.S. government agreed to furnish a subsidy of $250 million spread out over six years. Almost immediately after EOSAT went into business, at the beginning of 1986, the U.S. government faced a mammoth budget deficit and the Gramm-Rudman-Hollings guillotine.[14] The Office of Management and Budget (OMB) moved to eliminate the FY 1987 tranche of the subsidy, although $27.5 million of the original $69.5 million payment was subsequently restored by Congress. In the wake of the loss of the shuttle Challenger, even the smaller amount was deleted, forcing EOSAT to suspend construction of LANDSAT 6 and development of LANDSAT 7.[15]

With LANDSAT 4 well beyond its predicted lifetime and its performance seriously degraded and LANDSAT 5's projected operational life nearing its end, many communities within the United States and its government recognized the irreplaceable nature of the multispectral data provided by the EOSAT satellites and the need to improve upon the spatial resolution of the system. Thus, in the fall of 1987 the government committed its share of the funds necessary to build and launch LANDSAT 6.

Remote sensing, as will be seen in more detail later, serves many purposes from mapping to the evaluation of soil and water use and the survey of territory of interest for military operations. It is useful, therefore, for a modern industrial power to support remote sensing on commercial (broadly viewed) grounds, as well as for reasons of national prestige. It is, therefore, altogether appropriate to consider subsidies for remote sensing operations. In the United States this takes direct and indirect forms. The indirect subsidy may be the more important. The United States government is probably the largest customer, worldwide, for images from both LANDSAT and SPOT. SPOT images are purchased by the Defense Mapping Agency as a central agent; LANDSAT images may be acquired more directly by the agencies using them. While such purchases may increase the revenues of the two remote sensing companies, it would appear no less justified a "subsidy" than that received routinely by defense contractors which would have no other reason for existing if the U.S. government did not buy their goods.

The direct subsidy for EOSAT is, of course, a way to provide development funding for a technology in its infancy and to keep current prices for imagery in line with what customers are able to pay. Even so, the steep price rises since the LANDSAT system went commercial have reduced the abilities of university-based researchers and teachers to purchase current pictures. At some point it is possible that the technology to support the space segment of the system will drop in price through a combination of lowered launch costs in some future era and greater rationalization or redesign of the production of the satellites themselves. It is therefore reasonable to support a vigorous and competitive U.S. remote sensing industry through the early years. Eastman Kodak, owner of KRS Remote Sensing, estimates that the market for imagery and value-added services may approach $7 billion by the end of the century.[16]

The national security consequences of improved satellite imagery will be discussed in detail below as they relate to space-based journalism.[17] Many analysts believe that no insuperable problems are presented, although in certain critical situations, such as the 1962 Cuban Missile Crisis, policymakers and crisis managers would naturally prefer to continue to be able to monopolize the sources of information in order to control its flow.

One important consequence for the United States and the Soviet Union of the wider availability of satellite imagery may have been a certain devaluation of the intelligence provided to smaller states by the two superpowers. If a nation could assess the extent of war preparations by its neighbors simply by ordering routine imagery from SPOT, it would not need to request such pictures from either the United States or the Soviet Union, and so would not incur whatever debt might have been owed for the provision of intelligence.[18] The cost of SPOT images is paltry ($1900 for a computer compatible tape in May 1988) compared to other national expenditures for intelligence collection—even for a minor power.

Market Forces

The EOSAT Corporation has recently begun the detailed planning for its LANDSAT 6 satellite, due for launching in 1991. LANDSAT 6 could have carried a sensor with a five meter resolution; however, a market survey in mid-1988 did not find any customers willing to underwrite the cost of the camera in advance. Accordingly, EOSAT declined to invest its own money in the hope of earning a profit from the capability.[19]

David Julyan, executive vice president of SICORP, the U.S. SPOT subsidiary, believes, however, that the future is not in higher resolution, but rather in lower resolution and wider area coverage (which LANDSAT does today) and perhaps in extended spectral sensitivity and resolution.[20] SPOT, according to Julyan, has no current plans for higher resolution instruments; at one time it appeared that SPOT 3 and SPOT

4 would be improved significantly over the present generation.[21] Julyan is looking, perhaps, at the markets he knows best and the one monopolized by his competition. Dr. Murray Felsher, a geologist who publishes the *Washington Remote Sensing Newsletter* and consults for companies in the remote sensing business, believes precisely the opposite. Felsher considers that the market will increase "exponentially"[22] as resolution goes up. He is probably correct because the number of obvious uses for the imagery increases rapidly with resolution.

Some observers have stated that there will never be a U.S. commercial remote sensing industry because the market is largely for pictures of direct relevance to combatants and to nations contemplating military action. Leaving aside the probability that the market will be far more diverse and far more peaceful a decade hence, such military uses are a strong reason why the United States should encourage a civil remote sensing industry in order to compete for the influence wielded by the supplier of such imagery. It is not enough to say that the information can come from American military satellites, because, in practice, it is difficult to get such imagery released.

Assuming that costs do not increase as rapidly as resolution does (and they need not), high resolution images should have a larger market than do today's SPOT panchromatic pictures. Containing costs while increasing performance requires the introduction of satellite designs which differ from the "gold-plated NASA-standard" ones in use today including the greatest possible use of "best commercial grade" equipment. It is not axiomatic that the multiply redundant individual satellites which are the basis of the present art will be cost-effective in comparison with simpler instruments where system reliability is achieved by the purchase and launch of a larger number of cheaper satellites. Because the technology to be incorporated into such satellites would, in fact, be off-the-shelf, their development costs should be much lower than for a state-of-the-art system.

If resolution doubles to five meters, it becomes feasible to inventory even densely populated urban areas to determine land utilization and, for example, the watering of lawns during dry spells. The number of houses, and their sizes, can be accurately and rapidly determined. This information should be in building permit and tax records but is often hard to pull together. At the same resolution level a winter picture will tell quickly which homes have poor insulation.

More humorously, swimming pools (including above-ground ones) can be counted, perhaps for tax purposes.

At five meter resolution the activity at industrial sites can be monitored with little difficulty. Trucks can be detected with relative ease, and something of traffic congestion can be seen. Military analysts have indicated to the author that the step from ten meter to five meter resolution is the critical one for detecting and identifying ground forces.

At one meter resolution homes can not only be seen but identified. It is even possible to discern fairly fine details of the architecture of larger buildings. The real estate industry as well as planning and zoning officials can use satellite photos for planning, for predicting the impact of development on open ground, and possibly for showing prospective clients the appearance of subdivisions. All of these jobs can, of course, be done in other ways today, but there is little substitute for a highly detailed satellite photo encompassing thousands of square kilometers in a single picture. Furthermore, the present cost of acquiring similar, but lower resolution, satellite pictures is already much less than obtaining the same kind of survey information by other means, including aerial photography. In agriculture and silvaculture the differences are enormous.

Typically, using aerial photographs of a large agricultural region to estimate crop yields requires three times the man-days as would the use of SPOT images. In addition, multispectral sensing permits the early identification of unhealthy crops, the construction of a "thematic" map on which such crops as barley, wheat, and soy beans can be distinctly and automatically identified on the basis of their individual reflectance spectra. Man-made structures can also be noted and mapped in the same operation, generally with better accuracy than can be easily achieved by ground surveys. Unhealthy crops can be unambiguously identified in multispectral imagery, usually earlier and with greater confidence than by ground survey. While aerial photography can be used instead of imagery from a satellite, the low-flying platforms do not capture as large a picture in a single pass as can a satellite. Consequently, the photo plane must make repeated passes, each at very precisely known places and altitudes in order for the user to piece together an accurate and precise image.

Modern forestry uses multispectral data to identify not only the kinds of trees in a forest, but also their ages and types. The number of board feet in a stand of timber can be reliably estimated in satellite imagery. The same complications which make aerial photography more expensive in agricultural uses also operate in evaluating forests. Similarly, the health of the timber crop can be readily estimated from above.

SPOT's panchromatic images permit the rapid construction of maps at a scale of 1:50,000 and, with some difficulty, 1:25,000. New maps can be drawn, or old ones updated, at a fraction of the cost of using either ground surveys or aerial photography. For perspective a 1:25,000 highway map would be highly detailed, but the same scale is insufficient for most street maps of large cities. Even using SPOT pictures, differences between precisely measured features and the best existing maps of well-settled areas in the United States are readily apparent.

SPOT's product literature demonstrates the uses of large-area high resolution imagery combined with three-band multispectral imagery for use in urban planning. Examples include, trivially, the ability to determine the exact uses to which the land is being put (forests, crops, man-made structures). It is also possible to use the data to construct accurate topographic maps, to determine the slope of each parcel of land, as well as its exposure to the sun. Geological maps can be prepared as well using standard techniques of remote sensing.

It is true that all these tasks can be done with aerial surveys and ground surveys, but it is equally true that it can be done more quickly and, if the construction and launch costs of the satellite are subsidized, far less expensively from space. In drawing maps the two key advantages of satellite imagery are the wealth of detail which can be seen and the fact that much of the process can be automated, reducing the labor which has been previously associated with cartography. The high altitude of the platform used to take the picture, as compared to aerial surveys, minimizes the corrections which need to be made for relief parallax. When stereo pairs are taken from high altitude, contour maps can be made, virtually without human intervention.

Improvements in resolution, both spatial and spectral, are keys to broadening the utility of remotely sensed imagery. While a wealth of detail can be discerned in today's images, the resolution makes it just barely impossible to identify individual houses, for example, within cities. Streets are frequently concealed by overhanging trees. If the resolution of the multispectral sensor is not good enough to detect small patches of pavement beneath the foliage, city maps can be more difficult to construct than they should be.

Geologists frequently use remotely sensed images to locate areas worth exploration for minerals, oil, or water. While much of the information needed is contained in the multispectral reflectance, it is desirable to get the highest possible resolution in order, first, to see the texture of the surface and, second, to ensure that the reflected signal is from the anticipated kind of soil and is not an artifact produced by the blurring of an image which includes two different soil types.

As environmental concerns become more important in public and political life, the practical applications of remote sensing increase. It is possible to use remote sensing satellites to survey large areas for the discharge of pollutants, particularly oil (well measured in the Persian Gulf),[23] and this might be extended to measuring the dumping and discharge of chemicals and sewage. SPOT imagery has been used to monitor the environment for floods and for the prediction of floods. With higher resolution images than are currently available, it would be easier to estimate the probable extent of the inrush of water and to predict areas of safety. SPOT and LANDSAT have both been used to study and monitor forest and grassland fires.

It probably does not pay to dwell overly long on the uses for improved images from space nor on their markets. Barrier-breaking new technology creates its own demand.

Cost Factors

SPOT 1 cost several hundred million dollars to build and launch. LANDSAT 6 is currently budgeted at roughly $220 million to build and launch (FY 86-87-88 dollars). Such "NASA standard" satellites are expensive, in part because they are multipurpose and in part because they are heavily redundant in order to ensure long service lives. Perhaps more important cost drivers are the small numbers in which the satellites are built and the large amount of original development which is always done for each satellite or small series. For example, SPOT always intends to incorporate only "state of the art" technology. In practice this means a substantial increase in total costs.

An alternative design scheme is to use "off the shelf" technology as much as possible. This involves the careful selection of reliable components which will perform the job but leaves to others the expensive chore of developing technology for the next generation. Such an approach is not only feasible but appropriate for commercial satellite applications. In any event commercial development of "new" technology for remote sensing largely repeats development already performed in the military sector. At some point it might even become possible for governments to make available some of their older sensor technology to the private sector. If one can judge by the ratio of resources available to a superpower's government and those available to even the richest company, it is likely that the capabilities of intelligence satellites can always stay comfortably ahead of those available to anyone else.

A third way to reduce costs is to obtain the redundancy necessary for reliable operation by building a relatively large number of inexpensive "lightsats" (or "cheapsats," as they are sometimes known). Instead of trying to construct a single satellite in which all of the vital systems were duplicated to ensure long life, the builder of a cheapsat selects "best commercial grade" components, tests them extensively, and selects the actual ones to be used with some care. He might then plan to construct three (or more) satellites, each of which will operate independently. Using this technique, one satellite builder estimated that a satellite delivering a true-color video signal, compatible with broadcasting standards and having a five meter resolution, could be built and launched for less than $10 million, including at least two specially built ground stations.[24]

A system of cheapsats could be orbited for vastly less than the cost of a single LANDSAT. The comparison is unfair because the LANDSAT will carry sensors which reach into the thermal infrared and which can scan a much larger area of the earth at one time. Nevertheless, a cheapsat system does have one significant advantage: it will be capable of observing far more sites on the earth at higher resolution each day than can any single LANDSAT instrument.

The many markets for images and ideas will determine which paths are followed. Newsgathering satellites are apt to be built as cheapsats or piggy-backed on other payloads, benefiting from orientation and communications equipment launched for other purposes. Satellites launched to seek out resources or monitor agriculture will require far more sophisticated cameras, and might well need to expand the state of the civilian art.

There is a final way to reduce the costs of developing future remote sensing satellites dramatically. It is virtually certain that the problems associated with building satellites with high and very high resolution capabilities were solved at least a decade ago by the intelligence communities of the United States and Soviet Union for military purposes. Unfortunately, none of the technology used to construct such satellites has been transferred to the civilian industry—apparently not even where the same firms have built both military and civilian reconnaissance satellites. Similarly, no part of the archive of pictures taken by military satellites has been made available for civilian use. This artificial barrier could come down, in whole or in part.

Some American intelligence specialists believe that older imagery, degraded electronically to a resolution of a few meters and chosen to avoid revealing any sensitive capabilities of the satellites could be released for use in constructing a historical data base of satellite images. Others resist, believing that any breach in the secrecy will lead directly to serious compromise of U.S. systems. Congressman George Brown (D-Calif.) has often suggested legislation to open the intelligence archives.

Given that the technology in the intelligence community has moved ahead at least as fast as that available to the civilian world, it might also be possible to declassify some of the techniques used in "spy" satellites of previous generations. The 1979 SALT II Treaty signed by the United States and the Soviet Union restricted the modification of existing types of intercontinental ballistic missiles (ICs). Such missiles could be enlarged by no more than 5 percent, according to the terms of the pact. Since national technical means were relied upon for verification of the treaty, one can estimate that the intelligence services of the two countries were confident that they could discern the difference between a (permitted) 4 percent lengthening of a missile and a (prohibited) 6 percent increase. Since a typical IC is approximately fifty meters long, 2 percent is about one meter, which sets a rough lower bound to the capabilities of military satellites in service a decade ago.

Much information about the capabilities of modern military satellites is necessarily secret. Were the properties of the satellites which monitor agreements to become generally known, it would be far easier for a potential violator to evade detection. Even so, some in the intelligence community have suggested that older technology might be transferred to the civilian side, provided that the United States were certain that the capabilities transferred to public use were inferior to those of the Soviets at the time of the transfer. No doubt, others in the same services would object to even this small breach in the existing barriers.

Some technological secrets of some older satellites could and should be made public. This would make it possible to construct additional satellites of higher resolution than those presently available to the remote sensing community without paying the large price needed to develop the capabilities from scratch. In turn, this could lower the required prices for remotely sensed data while improving the quality of the product of the industry.

Transparency: Good or Bad?

The spread of satellite imaging technology has made it possible for many systems to view the entire earth. This has transformed closed societies into ones which are relatively transparent and which must, to some degree, accommodate to scrutiny from space. The change occurred first in the military arena, primarily between the United States and the Soviet Union, but has now been extended to civilian activities. These include the search for and exploitation of natural resources (indeed, the name originally given to the LANDSAT series was ERTS—Earth Resources Technology Satellite) and to the prediction of crop yields in competing nations. One area where satellite imagery has been particularly important is arms control.

Arms Control

During World War II weather reports from ships at sea were kept highly classified; weather satellites today provide many countries with more data of higher quality from virtually every point on the globe. In more subtle areas the situation today is at least as changed: satellite photography has markedly increased the transparency of human activities. No longer do high fences or inland locations prevent one nation or industry from peering closely at the activities of another. This transparency has almost certainly been beneficial in the field of arms control. Without the ability to monitor potential violations from space, it is unlikely that either the United States or the Soviet Union would have agreed to even the minimal restrictions contained in the Limited Test Ban Treaty of 1963, which simply forced nuclear testing to be conducted underground. Since 1963, of course, satellite monitoring has made possible more significant arms control achievements, including the ABM Treaty and the Interim Agreement on the Limitation of Strategic Offensive Arms (SALT I) of 1972 and the SALT II Treaty of 1979. Despite the useful onsite inspection provisions contained in the INF Treaty of 1987, compliance with the agreement could not be satisfactorily verified without the use of satellite imagery, at least to give warning of suspicious activity.

All strategic arms control agreements since 1972 have contained provisions banning interference with the euphemistically named "National Technical Means (NTM) of Verification"—spy satellites. If arms control has reduced international tensions, the risk of war, or the consequences of conflict, then transparency has been a benefit.

Transparency has apparently worked to advantage in at least one other situation. It is reported that in 1977 the South African government was nearly ready to test a nuclear weapon, but that unmistakable evidence of the test preparations was detected by a Soviet satellite. The Soviets informed the United States, which confirmed the report using its own satellites, and the South African government was persuaded that carrying out a nuclear test was not in its own best interest. The test explosion, apparently, never took place.

The Civil Sector

We have entered a new era in satellite reconnaissance. Pictures heretofore only available to superpower governments or their nation-state clients have now become available to anyone—person, corporation, and government—with only a modest budget. This has the power to change the way in which we enforce our rights to personal, corporate, and national privacy.

Satellites do not respect national boundaries. Nor do they respect property lines, and thus several questions arise. The first is simply one of technical feasibility of the detection and identification of activities on the surface. At the present practical resolution limit of ten meters very few industrial processes can be analyzed in detail; essentially no private activities of individuals can be detected, let alone identified or analyzed.[25] For the moment the only practical legal barriers to the dissemination and use of satellite imagery are, for U.S.-licensed systems, the LANDSAT Commercialization Act and, for U.S.-based users, the Espionage Act. The LANDSAT Act requires satellite systems to be operated consistent with U.S. national security interests; the Espionage Act prohibits U.S. citizens from disseminating pictures of certain sensitive military installations without advance permission. It is an open question whether American citizens can distribute SPOT or Soyuzkarta pictures of American military facilities, since those pictures were inherently acquired by a foreign power and then distributed to U.S. citizens, or whether such distribution is prohibited by the Espionage Act.

The questions of personal and industrial privacy, however, appear to take on a new dimension as satellite resolutions improve. These questions fall roughly into three categories: the cosmic Peeping Tom, able to observe private and personal activities; industrial espionage; and warrantless inspections by law enforcement or regulatory agencies. The first category of problems will profit from a degree of neglect: at least for the foreseeable future no satellite system is likely to have the capability to detect an individual person (covering, when standing upright, an approximate area of .40 by .60 meter seen from directly above or an area of about 1.75 meter by .6 meter if prone), let alone to permit the person to be identified and his or her activities characterized. Any pictures which might potentially infringe on personal privacy remain for now in the realms of either military intelligence or science fiction. In the United States the question of warrantless inspections has been settled by the Supreme Court in a question involving aerial photography of Dow Chemical Company by the Environmental Protection Agency. Dow argued, first, that the photography constituted an illegal warrantless search and, second, that such photography could reveal its trade secrets to its competition. The Court ruled that any person flying overhead could see and photograph Dow's facility, so there could be no constitutional objection to a regulatory agency chartering an aircraft for the same purpose.[26] The Court did, however, state that ''It may well be, as the Government concedes, that Government surveillance of private property by using highly sophisticated surveillance equipment not generally available to the public, such as satellite technology, might be constitutionally proscribed absent a warrant."[27]

As satellite photographs become generally available to the public through commercial providers, such as SPOT and EOSAT and the value-added firms working with them, the Supreme Court's caution as specifically applied to satellite inspection might lose its force. Nonetheless, if the government were to use its own proprietary systems, such as intelligence satellites, to observe private property, a warrant might well be required even if other kinds of satellite photography were commercially available. The fact that the Court stated that the photographs used by the EPA were "not so revealing of intimate details as to raise constitutional concerns" indicates that at some level of detail satellite images could raise such concerns. It is also worthwhile to point out that the Court, in the same opinion, indicated that personal and private activities within "the curtilage area immediately surrounding a private house has long been given protection as a place where the occupants have a reasonable and legitimate expectation of privacy that society is prepared to accept." Justice Lewis Powell dissented from the ruling, arguing that the degree of sophistication of the camera used put the EPA's monitoring of Dow in a class different from simple observation from a passing commercial airplane. Justice Powell argued that the Fourth Amendment restricted the government from surveilling Dow from the air.

Trade secrets, as opposed to governmental searches for evidence, are protected primarily by state laws against industrial espionage. While the use of satellite imagery to spy out the secrets of a competitor might well be actionable as a tort in state court, there are probably no federal statutes making it a criminal offense.

"Third Systems" for Arms Control

The superpowers rely on satellite observation for monitoring and verification of arms control agreements. Other nations also are parties to arms control treaties, often of a regional character, and to agreements on confidence building measures. They must rely on their own intelligence services or crumbs from the tables of the superpowers for the information needed to assure themselves that their agreements are being scrupulously observed. This has proved to be a satisfactory arrangement in the past but is not likely to continue to satisfy in the future.

The technology for satellite observation is now proliferating worldwide. In addition, future agreements binding smaller powers will probably acquire more central importance for their security than existing agreements such as the Nuclear Non-Proliferation Treaty. Such future agreements might include regional arms limitation treaties, demilitarized border zones, and nuclear free zones. At present nonintrusive monitoring of regional agreements would have to be performed by superpower observation satellites. This would probably be distasteful to the States Parties because it would mean that the necessary data for their security decisionmaking processes were under the exclusive control of other nations. The political imperative to take back a measure of national independence from the nuclear powers is likely to be irresistible. Finally, the increasing number of developing and smaller nations—India, Israel, Brazil, Japan, Canada, and Sweden—seriously interested in constructing their own remote sensing satellites indicates that the possession of independent National Technical Means may well turn out to be an internationally acceptable surrogate for nuclear weapons as a way of demonstrating military prowess and technological maturity. There are, of course, limits to the analogy with nuclear weapons: remote sensing can only provide information about the activities of others; by itself it cannot kill tanks, soldiers, or civilians.

For purposes of further discussion "monitoring" refers to gathering data; "verification" is the process of assembling data, perhaps from many sources, and arriving at judgments about the compliance of a party to an agreement with the terms of the agreement; a "third system" monitoring agency is any governmental, private, or quasi-governmental body (possibly an international organization), except one of the superpower governments, which operates an observation satellite used for monitoring of international agreements or behavior; an "independent" analyst or verifier is a nongovernmental person or group which uses information of the sort provided by imaging satellites to reach judgments about national behavior. "Third parties" are those who verify agreements to which they are not signatories; they may attempt to verify or certify compliance or noncompliance with those agreements; the operators of third systems become third parties if they do inject the subjective note into their descriptions of compliance with agreements which they have not themselves joined.

Third system (or third party) monitoring or verification is not an area which is likely ever to be served by dedicated commercial satellites. It is far more likely that third system monitoring will be performed either by governments or international organizations using national or international systems or by the same groups using images purchased from commercial satellite operators, in business to serve a wider market.

What legitimate functions can dedicated "third system" monitoring satellites perform and who should operate such systems? What can independent and third party verifiers usefully accomplish?

Any third party or independent monitoring system will be a very small actor sandwiched between two or more relative giants. National and international third system reconnaissance must operate with a certain degree of discretion and in a way which can be viewed by the superpowers as enhancing their own security as well as that of smaller states. Nongovernmental satellite operators and users of satellite images might be somewhat freer to choose their activities.

Since "verification" is but a euphemism for intelligence collection (particularly in this context), it is important that a national third system recognize its limitations and the proprietary interests asserted by others. Third party verification—as opposed to simple monitoring and provision of imagery—may never be appropriate since it may well be seen as interference in the national affairs of others. Third system monitoring, however, is appropriate when several parties have an explicit stake, sanctioned by treaty or agreement, in the behavior of others. Of course, any nation may operate a remote sensing system or an intelligence-collection satellite.

Some third party efforts to verify a treaty or to pass judgments on the acts of treaty signatories would be neither appropriate nor welcome: the U.S.-Soviet bilateral strategic arms treaties, in particular the Anti-Ballistic Missile Treaty of 1972, the SALT I Interim Agreement on the Limitation of Strategic Offensive Arms, and the 1979 SALT II Treaty.[28] Both parties to these agreements believe that they have adequate capabilities to monitor the compliance of the other side. Furthermore, any system based on moderate resolution instruments (such as SPOT) must provide data of far lower quality than is available through National Technical Means.[29]

Under almost all circumstances it would be inappropriate for a third party or third system, even one operated by another government, to attempt to pass judgment on the compliance of the United

States and Soviet Union with these treaties, although it is perfectly reasonable for independent and third party verifiers to collect data which bear on superpower bilateral agreements. It would be almost impossible for the user of a lower quality system to dispute judgments made on the basis of information from a higher quality system including elements other than simple photointelligence.

A "third system" of remote sensing satellites could, however, be used to demonstrate the truth of assertions made by one country about the behavior of another without provoking hostile responses by the nations concerned and without compromising the capabilities of secret intelligence collection systems. Third system images can perform another useful function: they may, at least to a moderate extent, be able to deter nations from making allegations which have no real foundation in intelligence data. Although it is difficult to disprove a charge using lower quality data, it is possible for an independent monitoring agency to state that its observations provide "no evidence" to corroborate an allegation.

The separation of collection from analysis and interpretation is an important characteristic of a successful third system or independent verification regime. Routine collection of images can thereby proceed without reference to political questions and on the understanding that the sensitivities of all concerned will be trampled upon equally. The system should respond in a nondiscriminatory way to target requests either from a list of subscribers or, preferably, any party whatsoever, governmental or private. This separation of functions is in distinct contrast to most proposals for third party monitoring schemes which integrate observation and analysis.[30] In particular, it is in strong opposition to the proposals for regional and international satellite monitoring agencies charged with certifying compliance or noncompliance (for example, ISMA). It is, however, a necessary condition in order to gain acceptance of the collection system.

As long as the pictures obtained by the third party system are made available to all parties, and as long as the satellite's camera can be pointed at targets in all countries, a third party satellite can provide data on an "open skies" basis. If the system is operated in a truly neutral and confidential way, it can serve as an intelligence collector for many countries not otherwise able to have the benefits of reasonable access to overhead imagery.

SPOT can, and may, function this way. Since its list of clients is confidential, we cannot know. It is critical that the satellite operator of such a system neither engage in image analysis nor serve the intelligence services of particular states in a favored way.

If, however, the operators of the monitoring system yield to the temptation to write their own intelligence estimates, it appears likely that the legitimacy of the collection will be called into question. Furthermore, if an international government-controlled system evolves, and if it engages in analysis which touches upon the sensitivities of its proprietors, the system will quickly find itself restricted in its action. If the analysis carefully avoids offending the operators but does criticize others, again the system will lose its credibility as a neutral source of data. Any attempt on the part of the satellite operator to offer analyses or pass judgments will destroy his function as a neutral verifier.

Specific Agreements

Agreements and treaties now exist in which many nations have explicit responsibilities and interests as well as the implicit interest which all members of the world community have in preserving peace. In particular the 1986 Stockholm Accord places responsibility for promoting confidence and security building measures on many countries.[31] Additionally, the INF Treaty has multilateral protocols, since the United States cannot, for example, authorize Soviet inspectors to visit Royal Air Force bases in the UK, nor can the United States pledge that the UK will allow such visits. Many nations participate in these two accords and are therefore interested in seeing that the agreements are honored.

The Stockholm Accord requires nations to notify the other signatories in advance of military maneuvers exceeding a certain size and to provide an annual calendar of such events. For exercises exceeding a certain level of military activity, signatories are required to invite observers and even to allow them to inspect from the air. These measures will surely prevent the misinterpretation of exercises as preparations for attack. The problem, however, is that, in order for inspectors to be sent, notification must be received. There is no explicit mechanism for ascertaining that activity close to, but not exceeding, the threshold at which formal notification is required did not, in fact, exceed permitted limits. Verification of compliance with the Stockholm Accord requires, therefore, nonintrusive inspection of a type not provided for in the agreement itself.

Such inspection can best be done through the use of reconnaissance satellites. To be sure, the United States and the Soviet Union operate satellites which can be used. It is reasonable and important for the smaller signatories, and particularly the neutral States Parties, to possess independent means for assuring themselves that all other states are in compliance. Hence, first use for a genuinely independent monitoring capability.

The Stockholm Accord is, in fact, monitorable with modest confidence using SPOT. A Soviet T-72 tank is about 9.1 meters long and 4 meters wide. While it does not quite "fill" a SPOT pixel, it comes close and so may be considered barely detectable given reasonable contrast between the vehicle and the ground. Other modern tanks are of comparable size. Armored formations are, however, much more readily detectable than individual vehicles. Because military units generally come in discrete sizes, it is likely that even relatively low resolution satellites can not only detect their presence, but estimate with high confidence their size.

Amphibious exercises also fall under the Stockholm Agreement; large ships can be easily seen from overhead. Because the unclassified data base on navies is extensive, and because it is possible to measure objects seen in SPOT images to moderate accuracy, ships which are detected can generally be readily identified as to class.[32] This fact permits monitoring of some aspects of the Stockholm Agreement to moderate confidence even with existing commercial satellites.

Utility for Monitoring INF

The INF Treaty will be verified by an extensive system of inspections and other intelligence means. Unfortunately for the NATO members who might be threatened by remaining but prohibited Soviet missiles, those states will not participate in such inspections. They will have no direct means of forming their own judgments as to Soviet compliance. (Presumably they will be able to monitor American activities taking place on their own soil and so assure themselves that the United States is in full compliance.) In matters regarding their vital national interests, states may justifiably seek independent information. This is a second, but weaker, situation where a third party monitoring capability may be of use.

Pictures of the Soviet SS-25 facility at Yurya and of the Saudi installation of Chinese-supplied ballistic missiles indicate that the basing installations can be readily discerned and identified using pictures with five to ten meter resolution.[33] It is possible that the mandated destruction of these facilities can be monitored at the present time. The INF Treaty's on-site verification provisions obviously permit the Soviet Union and the United States to check on one another's behavior in more detail than will appear in any satellite pictures —but the information gleaned during those inspections may never be available to the public in the United States and the basing nations.

Future Uses

It is often supposed that cross-border conflicts, such as between India and Pakistan or between Iran and Iraq, provide a third situation where a third party system might have utility. It is generally believed that the diffusion of information about capabilities and actions should serve to reduce tensions and, under some circumstances, deprive an aggressor of surprise.

A public-access satellite network might provide the necessary intelligence but would be acceptable to all parties only if the data were made available to all on an equal basis. Because national capabilities to build and operate reconnaissance satellites vary so much—India has orbited its own remote sensing satellite but Pakistan has no space capabilities—some international system might be desirable as a kind of "spy for hire," provided it were available to all.

Media Satellites

Remote sensing has proven its value as a tool in the gathering of news in four situations: when access to the surface is denied by authority; when access is dangerous; when access presents great difficulties so that the story cannot be reached in time; and when the story itself extends over enormous areas so that it only becomes apparent in a view from the sky encompassing thousands of square kilometers. Coverage of Chernobyl on the surface was forbidden by the government and presented deadly hazards as well. A follow-up story on the environmental damage caused by the accident requires a camera in space to be able to see the whole of the Ukraine in one view. Since Chernobyl many stories have been covered from space—primarily, but not exclusively, of military installations in the Soviet Union.

SPOT images have been used by news organizations to confirm assertions made by the United States regarding Soviet compliance. Pictures of Soviet facilities such as the Krasnoyarsk radar, the Sary Shagan laser facility, and a construction site for an electro-optical facility, probably including high-powered lasers, near the Nurek Dam have been published recently. Most of these pictures tend to demonstrate the validity of American statements, for example, that the Krasnoyarsk facility is a clear violation of the ABM Treaty and that the Soviets have an active research program in directed energy weapons.

The Soviet Union responded to the story on the Nurek electro-optical facility in an almost astounding way. *Pravda* published a picture of the facility near the Nurek Dam on the front page of its 22 January 1988 issue together with an article specifically mentioning the ABC TV news story on the site and then stating that the observatory was solely intended for tracking space objects.

The 1988 edition of the U.S. Defense Department's publication *Soviet Military Power* then reproduced the *Pravda* picture but suggested that the amount of electric power available to the site was far in excess of that needed for astronomical use.[34] It is doubtful whether either *Pravda* or *Soviet Military Power* would have published a picture of the Nurek site if Space Media Network (a Swedish corporation which takes pictures using SPOT and LANDSAT and then supplies the images plus analyses to the news media) had not first released SPOT pictures to the world's press. Some media observers believe that the visit of American representatives to the Krasnoyarsk radar facility in the fall of 1987 was, at least in part, a Soviet reaction to the publication of imagery of the site.

In the cases to date SPOT images have been used in a way which generally supports U.S. positions, and so the actions have not come into conflict with the U.S. government. Despite the fact that most of the pictures which have already appeared in the press have been used in ways critical of the Soviet Union, the Soviet government has made no protests either to SPOT, Space Media Network (the principal purveyor of such pictures), or the French or Swedish governments.[35]

Despite the generally good track record of the American media operating from space, the Reagan administration has shown a deep distrust of such efforts. The combination of the old space policy and the LANDSAT Commercialization Act has led to a situation where MediaSats must be licensed and must "operate in support of U.S. national security," broadly defined—or more precisely, undefined. The LANDSAT Act gives the secretaries of defense and state the power to suspend or revoke the license to operate a remote sensing system if either is dissatisfied with the images which are released. In effect the signal cable runs through the offices of the two secretaries, each of whom has a switch to break the connection.

This is a clear situation in which the government has established a form of prior restraint on the media. The restrictions will almost certainly be litigated in the Supreme Court as a test of the First Amendment. The question will turn on whether access to information is a necessary part of journalism and whether the government has the right to deny access—particularly when the system being used to observe the earth is privately owned or owned by a foreign concern. The case runs deeper than the famous case in the late 1970s when the *Progressive* magazine wished to print an article describing in modest but useful detail the principles which govern the design of thermonuclear weapons. In the *Progressive* case the magazine already had the information but might have been prevented from printing it under the terms of the Atomic Energy Act.

Today, the issue of freedom for private individuals to observe from space is dormant, for no American-operated system has sufficient resolution to make acute the problem of government security versus the public's right to know. It remains, however, an important issue to settle in advance because the dichotomy between the First Amendment and the LANDSAT Act is an important deterrent to potential builders of a MediaSat system.

Future Fears

Remote sensing satellites, particularly the improved ones which will be in orbit twenty years from now, will open up activities of governments and industries to the kind of scrutiny now reserved to the superpowers. One might hope that awareness of this transparency would, itself, act as a powerful deterrent to misbehavior. Realistically, however, observation satellites will not usher in an era of particularly greater stability than we now have, and we must suppose that tensions will continue to produce international crises. Some of these will involve the superpowers; some will involve only smaller nations. But observation satellites will make it at least conceivable that outside parties, the press or other nations, will find themselves in the possession of information about a crisis before the parties involved want to see the information made public.

If the press had obtained a picture of a Soviet missile in Cuba at precisely the time President John F. Kennedy and the Executive Committee of the National Security Council including, among others, Secretary of State Dean Rusk, Secretary of Defense Robert McNamara, and CIA Director John McCone, were considering the appropriate actions to take, the president could have been forced to take more violent action than he did.[36] We cannot pretend that there are no risks involved when private citizens or other governments gain access to what has previously been national intelligence. Government officials are properly concerned that the spread of such intelligence might affect their ability to manage crises successfully.

But there are also risks that journalists will gain access to similar information using the tools historically available to them. The principal national security risks are in no way unique to satellite images. There is little reason to expect the American press to act against American interests, but there is equally little reason to expect foreign journalists to act in support of our interests. For example, the plans for the 1961 Bay of Pigs invasion were known all over Washington before the action began but did not appear in the press; many top reporters were aware of U.S. concern about missiles in Cuba during the time between the U-2 discovery flight and President Kennedy's announcement, but the situation was not reported. For this reason it is surely preferable for the United States to take a position of leadership in the remote sensing industry, rather than to have the information flow entirely in the hands of foreigners. It is no longer possible to halt the momentum driving improvements in satellite technology; surely it is better to lead than to be moved by a tidal wave.

In fact, however, few of the problems alleged to be important appear to be either intractable or to have much effect on normal peacetime activities of any nation. If military forces are deployed for action, their location and disposition become a matter of real concern both to the operator of the forces and to his adversary. News-gathering satellites clearly provide a channel, but not a unique one, by which information of military significance can reach both the public and the parties to a conflict. The issue is not only one of whether or not the press would reveal information which would jeopardize American lives but also whether revelation of such data about third countries by U.S.-operated systems could jeopardize American or other friendly interests. Some potential for complicating American foreign policy clearly exists, and some observers with their roots in military reconnaissance believe that satellite imagery has an unusual potential for journalistic mischief in a field historically under firm government control.[37]

It is unlikely that information which qualifies as "intelligence" will be discovered by newsmen with cameras in space. Before sensitive information can be revealed it must be collected. Before data can be useful, they must be interpreted.

Obtaining images from space is not a trivial task. Not only must a satellite be in position to take the picture, which may occur only once or twice a week with existing commercial systems, it must be commanded to do so—on a pass where both weather and illumination cooperate. For SPOT and LANDSAT the delay between a programming request and acquisition of the picture by the satellite is at least twenty-four hours; a dedicated and properly designed media satellite system could reduce that to as little as twelve hours, but it is difficult to imagine a practical system in which the cycle time could be brought down lower. Existing satellites are in "sun synchronous" polar orbits. They see the polar regions several times a day but can view targets in the temperate zones, where most news is likely to occur, on a regular, but infrequent, basis. The "revisit interval" for SPOT is between two and four days at latitudes of interest; this functionally rules out coverage of breaking news.

A real difficulty is in knowing where to look. Close-look pictures which might reveal intimate details can cover only limited areas at a time; it is easy to miss a target whose location is known only approximately. It is equally difficult to locate a target which approaches the limits of resolution obtained in a wide-field picture, particularly if there is any uncertainty in its location. The history of the SPOT image of the Krasnoyarsk Radar, a picture discovered and processed by the Stockholm-based Space Media Network, broadcast by ABC, and reprinted in several defense-oriented publications is more illustrative.[38]

The radar is not at Krasnoyarsk, but near a village called Strelka. The entire facility covers an area only about 1000×750 meters, comprising only .02 percent of the picture. The Swedish analyst who located the radar did not know where in the image to look nor what was the layout of a Soviet "bistatic phased array radar"; he had to scan the picture for a target whose shape and location were both uncertain. The frame on which the radar was found was not the first he examined in his search. Without the near certainty that a newsworthy facility was located somewhere in the Krasnoyarsk region of the Soviet Union, no news organization would have invested the time and resources to acquire and study pictures of central Siberia.

A commercial observation satellite will rarely if ever provide its operators with the first information about actions which are newsworthy or of intelligence significance. Strong collateral information will have to be there first, information strong enough in most cases to form the basis of reportage. Acquisition and exploitation of a satellite image entails a significant commitment of resources. The difficulty of scanning an image pixel by pixel in the hope of finding something of interest, somewhere, should not be underestimated. Furthermore, satellite images require a great deal of study and interpretation to extract exciting information.

Another case illustrates the problem of timeliness. On 8 August 1987 a convoy of U.S. flagged Kuwaiti oil tankers escorted by American warships secretly entered the Straits of Hormuz. This is a situation where, one could imagine, the United States government might attempt to restrain coverage by a newsgathering satellite. Such restraint would have been largely irrelevant. It would have been unlikely that a satellite would have been in position to observe the initial movement of the vessels. After the first movement of the convoy the Iranian navy was presumably alerted by messages from its picket ships, signals from radar, or observation from the mainland. It is improbable that a commercial satellite will be in position to see an event and able to downlink the information quickly. This means that the imposition of serious restrictions on the operation of remote sensing satellites with resolutions on the order of a few meters is unwarranted except for events the very existence of which is sensitive for hours or days.

In short, the notion that commercial observation satellites, dedicated to the media or primarily used for other purposes, pose a serious threat to national security has been considerably exaggerated.

Operating a System

There is no future for a dedicated media satellite as long as only NASA-standard construction techniques are used. The media require high resolution, frequent coverage, and off-nadir viewing. Even more importantly, they need affordable "birds." They do not require high data transmission rates, since events of interest to satellite journalists will not occur with great frequency. Consequently, very few pictures will need to be taken on each orbit of the satellite, so on-board storage and intermittent transmission are feasible. It is also unnecessary for a media satellite to photograph an area as large as LANDSAT or even SPOT at one time, further reducing both the demands on the camera and the demands on the communications gear.

The stories which have already appeared based on satellite journalism have, with the single exception of the Chernobyl disaster, been investigative in character. It is important to recognize that the most important potential applications of media satellites are stories which require investigation and research and that breaking news will be difficult to cover. Consequently, an operator of a commercial and dedicated media satellite system might also find more conventional remote sensing applications for his images attractive. So long as the media can preempt other orders when necessary, there is no strong reason why the high resolution satellite news camera cannot be used by many customers.

Conclusion

In 1988 the best remote sensing satellites in reliable service can see objects between ten and thirty meters across. This is good enough for even untrained viewers to see and identify large installations. Identifying, recognizing, and describing smaller details remains the province of the expert photo-interpreter who must serve as an essential component of the analysis. But it is still possible that LANDSAT 7, to be launched late in the 1990s, will carry a camera which can resolve objects only five meters across and do it in natural color. There is reason to believe that future versions of SPOT, perhaps the fourth or fifth satellite in the projected series, might carry cameras at least that good and possibly better. Some military analysts believe that this is the critical quantum jump to make commercial satellite pictures readily useful in the military arena. As space launches become routine, and if the cost of lifting objects into orbit declines, the time for entrepreneurs—national and commercial—to enter the business will arrive, and the consequences will be profound.

At present a remote sensing satellite must serve many purposes with products which can be sold to a wide spectrum of clients. In the future we should be able to afford specialized and dedicated cameras in space, some devoted to studies of urban land use, others to agriculture, silvaculture, and geological exploration. By the early part of the next century commercial cameras capable of recording objects only a meter or two across should be in orbit—there is no technical reason why they should not be—making the sky transparent and opening many actions of the kind which are now shrouded by governments to the scrutiny of the world.

The enormous utility of space-based remote sensing, combined with the transparency of human activities which will inevitably accompany development of space, poses political and regulatory dilemmas for the governments of the world. To the extent that governments fetter the technology of remote sensing, they will sacrifice the benefits which it ought to bring. Furthermore, regulation of resolution, target coverage, and timeliness of publication of imagery must be totally international, and "leak proof," or it will prove to be ineffective. Since the technology of the present class of satellites is demonstrably within the reach of many countries, including some normally classed as "developing" rather than industrialized, it is questionable whether any kind of international regulatory scheme can evolve in opposition to market forces. It may become too easy for too many actors to enter the market for any form of regulation to be effective or desirable.

Instead, it is desirable for governments to recognize the utility and inevitability of a civil remote sensing regime and to adopt policies to foster private and truly commercial endeavors. Where necessary, governments ought not to shrink from indirect or even direct subsidization of improved systems. These subsidies can be justified by noting that remote sensing information has political and military utility (and hence the potential to allow its disseminators to exert influence or power) as well as ultimate economic value far in excess of the cost of the system. The subsidies are necessary at the present time because the market for space images is only now shifting from academic researchers to industrial and local governmental customers. Only in the past year or so has the value of satellite imagery been distinctly clear to users outside of the narrow fields where the science of remote sensing was developed.

The United States, in particular, has a tradition of free access to information. For that reason it is particularly inappropriate for this country to limit access by the news media to civilian satellite data or to attempt to restrict the technical abilities of U.S. built, launched, registered, and operated observation satellites.

A satellite goes where few men can, and where even fewer can interfere with its operation. Inevitably, as the price of images goes down and their sharpness improves, space will be a new staging ground not only for reportage and journalism, but also for science, for resource exploration, and for commercial development in ways which can only be guessed at today. Indeed, this entire paper has concentrated only on the easy applications, the ones which are not merely foreseeable, but practically obvious. Just as the many uses of the desktop computer were not predicted by its developers, so we can do no more than guess at the consequences of the information revolution which will be the result of the opening of the skies of earth to all.

ECONOMIC POLICY

New Technologies
Research and Development
Foreign Economic Policy
Third World
Finance

New Communications Technologies and Services

Walter S. Baer

Technology will be the principal driving force behind the introduction of new communications systems and services in the 1990s. Powerful communications satellites, fiber optic transmission links, digital switches, advanced television systems, and electronic information services are under development in many parts of the world. Technology is often considered an independent, exogenous force whose pace cannot be predicted; but like other human endeavors, technology develops in a particular social and political context. Regulatory, economic, and other public policies influence technology just as technology impacts policy.

This essay examines technological trends and developments expected over the next decade and explores their likely interaction with communications policy in the United States. The focus is on new communications products and services, with particular emphasis on consumer rather than business applications.[1] High definition television (HDTV) and broadband distribution networks are discussed in greater depth, both because they appear high on policy agendas and because they illustrate the interactions between technology and policy.

Technical Trends in Transmission and Processing

The technologies driving new communications and information services continue to advance, with no early saturation in sight. "More, better, and cheaper" characterizes the technical trends for both transmitting and processing information, introducing new trade-offs in system design and utilization.[2]

Among transmission technologies, digital fiber optic systems show the most spectacular gains. The fiber pairs installed in Los Angeles during the 1984 Olympics carried 45 megabits per second (45 Mbps), enough capacity for 672 digital voice channels. Fiber systems installed in 1988 can carry 565 Mbps, a twelvefold increase in four years. They have become the transmission medium of choice for nearly all new links between telephone central offices. Fiber optic systems planned for the 1990s will have capacities in the thousands of megabits. Nonetheless, while fiber optic are advancing most rapidly, satellite, coaxial cable, and microwave, and other terrestrial transmission systems are improving as well. They present moving targets for performance/cost comparisons with fiber.

At the same time the processing of information is becoming faster and cheaper. The pace of development is particularly striking in the underlying technologies of semiconductors, optoelectronics, and computing:

- Semiconductor very-large-scale integration (VLSI) largely follows the path predicted over a decade ago, with more than a fiftyfold improvement in the state-of-the-art in ten years.[3] Silicon VLSI circuits now contain more than one million logical components (gates) on a single chip, with more computing power than most computer mainframes of the 1970s.
- New technologies of chip design ("silicon compilers") enable low cost production of communications components such as digital coders/decoders (codecs) and signal processors. Although VLSI chips today are from silicon, gallium arsenide and related compounds promise even higher speed performance for digital switches and integrated optic/electronic devices.
- Parallel processing computer architectures are becoming commercially available and should find important applications in telecommunications switching and information retrieval systems.
- New discoveries in superconductivity may result in even faster, more efficient switches and processors in the long run, although superconductivity does not seem likely to play a significant role in communications systems in the next ten years.

These developments feed directly into improved telecommunications switches, private branch exchanges (PBXs), facsimile scanners, cellular telephones, and virtually all other communications equipment. One result of advances in integrated circuits for consumers will be the introduction of a wristwatch pager in early 1989.

Software engineering is also advancing but not as rapidly as hardware technologies. Software development dominates the cost of most new communications systems; more than half of the technical staff at AT&T Bell Laboratories and Bell Communications Research work on software problems. Software trends include distributing intelligence throughout complex networks, and developing "expert systems" for routine network operation, maintenance and control.[4] Software improvements also make it easier to interact with communications or information systems. For example, voice response systems let callers use push-button telephone to access computer-based information such as stock quotations, airline schedules, and theater ticket offerings. Software that could recognize human voice commands would be much more powerful, but the technology of general-purpose voice recognition is still not commercially available. Developers hope that voice recognition software will be integrated in communications systems sometime in the next decade.

Technical advances in information transmission and processing accelerate the trend to digital communications which began in the 1960s. Although the United States telephone network remains a mixture of analog and digital facilities, it continues to evolve in the digital direction toward the planned Integrated Services Digital Network (ISDN). As currently conceived, the ISDN will provide customers with end-to-end digital service at 144 kpbs—specifically, two 64 kpbs circuit-switched channels plus a 16 kpbs packet-switched channel. Although implementing this "narrowband" ISDN will take years and billions of investment dollars, it can utilize existing copper wires, and the 64 kpbs switching technology it requires is commercially available today.[5]

However, the narrowband ISDN concept may already be too restrictive for some business customers who want higher speed data and voice capacities.[6] International standards groups are now working on a "broadband" ISDN that would provide end-to-end digital communications at speeds of 150 Mbps or more—1000 times greater than the narrowband ISDN.[7] Fiber optic transmission systems can readily handle these data rates, but high speed switching in the megabit-per-second range is still a laboratory phenomenon. Broadband ISDN services presumably would be implemented first to commercial customers with dedicated fiber optic links. Switched broadband ISDN services to businesses and homes remain a telephone company vision for the late 1990s or beyond.

Transmission and Processing Trade-offs

Communications system designers have always had to consider trade-offs between transmission capacity and information processing at the sender's and receiver's ends. Telegraph lines in the nineteenth century had little information carrying capacity, so that operators encoded messages into a series of short and long pulses (dots and dashes) and decoded them at the receiving end. Today, computers process information at rates measured in millions-of-instructions-per-second, and transmission lines operate at hundreds of megabits per second, but trade-offs still are necessary.

Facsimile transmission provides a good illustration. Facsimile (fax) requires equipment to scan a document and convert the information to analog or digital signals, a transmission link from sender to receiver, and equipment at the receiving end to process the information and print it on paper. Before 1980 facsimile scanners produced analog signals for transmission over analog telephone lines. Sending one page of text took from three to six minutes. Advances in processing led to digital fax machines that transmit one page over the same standard telephone lines in less than one minute. The next advance has been to use digital transmission lines with higher data rates, requiring only a few seconds to transmit a fax page. Fax transmission speed in the past decade thus has increased by about a factor of fifty, both from improvements in fax signal processing and from the greater transmission capacity available on new digital lines. The cost of facsimile equipment has also decreased dramatically, increasing the number of fax users and opening up new markets.

Another example of information processing/transmission trade-offs is the growing use of local information retrieval systems, based on optical storage devices and more powerful personal computers. In the past large databases were expensive to store and replicate. Consequently, users accessed them at a central site over telephone lines and incurred both communications and processing charges with each inquiry. Development of CD-ROM and related optical devices capable of storing hundreds of megabytes can now bring these databases to the user for local searching on his or her personal computer (PC).[8] The cost of the database and its updates will generally be fixed, with no additional charges per inquiry. As a result, frequent database users will increasingly substitute local retrieval for long distance access of remote databases in the next decade.

Video transmission provides a third illustration. Transmitting a standard television signal in the United States requires a six megahertz (6MHz) analog bandwidth. Using straightforward digitizing techniques, the same signal requires a digital transmission rate of ninety megabits per second (90 Mbps). However, processing the picture before transmitting it can reduce the effective bandwidth or bit rate required. Bandwidth compression equipment has been available for several years to process analog television signals in a way that two television programs can be transmitted over a single 6MHz channel.[9] The cost of the processing equipment at either end must be compared with the cost of an extra transmission channel. Generally, for coaxial cable systems that have large channel capacity, "two for one" analog signal processing has not been worth the cost. This approach might be economic, however, for some microwave or satellite transmission applications where bandwidth is at a premium.

Digital processing of television signals, using data compression techniques that remove redundancies in the signal, can reduce the transmission bit rate by a factor of two-to-four with no loss in perceived picture quality. Further compression requires some compromise in the amount and quality of motion displayed. Slowly moving pictures adequate for most teleconferences can be compressed to 1.5 Mbps or even 64 kpbs, data rates that are now becoming widely available throughout the United States telephone network, but these compression schemes are not suitable for the degree of motion required for entertainment television. Still pictures can be readily compressed and transmitted over standard telephone lines in under a minute. Japanese manufacturers have developed such "slow scan" terminals, selling for under $500, for consumer as well as business markets.

The trade-offs between communications transmission and processing are dynamic ones. There is no final answer. In his 1987 report on telephone industry competition, Peter Huber emphasized the technical trends favoring communications processing and switching:

> In the past hundred years, the basic low-density transmission technology—twisted copper wire routed through underground conduits or via overhead poles—has not changed much, nor has its price. Fiber-optic cable has slashed transmission costs for high-

density applications, but the last mile of the network, where about half the transmission expense arises, carries mostly low-density traffic. In the past fifteen years, on the other hand, revolutionary developments in electronics have slashed the costs of switching and other forms of network intelligence. The inexorable trend is therefore to move switching out toward the end user. Making connections at a distance costs more in increased transmission than it saves in lowering the number of connections needed.[10]

These trends have indeed resulted in distributing intelligence within networks and substituting processing for transmission. The rise of packet switching provides one illustration. But advances in transmission technologies may change the balance again. With the carrying capacities of fiber optic (and other) transmission systems increasing so rapidly, packet switched services may lose some of their appeal. Similarly, we may see a glut in long haul transmission capacity in the next several years that will bring more price competition and accelerate the shakeout among long distance carriers.

Adoption of Communications Technologies

Technology's advance has brought new products and services to the marketplace over the past decade. The first large-scale test of cellular mobile telephone service was begun in Chicago in 1978. Commercial service started in 1983, and by 1988 more than 180 cellular systems were in operation serving more than one million subscribers.

Cable television's reach has expanded from fewer than 20 percent of United States households in 1978 to more than 50 percent today. The penetration of videocassette recorders (VCRs) has grown even more rapidly than cable. VCRs are now found in well over half of American households. For many families, watching a videotape has replaced Saturday night television viewing and moviegoing. Videotape sales and rentals have, in fact, become the largest source of revenue for motion pictures, surpassing theater box office receipts.[11]

The personal computer has changed from a curiosity ten years ago to a fixture in offices and a significant number of homes. Although personal computers themselves are not yet part of the normal home routine, microprocessors have been integrated into a wide range of consumer products. Telephone answering machines, VCRs, television receivers, and addressable cable converters all contain sophisticated microprocessors that control their increasingly complex functions. Microprocessors are also widely used as control devices in refrigerators, microwave ovens, washers, dryers, and sewing machines. Automobiles now incorporate microprocessors for control functions from adjusting the correct fuel mixture to remembering the proper seat adjustment for each driver. And during the 1980s consumers have become accustomed to using computers disguised as automatic teller machines (ATMs), in-store ordering kiosks, and pay telephones.

Just as Molière's bourgeois gentleman expressed surprise at his ability to speak prose, consumers might now be astonished by the number and variety of microprocessors they use in everyday life. The situation is analogous to the development and diffusion of electric motors. Sixty years ago, electric motors were too large and too expensive for most consumer applications. The development of cheap, fractional-horsepower motors led to the proliferation of small motorized appliances after World War II. Today, American consumers typically own dozens of electric motors in power tools, can openers, knives, mixers, blenders, toys, and toothbrushes. Similarly, microprocessors are proliferating quietly and unseen through the consumer economy.

A look back at these developments over the past decade suggests some general points about how consumers adopt new communications technologies. First, changes occur incrementally over a period of years after a new technology or service has been introduced. Even color television, which nearly all television viewers wanted when they saw it, took more than ten years to reach 50 percent of American households (see table 1). Cable television took four decades to achieve 50 percent household penetration. The most rapid adoption occurs for new products, like color television sets or VCRs, that can be purchased as individual units. Technologies that must be integrated into networks, like digital PBXs, packet switching, or fiber optic distribution systems, take much longer to diffuse.

Second, consumer adoption of new technologies and services typically follows a top-down pattern. More affluent, better educated consumers are the first to try a new technology or service—not only because they have more money to spend, but because their life styles prompt them to be early adopters.[12] The rest of the market follows in

Table 1 Adoption of Communications Technologies

Technology	Approximate Year of Commercial Introduction	1 Million U.S. Households by
Telephone	1876	1899
Pushbutton Telephone	1964	n.a.
Answering Machine	1970	1982
Cellular Telephone	1983	1988
Television (Black and White)	1946	1949
Television (Color)	1961	1963
VCR	1975	1979
Cable Television	1948	1964
Satellite TV Receiver	1976	1985
Compact Disc Player	1983	1986
Personal Computer	1976	1981

Sources: Historical Statistics of the United States; Electronic Industries Association; AT&T Bell Laboratories; Paul Kagan Associates.
n.a. = not available; x = not yet achieved.

the predictable "s-curve" pattern shown in diffusion studies. Compact disc audio players and telephone answering machines seem to be following that diffusion curve toward mass market acceptance. Other new products like home banking and videotext have yet to show much appeal beyond a limited, elite audience.

Many communications innovations also meet with early consumer resistance, even when they find wide acceptance later. Telephone answering machines provide a good illustration. When introduced to the consumer market in the early 1970s, many people found them "inhuman," "insulting," and "intimidating." "I would never talk to that machine," was an often heard comment ten years ago. Most of us were uncomfortable leaving a recorded message on an answering machine without the familiar interaction with a human respondent (some of us still are). Yet today, telephone answering machines have become a way of life in urban upper middle class households. Lifestyle changes, resulting in many more households with no one home during the day, certainly contributed to their acceptance, but so did the familiarity from more than a decade of use. Now many people consider them necessities. As one observer notes, "I would much rather

20 percent of U.S. Households by	50 percent of U.S. Households by	No. of years to 50 percent of Households
1907	1946	70
1976	1986	22
1988	x	x
x	x	x
1950	1953	7
1967	1972	11
1985	1988	13
1979	1988	40
x	x	x
x	x	x
1986	x	x

leave a message on a machine than have to call back again and again. In fact, I'm annoyed now when someone does not have an answering machine on the line." Objections that we hear today about cellular telephones and interactive voice response systems may similarly be transitory, so that these services may find widespread acceptance in the 1990s.

On the other hand, the promised benefits from new technologies and services are often overstated when they are first introduced. Promotional hyperbole accompanying a new development may lead to a counterreaction gainsaying its advantages. The expansion of television program choices brought about by cable represents a good example. During the 1970s cable proponents often talked about 100 or more new television channels, bringing subscribers everything from grand opera to local zoning hearings. Extravagant hopes for specialized, high-brow fare did not materialize, and some attempts to develop arts and cultural channels, such as a failed CBS Cable venture, suffered heavy losses. This has prompted some critics to decry cable's "failure" to provide "true diversity" of program choices. However, these criticisms should not overshadow the fact that cable does deliver many specialized channels of programming that are not found on broadcast television. They include (among others) channels dedicated to news, sports, weather, financial information, children's programming, rock music, country music, and live coverage of the United States Congress. While these offerings may not satisfy critics who want noncommercial, high-culture programming, they have clearly increased the range of program choices offered to United States television viewers. Looking ahead, we should allow neither overblown promotion claims nor critical cynicism to obscure the real benefits that may come from new products and services in the next decade.

Regulatory Influences on Innovation

The pace of innovation in telecommunications also depends strongly on regulatory policies. Despite the sharp turn toward deregulation during the past decade, telecommunications remains highly regulated compared with other high-technology industries.[13] Under the authority of the 1934 Communications Act the Federal Communications Commission (FCC) grants cellular telephone licenses, approves telephone company investments in long distance transmission facilities, allocates and assigns portions of the radio spectrum for commercial uses, sets detailed technical requirements for radio and television broadcasting, and generally develops, monitors, and enforces technical standards for all spectrum uses.[14]

Regulation generally is more effective in stable industries than in those where technologies and markets are rapidly changing. Under the 1946 Federal Administrative Procedure Act the FCC must adhere to elaborate rulemaking procedures and give all interested parties time to review, comment on, and challenge proposed changes. These procedures significantly increase the time between development of an innovation and its commercial introduction, as well as the cost of bringing a new product or service to market. Cellular radio technology was developed by Bell Laboratories in the 1960s, and AT&T was ready to begin cellular telephone service by 1970, but opposition by competing interests delayed its commercial introduction for some thirteen years.[15] Developers of other communications services can tell similar stories.

Spectrum allocation and assignment probably raises the most formidable barriers to new service introduction. The FCC, charged with management of the broadcast spectrum, allocates specific frequency bands for specific uses and then assigns particular frequencies bands within those allocations to particular users. This worked well in the 1930s when there were relatively few uses of the radio spectrum, but the explosion of technology and applications since World War II has created a hodgepodge of narrow, rigid frequency allocations. Various mobile communications services, for example, are allocated narrow bands of spectrum at different frequencies. With demand burgeoning, mobile communications suppliers are seeking to use bandwidth allocated for other services, such as FM radio subcarriers and portions of the UHF television spectrum.[16] In this fragmented environment a developer of a new digital paging service (for example, sending stock quotes to portable, pocket-size receivers) may find it difficult to obtain compatible frequencies in different cities in order to distribute the service nationally. In hindsight allocating a wider band of spectrum for mobile communications would help designers serve more users more efficiently.[17]

In the interest of fairness to all prospective users the FCC holds comparative hearings or lotteries to assign frequencies or grant licenses when there are many competing applicants. This process, however, may hamper entrepreneurial efforts to develop new communications services. For example, Airfone, Inc., started airplane to ground telephone service in 1977 under an "experimental" FCC license. The experiment proved successful, and commercial demand for air to ground telephone service clearly emerged by the early 1980s. The FCC, however, could not assign permanent use of needed spectrum to the company that had pioneered the service. Instead, it proposed in 1984 to award frequencies by lottery, allowing other companies to compete without incurring Airfone's development costs. Without the assurance of needed spectrum, Airfone was forced to sell out two years later to a larger company. Clearly, the FCC is faced with conflicting objectives of encouraging innovation and assuring equal opportunities for competing users of scarce spectrum. The frequency assignment procedures now used tend to favor large, established companies over small, entrepreneurial developers of new services.

Technology's Impact on Policy

Technology influences communications policy in three principal ways: first, it opens new possibilities and expands the range of choices, which may require government action, approval or coordination; second, it may bring unforeseen problems as it is widely adopted, demanding governmental response; and third, it may disturb the boundaries drawn by legislators and regulators to separate communications services and the industries providing them.

Expansion of consumer choice comes about from improved variety, higher quality, and reduced cost—more, better, and cheaper. Some technical advances offer wholly new choices not previously available; for example, VCRs allow viewers to record television programs for viewing at a more convenient time. Communications satellites introduced in the 1960s permitted transoceanic television transmission for the first time. Most technical developments, however, represent incremental improvements in quality, convenience, and cost. Fiber optic systems improve the quality of telephone transmission; push-button telephones make calling more convenient (and open possibilities for new voice-response services); telephone answering machines provide lower cost alternatives to answering services.

Here the policy goal is to maximize the flow of benefits from new technology while preventing market or government failure. For example, the FCC has decided to license two cellular telephone companies in each metropolitan area in order to ensure orderly development of cellular services while providing some benefits from competition. In cases such as high definition television, government policymakers may decide to play a leading or supporting role in setting standards. Defining the appropriate government role in standards is a tricky business, since the competitive marketplace may be better able to deal with system compatibility issues. Premature government action to set standards often proves counterproductive. Nevertheless, government action or coordination may be necessary to avoid policy gridlock, which would inordinately delay public benefits from technological development.[18]

Most technologies generate unforeseen problems when they are widely adopted, even if initial uses seem relatively benign. Electronic bulletin boards, for example, make information widely available to PC users and encourage the exchange of messages among like-minded users. But bulletin boards have also created problems of fraud, libel, and obscenity.[19] Unscrupulous individuals have posted credit card numbers on electronic bulletin boards, thus encouraging fraudulent long distance calling or credit card purchases. In a few instances electronic bulletin boards allegedly have been used to coordinate criminal activities by political fringe groups. In fact, the more effective the new technology, the more likely it will be used for antisocial or illegal purposes. Public policy must then deal with these unexpected consequences of technological development and diffusion.

New technologies, however, probably influence communications policy most by creating conflicts between previously separated industries. The 1934 Communications Act established clear boundaries between common carrier service, broadcast services, and other telecommunications services and generally set different rules and regulations for each sector. Rapid advances in communications technology during and after World War II began to play havoc with these regulatory boundaries. Microwave transmission made it feasible for companies to establish private communications networks in the 1950s, bypassing the telephone common carriers. Coaxial cable technology, in a continuing state of development since the 1940s, permitted local cable television distribution in competition with the established broadcasters.

The development of electronic computing resulted in a collision between the information processing and telephone industries. The conflict was recognized in the 1956 AT&T antitrust settlement which prohibited AT&T and Western Electric from entering the burgeoning computer business. Technological development continued nonetheless. Telephone switches essentially became computers, while computer manufacturers saw lucrative markets for their products in telecommunications. By 1969, when the FCC held its first Computer Inquiry, the technological convergence between the unregulated computer industry and the regulated telecommunications carriers was clear. This collision between two large technological industries, highlighted by the battles between AT&T and IBM, dominated much of communications policymaking during the 1970s and was a significant factor in the 1981 decision to break up the Bell system.[20] Today, the convergence of telecommunications and computing is widely recognized, but its political and policy reverberations still echo.

Technology's march ensures similar collisions between entrenched business interests in the next decade. The development of high definition television threatens to leave over-the-air broadcasters behind cable television, direct broadcast satellites (DBS), and other technologies with fewer spectrum constraints. Fiber optic developments bring new competition between the cable and telephone industries for delivering video programming to the home.

High Definition Television

Television technology has advanced far beyond the National Television System Committee (NTSC) standard adopted in the United States nearly fifty years ago. High definition television (HDTV) promises picture quality comparable to 35mm film, with sound as good as that from a digital compact disc. The path from NTSC to HDTV in the United States, however, seems a long and bumpy one, with many obstacles along the way.

The Japan Broadcasting Corporation (NHK) has been the world leader in developing HDTV since the early 1970s. NHK has adopted a "studio production standard" with 1125 scanning lines and a 16:9 screen width-to-height aspect ratio. The NTSC standard is based on 525 scanning lines and a 4:3 aspect ratio. HDTV's wider screen, as much as its higher resolution, contributes to viewer perception of a superior picture. Each HDTV frame has more than five times as many picture elements as an NTSC frame.

The NHK HDTV studio production standard has been endorsed by the Society of Motion Picture and Television Engineers (SMPTE) and is now being used for movie and television production in North America. It offers picture quality comparable to 35mm film with the advantages of videotape for easy editing and fast turnaround. *Chasing Rainbows*, a mini-series presented by the Canadian Broadcasting Corporation, and *Innocent Victims*, a television movie produced for CBS, were both shot using HDTV videotape and then converted to the NTSC standard for broadcasting. The NHK 1125-line format seems likely to be used widely for movie and television production in the 1990s. Within a decade extensive HDTV production could encourage the studios to replace film prints with satellite distribution of HDTV movies for theater projection.

NHK demonstrated its HDTV system last summer by transmitting the

Olympic games from South Korea to various demonstration sites in Japan via satellite. HDTV broadcasting to Japanese home viewers will begin in 1990 when Japan launches its BS-3 direct broadcast satellite (DBS) service. The DBS service will use a bandwidth compression technique known as MUSE to reduce the transmission bandwidth from the 30MHz required for the studio production system to about 9MHz. Japanese manufacturers will also introduce HDTV television receivers, VCRs, and videodisc players commercially in Japan by 1990, and they have announced plans to bring this HDTV consumer equipment to the United States in 1991 or 1992.

The NHK HDTV system is not compatible with NTSC (or with the PAL or SECAM 625-line television standards widely adopted in Europe and other parts of the world). Viewers will have to purchase new, expensive receivers to get HDTV; prices in the early 1990s are expected to fall in the $3,000–$3,500 range. Moreover, the 10MHz MUSE system planned for DBS broadcasting in Japan cannot be carried over the 6MHz United States broadcast television channels assigned by the FCC.

Various alternative advanced television systems that would be more compatible with NTSC have been proposed for the United States.[21] Most of these alternatives are in the conceptual or prototype stages and have not yet been field tested. "Advanced television" (ATV) is a more appropriate rubric for these systems than HDTV, since some of them involve improving the 525-line NTSC signal without providing more lines of resolution or wider aspect ratios. Table 2 shows the leading ATV concepts proposed as of this writing.[22] They are listed in three categories: systems that can be carried on a single 6MHz channel, systems that require a second channel to augment the basic NTSC signal, and wideband systems that require transmission bandwidths greater than 6MHz. These are all analog systems. Digital transmission of HDTV, or of television signals in general, awaits the development of broadband fiber optic networks to the home.

One ATV approach is to use today's technology to clean up the 6MHz NTSC signal as much as possible. Some of the NTSC viewing defects or "artifacts" stem from the way color information was added in the 1950s to the black and white "luminance" information, resulting in interference between the luminance signal and the color signal. Other artifacts arise from the interlaced scanning adopted as part of the NTSC standard which requires two scans ("fields") to build each pic-

Table 2 Advanced Television Transmission Systems

System Name and Developer	Scanning Lines per Frame	Aspect Ratio
Single Channel Systems		
Super NTSC: Faroudja Labs	525/1050	4:3
HD-NTSC: Del Rey Group	525	5:3
ACTV I: Sarnoff Lab (RCA/GE/SRI)	525	5:3
MUSE 6: Japan Broadcasting Corp. (NHK)	525	16:9 or 4:3
Narrow MUSE: NHK	1125	16:9
Dual Channel Systems		
VISTA: Glenn/NYIT	1125	16:9
HDS-NA: North American Philips	1050	16:9
ACTV II: Sarnoff Lab	1050	5:3
MUSE 9: NHK	1125	16:9 or 4:3
Wideband Systems		
MUSE: NHK commercially in Japan	1125	16:9
HDMAC-60: North American Philips	1050	16:9

*ATV signals on NTSC receivers will show some degradation from standard NTSC and the wide aspect ratios accommodated by masking the top and bottom of the screen or losing the sid

ture. Signal processing techniques can remove or minimize these artifacts, giving a cleaner NTSC signal for broadcast or cable transmission over a conventional 6MHz channel. Television receivers with the appropriate decoders, either built-in or added as an adaptor unit, will show an improved picture. However, standard NTSC receivers will still be able to display the standard NTSC picture with relatively little degradation.[23]

Faroudja Laboratories has developed its "Super NTSC" system using improved scanning, filtering, and signal processing techniques. A proprietary encoder must be added to every NTSC camera to give the improved signal, which is then transmitted over conventional 6MHz channels. Special receivers with line doubling, frame storage, and signal processing circuits can display a 1050 line picture. This equipment has been built and successfully demonstrated, but it is expensive;

Transmission Bandwidth (MHz)	Compatible with NTSC Receivers?	Status
6	Yes	Demonstrated
6	Yes*	Computer Simulation
6	Yes*	Computer Simulation
6	Yes*	Computer Simulation
6	No	Computer Simulation
6 + 3	Yes*	Prototype Demonstrated
6 + 3	Yes*	Prototype Demonstrated
6 + 6	Yes*	Computer Simulation
6 + 3	Yes*	Computer Simulation
10	No	To Be Introduced in 1990
9.5	No	Prototype Demonstrated

panels of the ATV picture.

coders and decoders now cost several thousand dollars each. Mass production could bring down the cost significantly, however, if the Faroudja Super NTSC system were widely adopted.[24] Matsushita and Hitachi have also developed systems of this sort to improve picture quality while retaining the NTSC transmission standard.

Other systems proposed by the David Sarnoff Laboratory, the Del Rey Group, and NHK use different technical approaches to transmit wide aspect "improved NTSC" signals over a 6MHz channel. For each system standard receivers would display a standard, perhaps slightly degraded NTSC picture. New receivers with signal processing circuits would show noticeably improved pictures. Better HDTV pictures can be transmitted over a 6MHz channel by sacrificing NTSC compatibility. NHK has proposed a "Narrow MUSE" system with 1125 scanning lines and a 16:9 aspect ratio providing, according to NHK's computer simulations, pictures superior to all the "improved" or "enhanced" NTSC approaches. MIT and Zenith, among others, have also proposed 6MHz "bandwidth efficient" systems incompatible with existing NTSC receivers.

The dual channel ATV systems augment the NTSC signal with additional picture and sound information carried on a second channel. Suitably equipped receivers process both signals and recombine them to display a higher resolution image. Prototype dual channel systems have been demonstrated by William and Karen Glenn of the New York Institute of Technology, North American Philips, and the Sarnoff Laboratory. Another dual channel system has been proposed by NHK as part of its MUSE family.

Finally, wideband systems such as the NHK original MUSE and HDMAC-60, proposed by North American Philips, offer high quality HDTV transmissions at bandwidths greater than 6MHz. Of course, they require new television receivers and are incompatible with NTSC. At present these wideband approaches seem most appropriate for satellite transmission and HDTV videocassette distribution.

There is really no way to compare the systems listed in table 2 at the present time. Only the NHK MUSE system has been fully developed and field tested. The others, including the variation on MUSE announced by NHK this spring, are still in the early development stages. Technically, one can say that systems using more bandwidth will generally provide better pictures and/or be more robust in various transmission environments. At the same time, maintaining compatibility with NTSC will generally lead to less efficiency in bandwidth utilization and/or compromises in picture quality. Dual channel systems require the greatest bandwidth but may not necessarily deliver the highest quality pictures. So far, comparisons among ATV systems have been made principally by computer simulation. Direct comparisons require operating hardware systems, which are still at least months and millions of research and development dollars away.

Policy Issues and Stakeholders

HDTV development in the United States raises all three kinds of public policy issues noted in the introduction:

- What should government policymakers do, if anything, to make HDTV available to American viewers as rapidly and inexpensively as possible?

- How should policy deal with the problems raised by HDTV's introduction or the unintended impacts of its widespread adoption? For example, should American viewer investment in NTSC receivers be protected in some manner?

- How will the existing stakeholders be affected? What role should public policy play in mediating among their competing interests?

This last question demands particular attention, since HDTV policy involves many major players with substantial stakes.

Broadcasters have the most to risk. Their 6MHz channel assignments and detailed technical regulations constrain them far more than other distribution media. Their worst-case scenario has American viewers responding eagerly to MUSE or another incompatible HDTV system in the 1990s. Broadcast stations might then see their audiences and revenues erode as cable and DBS distribute HDTV programs. The broadcast industry thus hopes to find some consensus favoring an NTSC compatible, 6MHz solution or a dual channel approach. But how would broadcasters obtain a second channel for HDTV transmission? With today's technology more broadcast channels could be squeezed into the UHF television band, but the existing regulatory regime makes spectrum reallocation or reassignment excruciatingly difficult.[25] Allocating more UHF bandwidth for television would be bitterly opposed by land mobile services and other prospective users of broadcast spectrum.

Cable operators see HDTV as an opportunity to offer subscribers new services and further differentiate cable from broadcast programming. Although state-of-the-art technology can pack more than seventy channels on a single cable, most cable systems do not have unused capacity and would have to displace some existing programs to carry HDTV. Moreover, distortion, reflections, and other transmission artifacts would show up much more strongly on HDTV than on NTSC signals. Cable operators thus will have to upgrade or technically "tune-up" their systems to carry HDTV. Still, cable companies have strong incentives to embrace HDTV when it appears in the American market—both because HDTV may attract new subscribers and increase revenues and because cable companies cannot afford to let videocassettes, DBS, or the telephone companies overtake them as the distributors of HDTV to the home.

Satellite system operators and programmers view HDTV as possibly the key to direct broadcast satellite (DBS) success in the 1990s. Although DBS has not been successfully launched in the United States, with several prominent failures during the 1980s, it technically is an excellent way to distribute HDTV signals. DBS systems are not constrained by the 6MHz channels assigned to terrestrial broadcasters. Consequently, HDTV could enable DBS systems to make an end run around their broadcast and cable competitors. Home Box Office, RCA/GE, and Hughes Communications show interest in backing DBS systems which would include high definition programming. Japan, of course, will demonstrate the technical feasibility of transmitting HDTV via DBS beginning in 1990 or 1991.

Telephone companies see HDTV as a way to get into the video distribution business and justify building fiber optic networks to the home. Although currently prohibited from offering video services themselves (but not from building facilities and leasing capacity on them to others), the telephone companies do not want to be cut out of the video distribution business in the long term. They believe in a "single fiber solution" that would ultimately carry all voice, data, and video services to the home. Broadband fiber optic distribution systems could carry HDTV without the 6MHz bandwidth limitations of broadcast channels. BellSouth demonstrated HDTV transmissions over fiber optics at the 1988 Democratic National Convention in Atlanta, and several telephone companies hope to begin field trials of HDTV distribution as soon as the technology is commercially available.

United States consumer electronics manufacturers see HDTV as the vehicle to regain a substantial share of the television equipment market lost to Japan over the last two decades. They strongly favor adopting a United States standard for HDTV different from the NHK standard, so that Japanese manufacturers will not have a head start in building HDTV receivers for the American market. "Let's not lose another market to Japan," say William and Karen Glenn in a recent *New York Times* article: "The American market for HDTV sets is estimated to be as big as $20 billion a year by 1997. The big question is where will those sets be made."[26] European consumer electronic manufacturers such as Philips also favor rejecting the NHK HDTV standard so they have a better shot at the American market.

Television viewers are the stakeholders most directly affected, since they have some $50 billion invested in more than 150 million NTSC receivers. While the early adopters will benefit from better television pictures and sound, other viewers will not want a new HDTV system to obsolete existing program services or their investments in television sets and VCRs.

No one in fact knows how eagerly American television viewers will take to HDTV. The system developers in Japan, Europe, and North America are optimistic that demand will swell once consumers compare HDTV pictures and sound with conventional television. The rapid market acceptance of compact disc audio players helps fuel that optimism. But there remain skeptics. A recent audience study by the Advanced Television Research Project at MIT reports: "Mass audience viewers prefer HDTV to NTSC in simultaneous, side by side comparisons. But the preference is not as strong as was expected and is highly influenced by the character of the programming and viewing conditions. We conclude that, to the eyes of the typical television viewer, the difference between NTSC and baseband HDTV is a subtle one highly dependent on environmental factors."[27] The MIT study also concluded that "viewers did not indicate a willingness to pay a substantial premium for an advanced video receiver based on what they saw in our tests." These results are not conclusive, as the MIT study makes clear, but they suggest that HDTV acceptance in the marketplace may not be as rapid as was the adoption of color television receivers and VCRs.

Setting HDTV Standards

Although HDTV has been under development since the early 1970s, American stakeholder and policymakers did not seriously focus on HDTV issues until very recently. Today, most participants and observers agree that agreement on standards that provide for an evolutionary path from NTSC to HDTV is essential. And because the issues are so complex, with so many competing interests, the federal government, through the FCC, should take the lead in setting HDTV standards.

In November 1987 the FCC created an Advisory Committee on Advanced Television Service. The committee's Interim Report, released in June 1988, recommends "establishing, at least ultimately, an HDTV standard for terrestrial broadcasting."[28] However, the committee faces formidable hurdles. Except for the Japanese NHK system, no other advanced television system has been tested thoroughly enough to warrant comparative judgments. Most are only technical concepts supported by computer simulations. Development and testing of even prototype hardware will not be feasible before 1989, and determining the full "spectrum impact" of the various alternatives may take at least another year.[29] By then, of course, the NHK system may be in commercial operation.

On 1 September 1988 the FCC issued a Tentative Decision that any broadcast HDTV service must be compatible with current NTSC receivers or simulcast with an NTSC signal on separate broadcast channels.[30] This decision rejects MUSE or any over-the-air system that requires more than 6MHz of continuous broadcast spectrum. However, HDTV transmission by cable, satellite, or other nonbroadcast means could use a noncompatible system. The FCC's Tentative Decision also requests comments about whether additional spectrum should be made available to broadcasters for augmented HDTV transmission on a second 3MHz or 6MHz channel. Comments were due by 31 October 1988.

In the short term, then, the FCC is the principal policy focus for developing agreement on HDTV standards and evolutionary paths. Broadcasters are supporting an Advanced Television Test Center to test the various HDTV concepts under development and are also funding an Advanced Television Research Program at MIT. The cable industry has its own HDTV committee and has established a Cable Television Laboratory to pursue HDTV developments. These programs could bring about the first real cooperations between the broadcast and cable industries in seeking a consensus on ATV and HDTV.

In the longer run policy should aim at making HDTV available to viewers without the constraints imposed by the fifty-year-old NTSC system. The FCC seemed to favor this viewpoint in its Notice of Inquiry on advanced television systems: "To the extent that such an approach is both technically feasible and economically efficient, we now incline toward the view that, in the event we establish improved broadcast television systems, they should be implemented in a manner that allows eventually for the complete replacement of the NTSC, so that the benefits of improved off air television service may be enjoyed by the nation's viewers generally."[31] This approach is likely to require a two-stage evolution. The first stage would include one or more advanced television transmission systems compatible with existing NTSC receivers but offering enhanced picture and sound quality to those who purchase new equipment. Developing a "smart" television receiver would contain signal processors to decode both NTSC and ATV signals. If the receiver has an "open architecture" that can process a variety of ATV signals, no single standard for ATV systems need be set in this first stage.[32] Competing single channel, dual channel, and wideband systems could compete in the marketplace.

Over time, as the population of smart receivers increases, consumer preferences may decide among the competing ATV systems, or a high-efficiency HDTV standard could be agreed on that could be received on the smart receivers but not on NTSC sets. The transition to the NTSC incompatible HDTV system would represent the second stage. It would not likely occur for at least a decade, but it would herald the arrival of true high definition television for the twenty-first century.

Broadband Distribution Networks

The debate over high definition television may be only a preliminary skirmish before the main event: who will provide broadband services to businesses and homes as we approach the year 2000? The principal contenders are the telephone and cable television industries, with terrestrial and satellite broadcasters having significant stakes in the outcome as well.

Today, telephone companies and cable companies run separate businesses over separate networks. The telephone companies operate a switched, two-way network that relies primarily on twisted pairs of copper wires to distribute voice and data service to home and business subscribers. Cable companies operate unswitched, one-way video distribution networks based on coaxial cable. But these separate networks and businesses are converging as fiber optic distribution systems improve in performance and cost.[33] Telephone and cable companies well recognize that this new technology has the potential to carry all video, voice, and data services on a single pair of glass fibers. Consequently, collisions between the two industries over who will own and operate fiber distribution networks seem inevitable in the 1990s.[34]

Telephone Company Scenarios

Within telephone company networks, fiber optics are beginning to move into the "local loop" that runs from the telephone central office

Table 3 Data Communications Requirements for Home Services

Service	Uncompressed Data Rate (KBPS)
Telephone	64
Alarm Services	0.1
Utility Meter Reading	0.1−1
Energy Management	0.1−1
PC Networks	1.2−64
Electronic Mail	1.2−64
Information Retrieval	1.2−64
Slow Scan Video	1.2−64
Video Teleconferencing	64−1500
NTSC Television	90,000
High Definition Television	200,000 +

to the subscriber. Transmission between telephone company central offices—the interexchange network—is rapidly becoming digital and mostly fiber. Fiber optics are also used in "carrier systems" between telephone company central offices and distribution points nearer to subscribers. Bell South estimates that 50 percent of new subscriber installations use carrier systems and 50 percent of those carrier systems employ fiber optics.[35]

For now, the final links to the home—the "last mile"—are still copper wires. Wire pairs are less expensive than fibers and remain the cost efficient choice for voice and most data services. As shown in table 3, home communications services such as security, utility metering, electronic messages, networking among personal computers, information retrieval, and slow-scan video do not require wide bandwidths or high data rates. These services can be provided over conventional telco copper wire local loops.[36]

Full-motion video, however, cannot. Distributing standard NTSC television requires 6MHz of analog bandwidth or 90 million bits per second in digital form. Processing the video signal to reduce redundancies can cut the required bit rate by a factor of four or more; but even with data compression, television signals cannot be distributed feasibly over narrowband, copper wire distribution networks.

Telephone company scenarios thus include two ways to bring fiber optics to the home. The cost of fiber local loops may become competitive with those for conventional copper wire loops, or the demand for new video services may justify building fiber distribution systems.

On the cost side Bell South has stated that by 1990 it can cost-justify installing fiber loops for new residential customers for voice telephone service alone.[37] Analysis by other telephone companies, consultants, and university researchers do not support that assertion, however.[38] A 1987 study concluded: "it is clear that running fiber to the home, even assuming significant future reductions in component costs, it likely to remain more expensive than copper, where current loop plant costs are roughly $700 per subscriber."[39] Moreover, optical fibers, unlike copper wires, cannot carry electrical current to make the telephone ring and provide other essential functions. Installing fiber optic local loops would thus require new telephones (powered by batteries or designed to be plugged into the subscriber's electrical sockets). Long-term power outages could then result in loss of telephone services as well.

Fiber networks are most cost-competitive if they can replace both the telephone wire and coaxial cable distribution systems, whose combined costs (in 1987 dollars) run about $1200–1500 per household. The cost of fiber distribution is much higher today, but costs are coming down steadily. By the mid to late 1990s many telephone companies believe it will be as cheap to build one fiber distribution network as to construct two separate telephone company and cable systems.

It is not clear what new services beyond those listed in table 3 will justify building fiber networks to the home. Coaxial cable systems are quite efficient for conventional television distribution, although the cable companies themselves are beginning to install fiber optics in their distribution networks. Cable amplifiers now operate at bandwidths of 550MHz, enough to carry seventy-two television channels per cable more than current fiber technology can handle in either analog or digital form. Cable systems should be able to find room for high definition channels when a demand for HDTV emerges in the 1990s. Fiber systems are not required for HDTV distribution.

Nevertheless, a number of American telephone companies have begun or plan field trials of direct fiber-to-home systems. They include BellSouth (Hunter's Creek and Heathrow, Florida), Southwestern Bell (Leawood, Kansas), Bell Atlantic (Perryoplis, Pennsylvania), U.S. West (St. Paul, Minnesota) and GTE (Cerritos, California). These trials generally use a mix of wire, cable, and fiber to carry different services, or they use separate fibers for voice and video. Broadband digital switching is not yet commercially available to integrate all voice, data, and video services on a single fiber to the home.[40]

Yet the telephone companies' ultimate goal is to provide broadband digital switching capacity so that their customers can connect to any source of video, voice, or data.[41] This would enable them to offer "video-on-demand" services qualitatively different from those available on unswitched cable networks. With video-on-demand, subscribers could order up a movie or another video program at any time, rather than be tied to a programmer's schedule. Bellcore researchers have outlined the technical requirements and projected costs of video-on-demand, and they appear optimistic that home viewers would prefer it to fixed schedule services or videotape rentals.[42] However, there is still no indication of real consumer demand for this kind of service. Video-on-demand, like Picturephone and videotex, may be yet another example of technology searching for a market.[43]

The situation seems quite different for business customers. Many businesses already generate enough voice and data traffic to justify building digital fiber optic links on the basis of current fiber costs. Future business video services, such as video conferencing or the exchange of video information among business work stations, may bring additional demand for broadband capacity. The regional Bell operating companies and other local telephone companies are moving quickly to provide broadband, mostly fiber links to their large business customers before they are bypassed at AT&T. Consequently, digital fiber optic distribution networks will reach businesses long before they get to the home.

Cable Scenarios

Cable companies are also testing fiber optics for video distribution.[44] For some years cable systems have used optical fibers for "transportation" links of several miles or more from satellite receivers to cable headends. Fibers are now proving competitive with coaxial cable and microwave for linking headends with the multiple hubs of large cable systems. These applications employ analog frequency modulation (fm) techniques to carry twelve to twenty-four television signals per fiber, so that handling the forty to eighty channels typically required means running several fibers in parallel. Fiber systems are chosen not for their capacities (coaxial cables can carry more channels), but because they do not require amplifiers and thus deliver higher quality signals to the hubs.

Deploying optical fibers in the distribution plant from hub to subscriber (trunks, feeders, and drops) presents greater technical and cost challenges. Coaxial cables now carry up to seventy-two television signals in analog form with amplitude modulation (AM) that is compatible with existing line amplifiers and home television receivers. Fiber systems operate best with digital or analog FM transmission requiring no amplifiers. Consequently, replacing cable with fiber implies converting the signals at some point from digital or analog FM to analog AM, which is too expensive today to be competitive with conventional cable distribution.

Research and development efforts to perfect multichannel AM transmission over fiber, and to reduce the cost of FM/AM conversion, are underway in several laboratories. If successful, they would quickly lead to greater use of fiber for video distribution. ATC, the nation's second largest cable company (80 percent owned by Time Inc.), has advanced a plan to use fiber optics instead of coaxial cable in trunk lines. The principal advantage is to reduce the number of amplifiers between the cable headend and the subscriber in order to improve reliability and deliver better quality television signals, rather than to increase the number of channels. The ATC design, like others under consideration by the cable industry, does not bring fiber optics all the way to the home. Coaxial cables are still used for the last links to the subscriber. It does, however, represent a significant step toward eventual all-fiber networks, for video distribution.

Policy Issues

Technology—in this case the development of broadband fiber optic networks—is again breaking down the legal and regulatory barriers between industries. In the short term the principal policy issues involve telephone company/cable cross-ownership prohibitions. Current FCC rules forbid telephone companies from providing cable television service within their telephone service areas. This cross ownership prohibition was made statutory in the 1984 Cable Communications Policy Act. In addition, the Modified Final Judgement (MFJ) in the consent decree governing the breakup of the Bell system forbids the seven Bell Regional Holding Companies from providing cable service anywhere.

Other telephone companies are seeking to buy cable systems outside their telephone service areas.[45] The telephone companies do not want to be permanently left out of the video distribution business, especially when they see fiber optic developments eventually making feasible a single, integrated network for all voice, data, and video services. The several telephone company field trials mentioned above indicate their interest in fiber-to-home distribution. In a controversial decision bitterly opposed by the cable industry, the FCC recently granted GTE a waiver of its cross-ownership rules to build a coaxial cable and fiber distribution system in Cerritos, California.[46] Another company partly financed by GTE will operate the cable system, but GTE will offer "experimental" services like video-on-demand over the fiber network.[47]

The telephone companies are seeking to overturn the current regulatory, legislative, and judicial cross-ownership provisions. They contend that consumers are being denied innovative services such as video-on-demand and that cable companies should not have a monopoly lock on local video distribution. In response the cable industry points to competition from videocassettes, over-the-air broadcasting, and the new DBS systems. Telephone company opponents also argue that the cross-ownership rules arose from past telephone company abuses of their monopoly power. Telephone company dominance of local exchange services will continue into the twenty-first century.[48] With the telephone companies having significantly more resources than cable companies—in 1987 each of the seven Bell RHCs earned more profit than the entire U.S. cable industry—the potential for unfair competition still exists.

Yet the telephone company attacks on the cross-ownership prohibitions have shown substantial success in recent months. The FCC has proposed broadening waivers of its cable/telephone company cross-ownership rule to encourage telephone company competition with cable companies in video programming as well as distribution. The commission also proposes recommending to Congress that it rescind the cross-ownership ban in the 1984 Cable Communications Policy Act.[49] The National Telecommunications and Information Administration (NTIA) has recommended that telephone companies be permitted to provide "video dial tone"—that is, to lease video channels on a common carrier basis to any program supplier, not just to franchised cable operators.[50] The video common carrier concept was first proposed by the White House Office of Telecommunications Policy in 1974.[51]

The cross-ownership issue will be high on the communications policy agenda in the years ahead. Technically, through the mid-1990s video and voice/data networks will remain largely separate. Video programs will be distributed on coaxial cables or optical fibers with little, if any, two-way switching capacity. Few economies of scale will exist in operating the video distribution network and switched wire network jointly. But the problem of possible cross-subsidy persists.

Dealing with the telephone company cross-subsidy issue should be far more tractable outside their telephone service areas than within. Consequently, removing the telephone company/cable cross-ownership prohibitions outside telephone company service areas seems an appropriate policy goal. Within their telephone franchises, however, the burden of proof should remain with the telephone companies to avoid cross-subsidies or other unfair competitive practices before the cross-ownership rules are changed.

In the longer run the development of switched fiber optic broadband distribution networks poses significant structural issues for United States telecommunications policy. If the technology and economics favor a single, integrated fiber network, who should own and operate it? Should it be run as a common carrier (the current telephone company model), or with programming and content rights protected under the First Amendment (the cable model)? If video, voice, and data services are combined on a single network, who should regulate it? Can video distribution continue to operate under municipal franchises, while voice and data services remain under state PUC jurisdiction? Policymakers still have a few years to consider these questions, but they will not disappear. Policy should encourage field trials that include the active participation of both telephone companies and cable operators and that make their findings about technical performance, cost, and demand publicly available.

Even if an integrated fiber network shows economies of scale, the economies may not be sufficient to justify monopoly provision of local distribution services. The benefits from technical and cost economies of scale must be weighed against the benefits of price and service competition. Unless the case for a single, integrated distribution network is overwhelming, the nation may be better served by two or more competing communications systems to the home.

Technology and Policy Choices

High definition television and broadband fiber optic distribution networks illustrate the complex ways in which technologies interact with communication policy. From many industry perspectives HDTV technology is an unwanted visitor from Japan that is upsetting the relatively stable relationships established in the United States among television programmers, distributors, and equipment manufacturers. HDTV shows how communications policy issues get tangled with issues surrounding trade, employment, and industrial policies. It also exemplifies how technology develops more rapidly than policy can respond. Policymakers usually find themselves behind the power curve, struggling to catch up. Yet in this example policy can influence technological development if it can be developed in a timely way, before the technical systems are conclusively decided. Agreement on technical standards and an evolutionary path toward HDTV in the next two or three years can accelerate the consumer benefits from the new technology.

The development of fiber optic distribution networks well illustrates how technology brings formerly noncompeting industries into contention. Fiber optic systems probably will not replace copper wires and coaxial cables, any more than television has replaced radio or satellites have replaced microwave transmission. Older technologies faced with new competition often find new niches. Fiber optic developments, however, challenge the different regulatory regimes that have been established at the federal, state, and local levels for telephone and cable television services.

Most of all, technological change makes life difficult for policymakers, as well as for the contending interests with which they must interact. Technical alternatives often seem overwhelming even to experts in the field, reminding them of the maxim proffered by a Chinese military commander two millennia ago: "In any situation where there are 36 alternative courses of action, running is always the best." Faced with technological advice, but running away from technology seems neither feasible nor desirable. Even though policymakers often must mediate among the interests that technology has thrown together, the problems need not have zero-sum solutions. Unlike the situation in many other policy fields, technological change in communications usually generates more gains than losses, with users generally among the winners.

Federal Policies for Telecommunications Research and Development

Linda R. Cohen

This essay investigates recent changes in the telecommunications industry and their likely effects on government research and development (R&D) policies. It analyzes the way changes in market structure —in particular the increased competition in the industry due to domestic deregulation and international competition—change the political economy of government research and development.

The analysis first considers the R&D problem, particularly in the context of international competitiveness. It then discusses reasons for underprovision of research in the telecommunications industry and for singling out telecommunications for special treatment by the federal government. Following this analysis, it considers the motivations of government actors concerning R&D and the differences between public and private sector R&D initiatives. After looking at government R&D, drawing examples from a variety of federal programs, it applies these ideas to the current telecommunications industry and to future federal intervention likely to be valuable for enhancing R&D and innovation in the telecommunications industry.

The Private Provision of Telecommunications R&D

By the mid 1980s American manufacturers lost market shares in fields they traditionally dominated, ranging from automobiles to steel to women's clothing. Exports in high-technology failed to keep pace with imports, and by 1986 the United States was for the first time a net importer, with a trade deficit in high-technology products of over $2 billion.[1] Competitiveness had entered the national vocabulary.

International competition adds fuel to discussions about the adequacy of investment in research and development. Two striking features of United States R&D spending emerge in international comparisons.[2] While the United States devotes a proportion of GNP to total R&D similar to Japan and the Federal Republic of Germany—2.69 percent of GNP, compared to 2.77 percent for Japan and 2.67 percent for West Germany—it devotes far less to civilian R&D. In 1985 total civilian R&D expenditures in the United States were estimated at 1.86 percent of GNP. The commensurate percentage is 2.75 percent for Japan and 2.53 percent for West Germany. Indeed, federal spending, which accounts for about half of United States R&D expenditures, has shifted from civilian to defense activities. In 1970 defense R&D expenditures accounted for 48 percent of the federal R&D budget; by 1987 it had risen to 64 percent. Federal civilian R&D expenditures dropped from $19.2 billion in 1970 (in 1982 dollars) to $17.1 billion in 1986.

Second, the rate of R&D investment has increased much faster among our competitors. Total annual R&D expenditures in the United States increased 55 percent in constant dollars between 1970 and 1985, from $62 billion to $96 billion. Japanese expenditures climbed 190 percent during the same period, from about $12.4 billion (1.85 percent of GNP) to $36 billion.

Public support for research has a solid economic rationale. Absent government policy, private firms are likely to invest less in R&D activities than is socially desirable. For a variety of reasons the private returns to R&D investment are typically less than the social returns. R&D results are frequently valuable to unexpected applications, for different products, firms, or industries. Research results may well be valuable, but to someone other than the firm that made the initial R&D investment. Furthermore, once a process or product is known, it can be imitated without duplicating the entire development effort. Unless the expected return is very large, the optimal strategy for all firms is to wait for someone else to do the R&D. In competitive industries research returns may be captured by competitors, by downstream firms, and by consumers. Finally, information from R&D is a public good, so that efforts to limit its dissemination and enhance appropriability are socially inefficient.

In the United States government policies to promote R&D investments have included patent protection and antitrust exemptions for R&D joint efforts, tax credits for private R&D expenditures, direct federal grants to industry, and direct federal research, development, and demonstration programs. One of the first examples of a government program to demonstrate new technology was in communications: in 1842 Congress appropriated $30,000 to construct a telegraph line from Washington, D.C., to Baltimore. It subsequently operated the line for a year at no charge to users.[3]

Communications technology is singled out for public support because of a number of special characteristics. First, communications and information technology is a key component for future generations of a variety of products. Communications and information technology plays a major role in new products by enabling new services and functions, and these technologies are expected to decline in cost in the future. Costs have declined dramatically in the communication/information field during each of the decades after World War Two, and this trend should continue. Similar cost declines are not anticipated for other factors of production to new technology. Energy, for example, is likely to become increasingly expensive, as will other resources that are depletable or fixed in total supply. Thus, the cost of new products will be lower to the extent that communications and information technology is incorporated or substituted for traditional factors of production. Consequently, competitiveness over a range of industries will to a considerable extent depend on technological competitiveness in the communications industry.[4]

Second, the government is itself a major consumer of advanced communications technology. The federal government is a major user of communications and information technology in all of its departments. As demands for government provision of services have increased, so have its demand for communications technology. This is of course critical in defense, where advanced defense technology relies on advanced communication technology, and where more broadly defined communications are key to the provision of traditional defense activities. Communications technology—the more advanced the better—contributes to the success of a number of government's more glamorous projects, including space exploration and other scientific endeavors.

Third, the federal government plays a major role in negotiations for coordinating international aspects of communications policy, such as spectrum allocation and international standards setting.[5] The dominant position of the United States in communication technology in the past contributed to both the government's ability to formulate a favorable position and to its influence in international negotiations. The federal government justified the National Aeronautics and Space Administration's (NASA) communications technology R&D role up to the mid-1970s by recognizing the contribution of communications R&D to American influence in international agreements.[6]

Finally, the telecommunications industry remains heavily regulated, despite the recent trend toward less regulation. With regulation comes two sources of uncertainty for the potential inventor: the invention may need regulatory approval, which can take an indeterminate amount of time to secure, and regulated firms may need approval of investment plans to acquire and use new technology. Regulatory delays for use of new technology can be very substantial, as was the case for cable television and domestic satellites during the 1960s and 1970s.[7] Consequently, government regulation may retard the dissemination of new technology and depress incentives to invest in R&D.

Juxtaposed to these factors are concerns that the provision of R&D may not be adequate. The overall balance of federal R&D funding between defense and civilian activities may be detrimental to civilian applications.[8] While the likelihood of communication technology spillovers in either direction is unclear (and will not be considered here), it can be argued that as military and civilian applications become specialized, the payoff from defense expenditures to civilian communications is increasingly small.

In particular, space communications R&D has been in disarray for over ten years. NASA's successful communication satellite R&D program during the 1960s ended in 1974. The follow-on program (Advanced Communications Technology Satellite — ACTS) has had a rocky history, and the extent of future NASA efforts are uncertain. The celebrated American reentry into space with the September 1988 shuttle launch provides access to space for the first time since the Challenger accident in 1986; however, there is currently a substantial backlog of payloads. Uncertainty over future launch schedules as well as prohibitive insurance costs have stymied private efforts to invest in new space communications technology.[9] Such uncertainty diminishes incentives to invest in R&D leading to innovations that will use future space launches.

Finally, and perhaps most important, the American telecommunications industry, and thus the private provision of telecommunications R&D, is in flux. The long-term impact of the divestiture of AT&T

and subsequent changes at Bell Labs on R&D and innovation is unknown, although major changes in the two years following divestiture were not evident.[10] Increased telecommunications competition has thus far created markets for new products, and enhanced incentives to invest in short-term, product-oriented R&D. However, we do not yet know the impact of changed market structure on investment in basic scientific research that has generally led long-term, fundamental innovations.

Congressional Politics and Government R&D

The way voters perceive the costs and benefits of government programs are included in their decisions about voting for particular legislators.[11] Three factors in the political calculus of program costs and benefits are important as background to discussions of government R&D: the distribution and definition of costs and benefits, their timing, and the likelihood that they will figure in voter assessment of the legislator at election time.

Distribution of Benefits. When a constituent is employed by a project, when his district receives substantial benefits that affect the overall economic health of the area, when he is a member of a group that benefits from a government policy, or when his business benefits from such policies, he is then likely to support that program and to want Congress to support it as well. Alternately, if a program imposes costs on a constituent, he is likely to oppose it, whatever the net social benefits. In either case two conclusions follow: first, program expenditures, which are economic costs, are perceived by some voters as program benefits; second, legislators are likely to consider the specific geographic distribution of program effects rather than, or in addition to, net effects on the country as a whole.[12]

Timing of Benefits. Since federal programs require annual appropriations, multiyear projects cannot be firmly committed at the outset. Because legislatures change over time, and because expected economic success is at best only one factor that determines political support, the survival of a program is uncertain, even if it appears to be successful. As a result, voters are expected to discount the present value of a program by a factor that reflects the necessary lack of legislative commitment. Furthermore, voters can more easily evaluate leg-islators on the basis of completed actions than on the basis of uncer-tain policy results. Finally, not only legislatures but individual congressmen lack commitment strategies: they need not deliver on election promises. Current votes are therefore likely to be based on an assessment of past performance rather than on campaign prom-ises. Thus, voters often evaluate programs on the basis of short-term effects, and legislators base current election strategies on short-term deliverables.[13]

Career strategies by legislators only partially mitigate this bias. Al-though they plan for future elections, including perhaps the election following the anticipated completion of the project, they first have to be reelected in earlier elections. As a consequence, the electoral sys-tem overall provides incentives for the extra discounting of future benefits.

Salience. Political saliency considerations introduce two asymme-tries into the calculation of costs and benefits: first, they create a threshold effect—programs are politically salient only when they ex-ceed some level of importance within the district; second, costs im-posed on constituents are likely to be more salient than benefits of equal size.

Three lines of reasoning contribute to the threshold hypothesis. First, voters only notice fairly major projects and vote on the basis of them. Small benefits or costs rarely effect individual voting decisions. Second, actions are taken in government to benefit organized interest groups, who assure the provision of public goods to all members of the group.[14] When the goods in question are public, individual be-nefits may not be large enough to make it worthwhile for a single person to shoulder the burden of organizing the group; furthermore, the cost of sharing the expense increases with group size, inhibiting group formation. The smaller the group needed—that is, the larger are individual benefits relative to the cost of organization—the more likely the group is to form and exercise political muscle.[15] The argu-ment applies at a district level as well. Politically active groups within a district are more likely to coalesce when the district distributional impact of a program is large.

Third, many actions taken by legislators are based not on expressed wishes of constituents, but rather on what they expect those wishes might be if their constituents ever found out about the program.[16] Programs with large distributional impacts are more likely to be the focus of congressional campaigns, and hence it is more important for legislators to adhere to the expected wishes of constituents on such matters. Moreover, if voters become aware of a political issue because some hopeful challenger brings it to their attention, then they are in general more likely to be aware of programs about which they are unhappy: dissatisfaction is the grist of challengers. Legislators are thus likely to be more sensitive to programs that impose substantial costs on their constituents than to those that grant similarly sized benefits.

Political Support for Research and Development

Models of government behavior predict the following general conclusion regarding R&D policy in the federal government: a federal R&D program is a shaky enterprise. The distribution and timing of its expenditures and economic benefits are not politically optimal; indeed, distributional consequences of a program can often be detrimental to the political calculus even if traditional economic cost-benefit analysis recommends pursuing the program.

At the start of an R&D program, expenditures are usually not politically desirable, and therefore these programs lack political appeal on pork barrel grounds. A typical R&D program starts out with the investigation of numerous concepts and relatively small expenditures. At the conclusion of this "research phase" the more promising ideas are investigated in a larger pilot plant stage. The second stage of R&D involves considerably more expense and the possibility of politically attractive contracts. Successful programs may proceed to demonstration. Demonstration plants incorporate important features of commercial sized plants or projects and are expensive. In most programs demonstrations are limited to one or very few separate projects.

Because of uncertainty in R&D, contract beneficiaries are not known at the outset and even if known will not receive substantial funds until later in the project. Consequently, expenditures alone cannot justify the programs, for alternate transfer programs with more attractive timing and greater certainty over recipients provide direct ways to target the distribution of federal largess.

Basing political support on ultimate economic benefits entails political problems, again owing to timing and distribution. To the extent that innovation benefits society these benefits are likely to be diffused rather than concentrated and thus fail a threshold test of political relevance. Future benefits are, of course, in the future and hence subject to additional political discounting.

To the extent that the benefits are interesting to industry R&D programs encounter two important problems. When a program involves discrete components (particularly at the demonstration stage), government may have to choose a winner from among firms bidding for primary contracts; the winner not only gets a profitable contract, but gets a leg up in the new technology and hence a competitive advantage. Such programs are therefore likely to create industry losers as well as winners. Because of political asymmetries in the evaluation of program costs and benefits, such programs are expected to be unstable. The United States government is usually very sensitive to charges of unfair advantages resulting from government intervention in the market.

More generally, to the extent that programs benefit all players within an industry, rather than identified subgroups, the program is more feasible politically. Market organization is consequently important to the discussion. If the market is regulated or monopolistic, so that firms are guaranteed sales whatever the outcome of the program, then discrete projects are feasible. If the market is competitive, then programs that work tend to have one of two structures. Either they include enough pieces that all players can participate in one of them, or they are centralized, with all players cooperating. Such cooperation has been more forthcoming in regulated industries, such as electric utilities, but more recently examples have occurred in the electronics field as well.

The second political problem with successful R&D programs is that fundamental innovation is likely to change the structure of the industry in which it is used. Industries that rationalize regulation on the basis of scale economies are likely to oppose projects that, if successful, would reduce the extent of relevant scale economies. Consequently, such industries are unlikely to be enthusiastic about some programs that are attractive from a social standpoint. The situation is not precisely symmetric with respect to competitive industries. Such firms will oppose a program that is anticipated to increase scale economies in the industry only if they believe that they will not be among the remaining firms after the shakeup. Thus, opposition to programs on these grounds is more likely to come from industries that are currently monopolistic.

NASA's satellite R&D program is a case in point.[17] On 19 August 1964 NASA successfully launched a geosynchronous satellite into orbit. The agency followed this feat with an acclaimed series of research satellites, laying the foundation for future applications in communications and meteorology. As a result, the satellite supply industry moved from a single provider—Hughes Aircraft, which had proposed and built the first series of NASA satellites—to a competitive industry with more than half a dozen firms interested in building satellites and participating in NASA's research program. NASA's second satellite series was thus subject to competitive bidding for prime contractors. However, because of the bulkiness of the technology—one reason the government was involved in the field—a single firm had to be chosen to be the prime contractor, and it was widely believed that this would give the winner a distinct competitive advantage for the next generation of satellites. The ensuing contract battle, involving lawsuits, government investigations, and substantial bad publicity for NASA, significantly reduced government enthusiasm for the program. The second phase was trimmed back, and the program ended in the early 1970s. Efforts to restart it have been plagued with similar squabbles among the satellite manufacturing firms.

At least at their outset (that is, before pork barrel support), major federal R&D programs tend to be associated with unusual political salience that inspires a national consensus in a particular area—energy in the 1970s and space in the 1960s. Such motivation, however, shifts over time, often unrelated to program success. For example, many critics were unhappy with the synthetic fuels program on efficiency grounds, but the rapid demise of the Synthetic Fuel Corporation in the early 1980s was a direct result of dropping energy prices which undermined public belief that energy independence was a national imperative. Consistent, long-term R&D support is relatively unlikely.

The rise and fall of the synthetic fuel program also demonstrates the importance of ideology in creating political support for R&D. When neither program expenditures nor economic results are sufficient to generate a majority coalition of supporters within a legislature—as is the case for most R&D programs—support coalitions are usually tied to ideological beliefs. However, the ideology that underpins public support for R&D changes with different stages of an R&D program. Appropriability concerns are paramount in the rationale for federal support of basic research and science, so that political support for such programs does not conflict with free market concerns or general opposition to government interference in the market. Government support for later stages of research, however, implies a more activist role. Ideological support for demonstrations rests on two factors, both of which are usually involved in public rationales for such programs: first, that the indivisibility of investments leads to particularly risky assessments by firms for demonstrations; second, that a national emergency has created a social imperative for speedy commercialization.

In the synfuel program ideological conservatives were more likely than liberals to support the more research-oriented work carried out by the Department of Energy. However, the situation switched following the 1979 energy crisis, when the program was reoriented toward short-term commercial development. The support coalition then rested on the liberal wing, who nonetheless defected with the decline in oil prices. The program relied on shifting coalitions and consequently lacked coherence in the R&D process. Equally important, later coalitions were not powerful enough to maintain the program, and, at least according to some assessments, valuable components were lost when the program was terminated in the early 1980s.[18] Ambitious, long-term projects intended to move through multiple phases of research are very unlikely to maintain a coherent, stable structure. The lesson for federal R&D programs in telecommunications should be clear.

Government R&D Program Management

An apparent contradiction emerges from studies of big government technology demonstration programs. Demonstrations, once underway, are extremely difficult to reorient or cancel even when the economics of the situation alter dramatically. Thus, the space shuttle program continued doggedly during the 1970s even though cost overruns and disappointing technical results clearly indicated that some program modifications were in order.[19] The federal program to develop a supersonic transport during the 1960s was eventually cancelled—as was a much bigger project, the Clinch River Breeder Reactor—but not until years after even the government's cost-benefit studies counseled program changes.[20]

These examples highlight project rigidity rather than program stability. Indeed, once a government R&D program gets underway, it can involve a project that is attractive for pork barrel purposes—big contracts to firms in a reasonable number of Congressional districts. At that point the project becomes viable based on pork barrel support, which depends on continuing that particular project plan, whatever the ultimate economic implications.

Indeed, a number of characteristics of R&D imply expected trouble on these grounds. Whenever a program involves a big contract, R&D results are uncertain. Any initial line of action is expected to be modified before a commercially viable alternative is chosen. Supply and demand conditions are likely to change over the course of the program. Recommended R&D plans entail tremendous flexibility. Juxtaposed to this flexibility recommendation is the observation that cost overruns are more likely to occur in government programs and that consequently the existence of pork barrel based rigidity at the demonstration stage is particularly damaging to R&D prospects.

This harsh assessment is based on several government biases that are likely to result in inefficient program management. First, government is likely to underinvest research, owing either to impatience by legislators or attempts by bureaucrats to bring a project to the major procurement stage, where, with additional pork barrel support, it is less likely to be cancelled.[21] Such impatience leads to cost overruns downstream because research results are needed to plan efficiently the next stage. Sometimes problems can be massive. Depending on where one allocates blame, the Clinch River Breeder was delayed for between four and eight years in the 1970s because of its inability to procure necessary safety and environmental licenses. Initially, the inability resulted from the Atomic Energy Commission's (AEC) lack of information: it could not satisfy licensing requirements because no interim results were available prior to construction of the large demonstration. With hindsight experimentation on a smaller scale was clearly in order.[22]

Second, bureaucracies, and especially scientific bureaucracies, control the research alternatives considered by Congress. Studies of NASA and the AEC suggest that the bureaucracies are motivated by concerns for scientific and technological sophistication rather than for commercial feasibility. Consequently, R&D alternatives considered by Congress tend to be biased in the same direction, further diminishing the likelihood of commercial success of direct federal R&D programs. In addition, bureaucracies often want to maintain or expand their programs and therefore have incentives to bias the information that they provide to Congress.[23] Bureaucratic optimism over program results is intensified to the extent that bureaucrats who work in a particular technical area tend to view the technological choices as favorable from the start.

In conclusion, experience over the past twenty years suggests that major commercially oriented direct federal R&D programs involving large commercial demonstrations are likely to be very inefficient and ultimately unsuccessful.

Coherent Federal R&D Policy

The federal government has been criticized for the incoherence of its communications R&D policy.[24] Conflicting and contradictory R&D policies have created disincentives for private planning and investment and have foiled government efforts as well. Perhaps the clearest example is in satellite development: during the 1960s NASA's successful efforts were prohibited from commercial application by the Federal Communications Commission. Overlapping civilian and defense spending clouds the assessment of R&D efforts because the government can claim, perhaps justifiably, that cutbacks in civilian spending are compensated by spillovers from defense. This incoherence is not only inevitable, but is likely to become more pronounced with changes in the telecommunications industry. Also, and somewhat paradoxically, multiple overlapping agencies are not necessarily bad for R&D and can parallel some of the strengths of competitive private sector research.

When citizen opinions diverge and are echoed among legislators, then federal policy is unlikely to be coherent. Congress divides itself into committees with responsibility for legislation, oversight, and appropriations in different areas of federal action. Congressional committees have disproportionate power over areas within their jurisdictions. While jurisdiction over specific bills is usually housed in a single committee, jurisdiction over policy is divided; one universal division is between authorization and appropriations. In addition, authorization for programs that have an impact on industry may be housed in a number of different committees. Energy policy in the 1970s was considered by thirty-seven different congressional committees and subcommittees. Each can propose legislation and bring it to the floor in such a way that it has a strong chance of prevailing, even though the policies, when taken together, appear to conflict. Several earnest legislators on opposing sides of a general policy can prevail in different committees and concurrently on the House and Senate floors.

Expected changes in the communications industry will create greater conflicts. Competition by definition increases conflict. Specifying internationally oriented policies will increase conflict between importers, consumers, domestic producers, and federal policy goals in other fields. Adding commercialization goals to science goals for NASA, for example, is bound to cause confusion in policy processes and outcomes. Congress is organized so that small bits of policy address concerns of different groups, resulting in conflicts that parallel those within the population, rather than producing coherent policy.

Nevertheless, this imperfect world is not all bad for R&D. It has been claimed that government is unlikely to choose winners among R&D proposals. In fact, no one can reliably choose winners in research. A celebrated example is Western Union's refusal to buy Alexander Bell's basic telephone patents in 1876 for what it considered to be a princely sum of $100,000.[25] The Defense Department turned down Hughes Aircraft's proposal to develop and launch the geosynchronous satellite that was later NASA's tour de force. Multiple sources for potential funding and development within government, as within private industry, create far greater opportunities for innovation and success. Government inefficiencies may well strengthen R&D opportunities.

Furthermore, coordinated activities require compromises that can constrain program choices to the point of infeasibility. When the Energy Research and Development Administration (ERDA) was established to coordinate energy research, it found its choices in coal research to be constrained by programs oriented toward Eastern coal use; programs that would develop products to substitute, as directly as possible, for imported oil; and programs that would quickly address the perceived national energy emergency. These constraints were incompatible, and synthetic fuel processes for gasoline and natural gas substitutes that use Eastern coal are still in the stage of fundamental research. Nevertheless, ERDA attempted rapid development of those processes rather than devoting resources to the processes that used Western coal and were much closer to commercialization, that would improve obtainable products from Eastern coal, or that would continue the more modest long-term research effort in advanced Eastern coal synfuels.

Telecommunications Research Policy for Government

The telecommunications industry is undergoing two profound changes: increased internationalization and increased competition. Both changes will involve realignments in political support groups for telecommunications and alter potential government R&D activities. Coordinated federal programs for research, development, and commercialization are too ambitious to be efficient and successful. More modest government programs, and alternate federal activities, must be considered.

As the industry grows more competitive, the government is unlikely to be successful with research programs that are designed to help specific firms or that include large discrete projects. Nevertheless, support for basic research is appropriate, even though innovation cannot be promised. Activities that do not single out particular technologies and particular firms are less likely to encounter debilitating political problems and are less susceptible to federal bureaucratic biases.

Of particular interest are policies that can encourage private firms to enhance their R&D programs. Certainly, the most important change on the current policy agenda is deregulation. Regulation is conceded to inhibit innovation, and deregulation has been hailed as an opportunity for private investment in research and for innovation.

Table 1 contains funding trends for the communications equipment industry and United States industries for all R&D expenditures and basic R&D expenditures. These figures should be interpreted with some caution, as they rely on company reporting and accounting procedures, as well as company interpretations of what constitutes R&D and basic R&D. The data give little guidance for future funding trends. However, they do suggest that the 1984 divestiture caused develop-

Table 1 R&D Expenditure Trends (in millions of 1982 constant dollars)

	Communications Equipment			All Industries		
	Total R&D	Basic R&D	Percentage Basic	Total R&D	Basic R&D	Percentage Basic
1975	4056	185	4.57	41132	1241	3.01
1977	4054	223	5.50	44374	1355	3.05
1979	4638	249	5.36	48764	1477	3.02
1983	6841	293	4.30	60991	2088	3.40
1984	7133	280	3.93	65771	2383	3.60
Average annual percentage change						
1975−79	3.6	8.5		4.6	4.7	
1979−83	11.9	4.5		6.3	10.3	
1983−84	4.3	−4.5		7.8	14.1	

Source: Figures are derived from National Science Foundation, *National Patterns of Science and Technology Resources, 1986*, NSF 86-309 (Washington, D.C., 1986), 54, 59; SIC Code 366.

ment work to be substituted for basic research at least in the short run in communications, as markets for products became, or were anticipated shortly to become, available. The 1984 figures, in addition, reflect uncertainty and chaos in the first year following the industry's reorganization and uncertainty in the few years prior to the reorganization.

Whatever the ultimate result of deregulation, uncertainty over the future structure of the telecommunications industry inhibits R&D investments. Of course, R&D itself contributes to uncertainty, and the nature of competition and entry in an industry creates uncertainty over the identity of future actors. Neither is the concern here; rather, it is uncertainty over what the rules for the industry will be—for example, the extent of competition and the extent of prohibitions to market solutions. Resolution of federal and state regulatory policies will hence remove an important source of uncertainty for R&D investments. Similarly, in the international arena, resolving issues of regulation in and access to foreign markets will rebound on domestic R&D decisions.

Cooperative research ventures like Sematech and the Semiconductor Research Corporation are a relatively new strategy.[26] The appeal to students of R&D is clear. Not only do they avoid classic free rider issues (assuming all firms likely to benefit are involved), but they do so without restricting results. However, they have a feature in common with government development programs that are likely to limit their ultimate success. As big, prestigious efforts, they are subject to distributive politics even if they do not receive big government grants. To the extent that government takes credit for the facilities, they may evolve into the same species of dinosaur created by other federal R&D bureaucracies.

For example, the Clinch River Breeder Reactor was at its initiation 80 percent funded by a cooperative industry effort. This figure quickly fell by the wayside, as did private management control of the enterprise. By the time the project was canceled it had not only consumed over $2 billion, but it had also diverted resources from other federal nuclear fission programs. The breeder reactor program itself was scaled back to accommodate Clinch River, which grew from an estimated 2 percent of the breeder budget at its beginning to over 40 percent later.

The power of this example is unavoidable. Sematech, for example, is currently authorized to obtain half of its funding from the federal government and has received appropriations of $100 million for fiscal years 1988 and 1989. If private firms lose the circle-the-wagon-train mentality that international competition has elicited, it is possible and even probable that the centers will come under increased federal control. Lack of sustained expected success, however, does not detract from their potential among the alternatives available.

Space communications research deserves special mention because the government is likely to remain involved in the critical launch component for some years and is inevitably party to international treaty negotiations. Relying on direct federal technology development programs contains a degree of futility. However, the government can use its control over launches to advantage to aid private research efforts. A recent study concludes that it would be technically feasible for NASA to allow some private R&D projects on unrelated satellite launches.[27] By doing so it would lessen one of the barriers to research —the expense, riskiness, and uncertain timing of dedicated R&D satellites.

The three cases discussed here—deregulation, cooperative private research, and satellite piggy-back launches—each address a response to market failure in the provision of research and development. The first case concerns the restraining influence of regulation and limited entry in a regulated market. The second concerns limited company resources and appropriability. Launch piggy-backs address a troubling feature of some types of R&D, which is that not only are substantial resources sometimes required, but some projects are indivisible —the whole can be lost when a component fails—so that investor risks are high.

We can extrapolate from these examples general recommendations for government policy. Actions by the government to clarify post-divestiture policies will rebound on private R&D investment decisions. Such actions are the most important component of R&D policy for the federal government, for increased competition in the industry has in fact reduced federal opportunities for effective direct R&D programs. Finally, a more narrow goal for government is to investigate ways to allow R&D experimentation by firms that do not involve large, discrete investment choices. The last involves specific products and clearly is not always possible; it is offered here as a general policy guideline.

Incoherence in government policy is unavoidable. Of course, specific instances of incoherence may be inexcusable and may indeed be subject to repair. However, when policy creates conflict between either different sectors of the economy or between different firms within a sector, the political system is designed to produce conflicting policies. A challenge for government, as for industry, is to use the conflicts to aid innovation.

Telecommunications and Foreign Economic Policy

Peter F. Cowhey

The unilateral opening of the American telecommunications market has offered major gains to consumers, but it has also placed American equipment makers under great competitive pressure without providing new export opportunities. Moreover, foreign governments often restrict United States providers of computer communications networks and the global operations of their American customers. While it is therefore tempting to define the United States telecommunications trade challenge as an effort to open foreign markets, this reading of international economics is a recipe for failure. It ignores another urgent challenge—facilitating the efficient interconnection of diverse new communications and computing technologies, the new information infrastructure for the world economy. The true challenge for the United States will be to build interconnection of the world's communications and information resources to increase competition. The task of assuring adequate and efficient interconnectivity will force a rebuilding of national communications systems as well as a rewriting of computer architectures. Crucially, international negotiators will have to agree on desirable architectures and technical standards for the interconnection of diverse systems. While the simplest way to resolve problems of international communications interconnection is to choose a single design and leave it to national monopolists to implement, such a solution would slow technological progress and less efficiently allocate resources than a competitive market. This was the fundamental insight of communications deregulation in the United States. American diplomacy for international communications must convince other countries that the network of the future will work best if designed to fit a competitive environment.

This difficult task requires the United States to rework its understanding of the world economy. International economic diplomacy has long assumed that there should be competition in the world economy for goods and monopolistic practices for the services and infrastructure to support a goods economy. At a time when the Gross National Product (GNP) of industrial countries is over 60 percent in the services sector and many of the competitive advantages in goods rests on services, a division of competitive frameworks is obsolete and counterproductive. In international communications negotiations the United States has the opportunity to set important precedents concerning restructured rules of competition for the world economy.

This essay reviews the economic stakes in the international communications negotiations—an issue as much about the emerging computer and information industry as about communications proper. It then examines divergent approaches to structuring the relationship between the communications and information industries, arguing that divergence in domestic frameworks entails disagreements concerning international communications and trade institutions and a potentially painful restructuring of domestic rules about competition and innovation. This analysis then offers broad alternatives for a world communications regime and details policies to modify traditional free trade frameworks to build a competitive regime for communications.

What Are the Economic Stakes?

Each country must consider communications policy as part of a broader strategy for improving its international competitiveness and for negotiating the future of world economic competition. Communications is at the heart of both the electronics and the service sectors and most countries have seen their communications industries as "national champions" for developing high technology information industries. The United States has been reluctant to formulate its policy this way; nonetheless, its trade policy must confront such practices elsewhere.

American trade negotiators have proposed to open international markets for its communication equipment and its services. Some worry that equipment interests are being sacrificed for gains in service markets, while others assume that the two are natural complements.[1] In fact, while the two sectors are highly interdependent, the relationship is not simple.

The world market for information and communications products and services is changing profoundly. The market for communications equipment proper roughly falls into two major segments. Network equipment, about two-thirds of the market, features items like central office switches and fiber optic cables, and customer premises equipment (CPE), including private branch exchanges (PBX), telephone key systems, facsimiles, and handsets.

The CPE market is becoming intermeshed with the computer market, which is growing much more rapidly than the market for communications equipment. The CPE market itself has several niches. At the risk of vast oversimplification United States manufacturers are best at producing network management CPE that allows individual users of communications networks to manage or duplicate many central network functions. So far, they also have produced the most sophisticated links between computers and communications. Although Japan ran its original trade surplus on lower end technology like telephone keysets, now developing countries are displacing Japanese firms in these markets, and Japanese companies are emphasizing CPE that uses advances in microchips and imaging technology to add value to inputs provided by public networks—for example, the image processing available on its new television and fax equipment. The Europeans, on the other hand, appear most interested in equipment that efficiently interconnects with sophisticated network services. These differences in specialization reflect divergences in strategies for the underlying communications network.

The total market for services far surpasses the one for equipment.[2] Only some service markets will prove contestable. Nearly half of telecommunications services consists of local phone service, which will be slow to open to major foreign challenges. The most promising segments for competition are international services (about $39.5 billion in 1984 for voice and data); data transmission services, ranging from circuits leased for data communications to value added services (less than 10 percent of all world communications services); and information and computer services proper.[3]

International voice services are the most profitable part of the market,[4] but data related services are the fastest growing and potentially very profitable. Hence, the computing and information side of this market, both equipment and in services, should be at the heart of future United States strategy. They also represent the market segments

Table 1 The World Market for Telecommunications and Computer Products and Services ($ billion; estimates not adjusted for inflation)

	1984		1990*		Annual Growth Rate (percentage)
SIC Item	World	U.S.	World	U.S.	
Telecom Equipment	60	(24)	95	(36)	8
Computer Equipment	80		195		16
Telecom Services	265	(103)	444	(165)	9
Computer Services	40		97		16
World Totals	445		831		11

Source: Reproduced from Jonathan David Aronson and Peter F. Cowhey, *When Countries Talk*, 7.
*Estimated.

where the political pressure for change in other countries is greatest.

A successful strategy for the high end of the market depends on changing the ground rules for the underlying public communications network. The underlying architecture and degree of competition in the public communications network strongly influence the feasibility and competitive advantages of different information services and computer equipment. Indeed, hardware and software defined services over a network are often substitutable.[5]

American telecommunications deregulation created a commitment to flexibility in the location of the most sophisticated control and value added features of a network (the network's intelligence). Customers can decide to rely on the central network to provide the intelligence, use their own equipment to provide intelligence, or rely on third party service providers. This experience in running a diversified and flexible network environment is a potential competitive advantage, but it depends on a new vision of the future network.

Commonality and Divergence in Regulatory Reform

The roots of international telecommunications change are in domestic politics and economics. Most major countries are reorganizing their communications and information markets. Still, telecommunications is an esoteric subject with its own arcane technical and economic logic. Busy political leaders cannot learn this business, but

Table 2 Estimated 1987 World Data Communications Market ($ billion)

	Services	Products	Total
North America	24.71	86.78	111.50
Europe (not USSR)	11.37	39.90	51.29
Asia (with USSR)	12.36	43.39	55.75
Oceania	.59	2.08	2.67
Latin America	1.38	4.86	6.24
Africa	.49	1.74	2.23
Total	49.43	173.57	223.00

Source: Jonathan D. Aronson and Peter F. Cowhey, *When Countries Talk*, 66.

they can select basic policy instruments and which government agency will oversee the market. No selection of an agency or policy instrument has neutral effects. The choice redistributes economic and political power in the favor of some classes of firms and consumers at the expense of others.[6]

Governments and interest groups also select domestic bargains with an eye toward the counterpart international arrangements for telecommunications. Highly regulated markets do not want intrusions from very competitive global markets. Countries introducing greater competition must seek changes in international arrangements to accommodate them. The particular bent of domestic reform will drive the priorities for international restructuring. The specialized bureaucracies and corporate arrangements enshrined in the domestic arena require international counterparts.

The Common Denominator of Reform

In the past most governments granted authority over communications to a single monopolist and merged their telephone company and the government ministry that regulated it. In addition, governments often mixed their postal and telephone services under one operation —Postal Telephone and Telegraph Authorities (PTTs). As a rule, telephone operations subsidized postal operations, long distance services subsidized both local telephone services and the post office, and telephone company services subsidized the manufacture of telephone equipment. Usually the telephone company did not own equipment makers, although the United States deviated from this norm.

The nature of regulatory reform in telecommunications generally affects different beneficiaries. Many important breakthroughs in information use have clustered in the relatively few large corporations and government agencies who are the largest users of communications systems (typically, 5 percent of all users constitute over half of the long distance traffic).[7] This group has both motives and resources to influence communications regulation.

Similarly, the microchip revolution introduced many important new companies into the electronics industry, particularly in the United States and Japan. Traditionally, a handful of older electronics firms dominated the production of communications equipment in conjunction with the dominant national phone company. Newcomers to the industry wanted to break this cozy relationship through changes in regulation. With recent changes in industry structure, the industry is now divided about how to balance goals of interconnectivity and proprietary technical advantages.

Finally, many service and equipment producers wanted to produce new information and communications based services. They did not want traditional telephone monopolies to ban their entry or exploit their monopoly over the basic telephone system to dominate the new services. Continuing debates about the scope and flexibility of regulation in these market-oriented areas are fueled by concerns over innovation and its direct and indirect beneficiaries.

Countries vary in how they sort out who wins and loses from reform. Still, the minimum common denominator has three major components.

Rationalized Regulation

Reformers want to rationalize the role of the dominant phone company. They often begin by separating postal and telephone services to reduce cross-subsidies. Many separate government policymaking from telecommunications operations and may privatize the telephone company to widen the gulf between regulators and the national phone company and bolster the rights of larger users and new competitors. In addition, many governments restructure their telephone company, commonly by dividing subsidiaries for basic and enhanced communications services, again to curb cross-subsidies.

Reform has not resolved the policy dilemmas posed by cross-subsidies for the average household and small businesses. Household voters and small businesses are numerous and sensitive to changing telephone prices, at least in the short term. Most governments try to appease them by retaining some cross-subsidies, even if they are gradually phased down. Remaining cross-subsidies, in turn, reduce the overall efficiency of pricing. Governments are often keen to promote international services as a source of extra income because these services are less visible to voters.

Partially Liberalized Equipment Markets

Most countries granted a monopoly for the sale of customer premises equipment (CPE) to their national telephone company.[8] The reform movement curtails this monopoly and liberalizes competition in the provision of installation and repair services. This opens the way to independent systems integrators (such as Computer Sciences Corporation and Electronic Data Services) which provide services, software, equipment, and enhanced communications services. Strikingly, major telephone companies are privatizing their own services by integrating customized systems for large customers.

The provision of network equipment is also being modified.[9] The new policy liberalizes procurement practices, in part to satisfy trade complaints about discrimination against foreign equipment supplies. However, no one anticipates liberalization to do more than open a larger minority share of the market to a greater number of foreign suppliers. Perhaps more important, trade negotiators have started to win acceptance of two principles: technical requirements must be transparent to all buyers and sellers, and the process of setting standards should involve participation by interested foreign participants.

Open Competition in Network Information Services

At a minimum all industrial nations agree that many information services should not become a monopoly of the telephone company and that the phone company should be subject to regulatory controls to curb unfair competitive advantages from its monopoly over the basic network.

Alternative Models for Reform

Reform means the possibility of increased international competition. At a minimum trade negotiations can progress on information services and equipment issues. The potential breadth for competition can take in far more. In general the troika of global financial centers —the United States, United Kingdom, and Japan—have moved farthest toward open competition; most of Europe has followed a more conservative course. In as much as the troika constitutes the bulk of the international telecommunications market, European models will probably require further liberalizing.[10] However, reforms need not be dictated by the prevailing American model. A Japanese-European understanding, particularly with an eye toward increased European economic integration in the next decade, could also shape the future. Differences among these national and cross-national approaches are crucial for trade negotiators.

Competing Visions of the Global Network

Every new telecommunications official quickly learns that Integrated Service Digital Networks (ISDN) are the wave of the future. This means that the network will use digital technology to deliver packages of voice, data, and video services. ISDN, however, is an internally complex concept.

"Dynamic centralization" expects the traditional telephone system to become a powerful public network for completely integrated voice, data, and video services available to everyone over broadband, high speed networks of fiber optic cables. Competition will play an increased role in providing specialized services offered over the network; the content will be competitive, but the pipe will be a public utility in order to capture economies of scale and scope while raising adequate capital for operation and investment. Pricing for network services will be more flexible for large users but still permit cross-subsidies to support expanded universal public service (UPS), including some enhanced services, to the household. Standardization will bridge the existing gaps among communications and computer systems around the world, with interconnectivity as the global watchword. In general, European authorities have favored this approach.

"Flexible decentralization," on the other hand, believes that technological innovation should occur in a world of sharply increased competition and flexible architecture for future services and equipment; the marriage of information and communications technologies is too important to be dominated by a central network. Every country needs one or more public networks that exhibit economies of scope in providing flexible service interconnection. Moreover, public networks require common understandings about the role of standards. The public network, however, should not exclude flexible specialization by other networks. Indeed, the optimal mix of services depends on market capacity to redesign the pipe (including the locus of command in the network) as well as to compete in content. In this view competition in the infrastructure of network facilities encourages innovation.

If dynamic centralization sees the public network as the highway of the future, flexible centralization argues for competing highways and modes of transport in the information infrastructure. The latter view has been the United States' ideal, and British policy approximates it.

The Japanese approach is a hybrid: it embraces competition in the flexible decentralization model while it creates a core public network that defines UPS and architecture similar to dynamic centralization. (Figure 1 compares the degree to which network intelligence will dictate the design of its services and the range of services that the public network must deliver universally.)

Competition in Services and Facilities

The troika accept the principle of multiple independent transmission facilities. They also permit substantial freedom in the resale and shared use of circuits rented from facilities providers. Only when transmission facilities are competitive can new entrants in communications and information services be assured access to low-cost, efficient transmission facilities.

The troika also embrace competition in most forms of services, although their common quest to allow for limited cross-subsidies for small users produces some restrictions in each country. The United States, for example, accepts unlimited competition in all services except those involving local basic services. Local monopolies can extract rent for the support of local residents from long-distance carri-

Figure 1 Network Strategy: Degree of Centralization of Network Intelligence

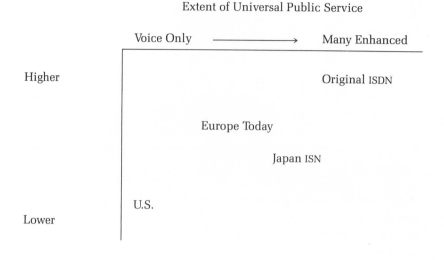

ers, although bypass facilities at the local level curb even this option. The United Kingdom has opted for competition in all services but presently restricts basic services to a duopoly. Japan allows unlimited competition in basic services in principle, but administrative practices restrict it in the local loop and restrict the total number of long-distance and international carriers. Figure 2 compares the degree of competition in communications facilities and services among industrial countries.

The European picture is more complicated because the European Common Market (EC) is setting minimum standards for telecommunications competition and market integration around a dynamic centralization model, with the hope that liberalization will grow. It endorses extremely selective competition in supplementary facilities for the underlying communications network. For example, Europe may accept independent competition in new facilities such as cellular telephones and some communications satellites in limited competition with Intelsat.

Western Europe endorses substantial liberalization of pure information services, but it is more cautious on services that combine value added (for example, packet switching) and information services.

Figure 2 Competition in Services and Facilities

	Europe	Japan	U.S.
Services			
Local Basic	No	In Theory	Bypass
International Long Distance	No	Yes	Yes
Domestic Long Distance	No	Yes	Yes
International Enhanced	Limited	Yes	Yes
Domestic VAN	Limited/Yes	Yes	Yes
Information	Yes	Yes	Yes
Facilities Competition	Low	Medium/High	High

Thus far, the traditional international value added networks—designed to help large users manage global interconnection and management of their internal information systems—have arduously established operating rights in most countries. In the future there are likely to be new networks open to specialized users; for example, a joint venture in France by IBM will serve interested financial institutions. Competition may also grow among services offered by each European telephone carrier by requiring all members to accommodate each other's enhanced services.

Control over licensing new entrants is at the center of prolonged political battles in Europe. Licensing can open the way to imposition of universal service obligations on some enhanced services, requirements based on local telephone company standards and pricing, and disclosure of proprietary information to local telephone companies.

Developmental Goals of Communications Policy

Communications policies influence competitive advantages in world markets, but the ways governments conceive their advantages differ markedly.

Deregulation in the United States effectively stalled public debate about public development policy until recently. The government assumes as a matter of policy that market competition will determine the most desirable technological developments, especially if the Regional Bell Operating Companies (RBOCs) gain more latitude in providing services, including on international services.[11] Perhaps the greatest effort has gone to promoting Open Network Architecture, a strategy to ensure that major common carriers configure their network such that they cannot use technological design to bar new entrants in advanced information services. The politics of the Federal Communications Commission (FCC) tend to emphasize conflict. Its quasi-judicial style puts a premium on adverserial behavior, and it controls no public spending programs with which to assuage losers. The continued rivalry of all interested parties has hindered efficient information exchange for designing the future network.

United States government policies influence the competitive advantages of American companies in the world market. United States equipment makers are especially sophisticated in network management equipment. Its specialized value added networks (VANs) remain world leaders, and its largest users also benefit. Meanwhile, the public networks no longer offer a universal menu of service at a single set of prices to all customers. They are privatizing their services by customizing them through specialized tariffs and software delivery systems designed to lock in large customers.[12] AT&T is installing these capabilities into its central office switches as a competitive advantage.

European policy has different implications for its industries. Larger users are better treated than in the past, but less so than the United States. Public policies assume that pricing and restrictive entry on value added services permits continued cross-subsidies and network economies for serving local households. Moreover, PTTs argue that cross-subsidy should extend from telephone services to some enhanced communications services, a significantly expanded universal public service.

They also promote European computer, electronics, and software industries. The Europeans consider themselves competitive in software but behind in computers. Liberalizing information services is good for software specialists. At the same time, the PTTs plan to use the public network's data services to standardize much more rapidly their computer systems. This strategy will give new competitive advantages in the computer industry to firms with intimate knowledge of the sophisticated public network services supporting computing. This will help European firms. It will also give new advantages based on the performance of the individual machine rather than on proprietary specialized architectures of families of products (which were the traditional advantages of IBM and Digital Equipment Corporation).

The process supports a small pool of favored suppliers of network equipment. Procurement policies favor international corporate alliances among the makers of European communications equipment in order to strengthen their position against AT&T, Japanese firms, and, to a lesser extent, Northern Telecom. The Alcatel absorption of ITT's European telecommunications holdings is one vivid example of this posture, and Pan-European research and development programs for communications equipment is another.

Japan has introduced both extensive competition and an ambitious developmental policy. It has tried to bring all interested parties into new public networks rather than bypassing public networks, as is happening in the United States.[13] Each new carrier has a consortium of electronics firms, large users, and major service companies (including owners of VANs) in their ownership. This consortium arrangement internalizes the bargaining processes and information sharing issues that normally divide special communications interests in the United States.

The Japanese government seeks to have new networks provide wideband fiber optic and satellite capacity to the general public as soon as possible, and it wants enhanced services to emphasize the role of functionally similar users (for example, machine tool companies). The purpose in part is to ensure that heavily used and competitively disciplined public carriers will open the new information society (a favored Japanese slogan) to large and small users, including small business.[14]

Japan is already a major exporter of telecommunications equipment and continues to emphasize innovation. Nippon Telephone and Telegraph (NTT) remains a principal source of research, network design, and procurement support for Japanese producers of telecommunications and information equipment, even while it has slashed purchasing prices that once subsidized suppliers. Japan has succeeded in certain segments of transmission equipment (for example, large satellite receiving stations and fiber optic cables) and the lower end of customer premises equipment (for example, key telephone systems and fax machines).

Although it has liberalized significantly, the Japanese market is far from open to foreign telecommunications.[15] Japan has abolished legal barriers to the sales of foreign telecommunications equipment, but many United States companies report some continuing informal barriers. Moreover, the Japanese broadband network seems designed to move the next generation of CPE to sophisticated network user equipment. Rather than emphasize large PBXs or minicomputers as a network organizer, flexible central networks, subject to competitive discipline, will interact with very smart CPE designed to query and tap all of the network's capabilities — such as very sophisticated fax machines in interactive networks. Equally important, broadband fiber will speed mass market penetration of the next generation of consumer electronics, including high definition television.

At the same time, Japan will soon become a major exporter of communications services. For example, the substantial Japanese accumulation of financial assets in the United States will almost certainly translate into a major flow of Japanese service exports in information and communications services to this country. The Ministry of International Trade and Industry (MITI) estimates that Japan's world exports in enhanced services will be $15 billion per year by the year 2000.

International Implications

Countries seek international rules for markets to reinforce their domestic regulatory arrangements. Reform means that most industrial countries want to tinker with international rules, but the divergence in reform sends them in somewhat different directions.

The troika has had sometimes tumultuous, sometimes cooperative relationships to forge common understanding for the international communications market.[16] United States-Japanese bilateral negotiations — the Market Oriented Sector-Specific talks that took place in 1985 — were particularly difficult, and some matters remain unresolved.[17] The troika nonetheless appears headed toward several common stands.

First, it has accepted competition in the provision of international basic services and facilities. The United States has three big international carriers and many smaller ones; Japan will have three, and the United Kingdom has two. Each has accepted "private" international fiber optic cables to compete for the traffic of specialized private networks. The United States and the United Kingdom accept private international satellites for specialized services. Japan has accepted a significant ownership role by a foreign carrier (Cable and Wireless) in one of its international carriers.

Second, the three countries have agreed to abandon traditional restraints on the shared use and resale of international circuits, making it much easier for providers of enhanced services to operate between countries. All three allow foreign ownership of domestic enhanced services. If completed successfully, these "I-VAN" agreements will open the way to freer and more flexible networks among the three countries and other interested nations.

Third, the troika agree that equipment markets should be open, although implementation may fall short of the goal. The United States-Japanese talks established important precedents on the crucial issue of technical standards.

Despite these agreements, important differences continue among the three countries. The United States government exercises fewer controls over enhanced services than the other two. Perhaps most crucially, the Ministry of Post and Telecommunications (MPT) retains control over Japanese telecommunications policy after a major challenge by MITI which represented the computer and general electronics industries. MPT is much more attuned to domestic politics and economic interests than MITI. The contest between MITI and MPT is not over, and MPT must write rules so as not to give MITI too much ammunition. MITI will raise a fuss whenever MPT rules appear to cause a trade conflict with the United States or hamper the ability of MITI's industrial constituency to match the communications strategies of their United States rivals.

Many analysts believe that MPT is using international deliberations to strengthen its hand in domestic power disputes. For example, MPT insists that all service categories be covered by explicit administrative rules: the Japanese want rules to govern emerging fax networks, while the United States insists that no rules apply or are needed. In 1988 MPT decided that all international VANs had to use the X.75 standard to maximize connectivity. The United States successfully protested that the rule prevented the right of specialized services from designing proprietary technical standards or choosing among available standard protocols.[18]

The Japanese government preference for oversight on network design is a counterpart to its campaign to open international competition in the equipment market. The government uses administrative oversight of services less to block service competition than to spur selected new service features, particularly the use of optical imagery in conjunction with voice and data systems. This trend continues to raise serious questions about administrative oversight of the computer industry, and some Japanese electronics firms want to reduce MPT's power.

European countries have looked for an international order more favorable to dynamic centralization. They saw an opportunity for such an international order at the special 1988 meeting to rewrite the telecommunications regulations of the International Telecommunication Union (ITU)—the World Administrative Telegraph and Telephone Conference (WATTC). Most European nations initially proposed to extend ITU regulations to "any entity" that uses the international network and to services not available to all interested users (that is, public services). They also championed more extensive standardization of public and private networks. Some countries suggest that traditional pricing procedures—the so-called accounting and settlements provisions—be applied to some enhanced services. These pricing procedures could greatly reduce the cost advantages enjoyed by many independent providers of enhanced services. Naturally, this vision also endorses strong restrictions on the independent provision of international facilities unless undertaken by a consortium of countries and companies approved by the national telephone authorities. This has been accomplished with the Eutelsat satellite.

American diplomats received encouraging signs in the summer of 1989 that the EC might become more receptive to international change. The Netherlands hinted that it might soon replicate British-style competition. In addition, bilateral talks with European countries had won concessions on the terms of market access for United States providers of equipment and enhanced services.[19] West Germany (FRG) has tentatively accepted United States satellite system competition with Intelsat. The Netherlands and Sweden also appear likely to enter into the troika's I-VAN agreements. Europeans largely supported a favorable draft paper on GATT rules on trade in telecommunications services at the Organization of Economic Cooperation and Development;[20] the Netherlands also floated a draft proposal for WATTC that approximated United States objectives.

In short, there are signs of change, but a significant gap remains between the United States vision for the future of the international communications regime and most industrial nations. Although several key countries now favor a more competitive model, the question is: what alternatives are available?

Models for International Change

Finding a common international framework for communications rules is an arduous task. Even if governments agreed on basic principles, perennial coordination problems remain. While the desire for reform may be broad, or even universal, both the nature and timing of reforms can impose significantly different rewards and risks for individual countries in the global adjustment process. It is also often hard to guarantee good faith adherence to intergovernmental agreements, a particularly difficult task when the market is highly imperfect, when rule violations are often hard to detect in dynamic technologies, and when the success of intergovernmental agreements is predicated on successful predictions of business initiatives and responses.

Of course, no agreement on principles exists. Future American choices are especially complicated because each international negotiating forum favors different economic interests and different configurations of political and economic relationships.

The United States has to reconcile strategies among multilateral negotiations and bilateral diplomacy, and among strategies based on GATT or the ITU. International communications has traditionally fallen outside the jurisdiction of the GATT, and thus beyond the control of national trade ministries specializing in building intersectoral trade coalitions. Instead, specialized communications ministries controlled national and international policy, and their political clienteles were national telephone companies and major telephone equipment manufacturers. They channeled their work through the ITU and later were the shareholders in INTELSAT (the International Telecommunications Satellite Organization).

The ITU has a mandate to foster the development and efficient operation of telecommunications facilities, ranging from development assistance to detailed regulations for accounting and revenues from international services. Its technological expertise also makes it crucial to the design of new international technical standards. Most important, its guidelines for international communications commerce largely conform to the old monopoly model for communications. For these reasons traditional telecommunications authorities and companies, especially in Europe, are comfortable with ITU methods and world view. Developing countries favor ITU commercial regulation because the ITU fits their preferences for strong government oversight over communications markets and because their governments have a greater voice in the ITU than at GATT.

When the United States telecommunications trade balance slipped into the red, it instituted bilateral telecommunications talks. Piecemeal success convinced the United States government systematic reform was desirable. The GATT became the vehicle for this effort in both equipment and services. These initiatives moved communications policy closer to the influence of trade ministries and their constituents, a different group from the ITU coalition. The trade specialists have proven remarkably successful in integrating world markets, but they suffer from limited expertise on communications and the uncertain fit of communications services under traditional trade concepts. Still, the integration of communications and information makes it increasingly practical for GATT to extend its purview to services.

The agenda of international diplomacy also posed a vexing schedule for American diplomats. The ITU scheduled conferences through 1989 that will influence orbital slots for satellites (Space WARC); more crucially, it tried to rewrite rules governing the regulation of international communications services (WATTC) and plans for the future of network design (the CCITT Plenary). At the same time, the GATT's current multilateral Uruguay Round was due for a mid-term review in 1988. Moreover, new trade legislation in 1980 forced the U.S. Trade Representative to accelerate the pace of bilateral trade talks on communications markets. Thus, bilateral diplomacy could dominate the United States agenda until the close of the GATT round in 1990 and perhaps until the next stage of integration of the European Common Market in 1992.

Because process is often policy, the United States must chart its global communications policy carefully. The GATT option does not preclude a significant role for the ITU or vice versa. Such stark choices are not the most important questions. Rather, the issue is the degree and terms for competition over the long term. GATT commitment means that a growing and significant part of the communications market will move to a competitive framework defined by GATT principles over

Figure 3 Options for Organizing the World Market: Efficacy of Multilateral Solution

	High	Low
GATT	Free Trade	"Mixed" Reciprocity
ITU	International Corporate Alliances	Grey Market

time; ITU practices would have to accommodate such a change.

Imagine two variants for each institutional scenario. The first assumes that the multilateral rules of the institution prove efficacious (a strong multilateral solution), while the second assumes that the multilateral rules prove inadequate (a weak multilateral solution). Each pair of conditions produces a dominant strategy for the market. Figure 3 captures these options.

The United States is best off under a GATT scenario. Depending on whether or not the United States can achieve a fully successful multilateral accord, it will choose either a new form of free trade or an emphasis on mixed reciprocity—a blend of plurilateral and bilateral agreements—within the GATT framework. If the United States acquiesces to an ITU dominated strategy, it is likely to end up with a grey market system, similar to those found in countries trying to enforce unrealistic currency exchange rates. GATT would then play a minor role for services and a larger one for equipment.

The ITU Options

Any evaluation of the ITU options requires a brief restatement of three central premises. First, the current international system reinforces the power of the traditional telecommunications carriers. The ITU remains basically an organization of and for dominant telephone companies despite ITU attempts to diversify the interests involved in its operations. (The ITU rules only permit national administrations and

Recognized Private Operating Authorities as CCITT delegates.)[21] Second, the ITU provides legal reinforcement for something akin to a loose cartel or strong oligopoly. It has virtually defied the laws of market gravity in its longevity and effectiveness but may not continue indefinitely, even if governments continue to pay it nominal allegiance. Third, the ITU has the primary technical skills for negotiating the global interconnection of networks. At stake now is the degree to which its designs must fit broader competitive criteria.

Even if the ITU retains its primacy, telephone companies do not necessarily agree upon the best strategy for organizing their interests, particularly as some countries introduce new international carriers. Moreover, domestic reform movements assure that some enterprises can challenge the dominant international position of the traditional carriers. This point is critical: even if traditional telephone companies retain primary control over policy, the terms of their victory may significantly impair their traditional harmony in international dealings. Thus, in a world where the ITU dominates the organization of the market one can imagine two outcomes—corporate alliances or a grey market.

International Corporate Alliances

European authorities prefer to rationalize regulation on a global level, much as they seek to do regionally. They hope that their case is sufficiently convincing to woo Japan and the largest American player, AT&T, to support their approach. They would retain the ITU and the ministries of communications as the preferred government agencies managing the world market. The GATT would play a minor role by enforcing the rules governing customer premises equipment and a loose set of guidelines for fair entry in enhanced services for interested states.

This strategy assumes a minimum common denominator for national reform, but governments will restrict international competition substantially to shift rents from the international market to subsidize the home market. It also assumes that the public network can create compelling economies of scale and scope through international collaboration on dynamic centralization. Once achieved, these new efficiencies will satisfy the claims of large users and the information industry.

In this approach reformed national telephone companies and larger telecommunications equipment firms (which also manufacture computers) are the preferred commercial interests. Large users could remove their most valuable value added services from the public network to private networks but would be hindered by start-up costs in administrative haggling and initial economic investments. In principle large users should agree to this strategy due to improved efficiencies in public network service and pricing.

Intergovernmental market management revolves around the following core ideas:

(1) Retain a monopoly on public network facilities and basic services even if there are competitive arrangements for enhanced services;

(2) Continue selective monopolies for some enhanced services and broadcast services;

(3) Create comprehensive technical standards and definitions of services to facilitate coordination of network design and pricing;

(4) Register under the oversight of telecommunications administrators all potential entrants into every phase of the communications and information markets;

(5) Rely on joint planning and investment in international facilities for telephone companies to reduce surplus capacity.

Much of the regulatory apparatus to implement these ideas maintains the status quo. However, technological innovations have so eroded the old system that most PTTs endorsed an early draft of new telecommunications regulations for the World Administrative Telegraph and Telephone Conference (WATTC) that tried to reinforce it.[22] In particular, the draft raised three subjects of concern.

(1) Who is covered by ITU regulations? Many PTTs want to extend coverage from services generally available to the public by "administrations" or "recognized private operating agencies" (for example, Western Union International) to all services and suppliers provided via communications networks. This would bring enhanced services under the scope of the ITU. This might, for example, require a private banking network to offer universal access to all interested users, or it might require a United States VAN to follow the accounting and charging policies of the public phone companies.[23]

(2) What constitute the obligations of service providers in interna-

tional services? Many PTTs want to establish requirements to govern quality of services (in light of CCITT frameworks, which include suggested network architectures).[24] This contrasts with the view that the chief requirements should only be "no harm to the network" and the ability to establish internetwork connections.

(3) Are the draft regulations stated to make them binding on domestic national laws rather than merely recommendatory (as is the case with CCITT resolutions)? Binding regulations would, for example, forbid the United States to declare many enhanced services outside the domain of national regulation.[25]

These draft rules reinforce effective control over network design and facilities by the major telephone companies. At the same time, it puts adjustment risks on would-be providers of independent services: new innovative service networks would have the advantage of known current standards, but would risk being reversed by public networks. For example, a provider might have to switch to a mandatory network protocol from its proprietary protocol. The registration and oversight requirement also opens the way to restrictive regulations.

Rationalized regulation also assumes that major national carriers can cooperate in developing, deploying and pricing services to meet global demands of large users who already seek integrated systems on a global scale. This implies that the telephone companies can overcome serious coordination problems among themselves. How can they do so? International public commercial alliances (IPCA) are one way to attempt coordination among national phone firms.[26] IPCA entail joint international business strategies among dominant national phone carriers for collectively producing and delivering key products to major customers, especially global customers. Can the major national telephone companies jointly design a market strategy for both monopoly and competitive services to win these customers?

IPCA make sense if there are a handful of clearly dominant players who will control the major marketplaces over time and share common interests about the development of technology, international facilities, and the control of customers. In particular, they reject challenges to each other's control over their core market, even though they contemplate selective competitive ventures in their partners' home markets. If massive predation is not practical, each benefits from sharing costs and technical efficiencies when competing against others for control of important global customers.

IPCA are already emerging. Ironically, the most important example —the announced alliance between British Telecom, Kokusai Denshin Denwa (KDD), and AT&T—involves the international market leaders of the countries with the most advanced experiments in national competition—the United States, United Kingdom, and Japan. This alliance assumes that competition will be constrained by the conservative wing of the Japanese MPT and the success of Europe in holding to its preferred strategy. Therefore, the market leaders in the troika seek to rationalize their hold on national customers while configuring their strategy to slowly increasing global competition.[27]

The objective of the new alliance is global information movement and management, the delivery of an integrated set of services for global customers originating from each of the three countries. A global customer can go to any of the three companies to acquire a single account manager to oversee billing and service provisions throughout the three countries. This requires extremely strong levels of coordination concerning pricing, marketing, and the design of technical services. It also assumes good faith among all players over time.

In short, IPCA acknowledge a vigorous competitive fringe but are confident that governments (for their own political reasons) will blunt waves of new entrants into the market, and large firms will coordinate a common framework.

How favorable is this outcome for the United States? Not very. It is generally acceptable for AT&T, traditional international RPOAs and network equipment manfacturers, because it may provide a new route into the international market for AT&T. The effects on the CPE and computer industries will be mixed. On the one hand, networking protocols are standardized, the chief basis on which the strategy might co-opt support from computer companies worrying about IBM's influence over standards. On the other hand, relative inflexibility of network design and pricing, as well as subtle tendencies toward concentrating value added services in the network or in network equipment are disadvantages. Clearly, consumers and providers of enhanced services stand to lose the most.

This scenario reaffirms administrative solutions for the world services economy. Moreover, it segregates telecommunications and information services from the broader reform of the world service economy, thereby weakening the effectiveness of competition in equipment.

At a time of transition in the management of the global economic system, these are troubling precedents.

The Grey Market

Even if ITU dominance is the initial international version of limited competition and rationalized regulation, the system will not necessarily function effectively. Rather, the battle for ITU primacy may be won precisely because many key actors expect the new system to be ineffective, enabling a grey market of private negotiations for telecommunications.

The closest analogy to this possibility is the black (or parallel) market in foreign exchange, particularly where developing country exchange rate parities are hopelessly overvalued. In such cases currency depreciation seems a logical policy alternative. Were government to take action to rationalize exchange rates, it would probably also impose exchange flow controls, providing temporary relief for such politically potent interests as small businesses. Controls are strongly opposed by finance ministries and banks; advocates of a more realistic exchange rate in finance ministries and the international financial institutions therefore join financial actors to advocate no action on currency values, in turn permitting parallel foreign currency markets. This parallel market devalues the currency, though not as effectively as a formal devaluation, while providing financial advantages for some actors in the new parallel market.

New technologies and new investments in international communication infrastructures made the existing monopoly model obsolete. There is already a thriving grey market, albeit not as efficient as an open market. It bestows special advantages to potential middlemen with extensive capital, technology, political connections, and customers, but who are not the primary objects of attention of regulatory oversight. The RBOCs, for example, might derive special advantages amidst the decaying global regulatory system.

In many ways WATTC was a response to the grey market. Whatever the rules created at WATTC, coordination under the ITU may stumble for several reasons. First, there is great diversity among market participants—new specialized service providers and customers with extensive private networks operating on a global scale. Second, telephone companies have changed and are now far less homogeneous.

The United States, United Kingdom, and Japan each have many international common carriers which now need to move global customers from the public network to private or quasi-private services. Many monopoly phone companies are more commercial and bend their own rules to win pieces of more profitable business. Third, the race to consolidate advantages in the provision of transoceanic communications facilities (such as the new Atlantic and Pacific fiber optic cables) has undermined old prices and restrictions on the use of communications facilities. Each international communications facility courts the vital market of large users by lowering prices and promising flexible use of circuits, thereby eroding old rules and prices.

Why don't those who discount a strong ITU simply initiate another system? In part, they fear that any governmental efforts to impose new rules will make things worse rather than better. The parallel, again, is to the problem of correcting exchange rate imbalances in currency markets. Some people envision the grey market as the most practical route for change in the international communications market: in a phrase reminiscent of cold war foreign policy, regulatory dominos will fall on their own. There is even some sign that the ITU bent (unconsciously) in a direction that favors the grey market in preparation for the WATTC.

Early in 1988 ITU Secretary-General Richard Butler circulated a proposed draft for WATTC regulations that distinguished between "telecommunications services generally available to the public" which would be subject to all ITU regulations (including separations and settlements processes) and "special arrangements for specialized telecommunications networks, systems and applications, including the underlying means of international telecommunications transport" for which countries could "make special arrangements" among themselves. This language would also officially recognize these new services and affirm the need to accommodate their access to basic network services (such as leased circuits).[28] The draft language on "special arrangements" opened the possibility of special deals outside the conventional ITU framework for countries wishing to introduce more competition. These provisions could be combined with the deletion of proposed article 1.7 that called for regulations to be extended to "any entity" that used the public network. Together, they would largely satisfy United States demands for competition. At the WATTC France and Italy led a large number of countries in backing the more restrictive regulations. The United States had the support of such countries as Sweden, the United Kingdom, West Germany, and the People's Republic of China. The result was likely to be an artfully ambiguous compromise.[29]

No one openly advocates a grey market because it is not politic to oppose constructive reform. Still, such a strategy could turn potential political failure into a source of commercial innovation. In a time of change this is no small benefit. It is far less efficient, however, than establishing a system in which everyone could compete more openly and threatens at the same time to erode financial support for existing cross-subsidies.

Grey market policy also creates unsatisfactory linkages between telecommunications services and equipment by encouraging ad hoc deals on services while providing little basis for government to leverage services with equipment or to trade one against the other.[30] Equally important, it may deepen divisions between AT&T and the RBOCs.

Many RBOCs fear continued reliance on AT&T hardware and software because they may one day compete against AT&T. They believe that AT&T gains significant advantages in services from its hold over software used in RBOCs' central office switches. The grey market game encourages RBOCs to break their reliance on AT&T equipment, but a grey market does little to assist AT&T in gaining access to foreign communications markets.

The grey market mode can provide a misleading sense of progress for policymakers. While specific deals and accommodations might be plentiful, the cumulative process might also create a market of many specialized commercial interests sheltered from full competition. The total level of innovation and reform would fall short of that imagined by domino theory proponents. Equally, the grey market retains a framework of limited competition, segregates communications and information services from other services, and encourages bilateralism and further grey markets—the worst precedent for working out the future management of the world economy.

The GATT Option

Another set of reformers favors placing telecommunications and information services, in whole or in part, within the framework of traditional free trade agreements. The GATT governs such arrangements.

This approach implicitly changes the institutional arena away from one built around communications companies to one emphasizing a full diversity of manufacturing, services, and general trading interests in industrialized countries, thus leveling the playing field for communications. The GATT is an especially effective "early warning system" for noncommon carriers concerning potential government barriers to the delivery of international communications services and equipment. A GATT strategy can increase both the level of reliable information for market participants and the role of communications services and sophisticated electronics firms.

Like the ITU option, the GATT framework may not work as intended; indeed, the most modest United States plan for the GATT may prove ineffective. If GATT dominance is inept, the likely alternative is a mixed bilateral and plurilateral (small groups of like-minded nations) negotiation, while new formulas for judging reciprocity in the competitive opening of markets would emerge under a GATT umbrella; a "mixed" GATT regime might produce a formula similar to the bargaining system in the international airline market. In the airline market governments bargain bilaterally over how many carriers from each country can serve the other and the number of cities that they may serve.

Free Trade under a Strong GATT

Who wins if the GATT plays a significant role in governing trade in telecommunications and information services? This effort serves the interests of the newcomers in the communications arena—for example, it serves the political interests of an electronics firm like IBM. It can also support large users who may selectively enter the supply side of the market, for example by selling internal corporate information systems. Indeed, some critics attack GATT's intrusion into communications as a ploy of large multinational corporations at the expense of smaller businesses and households.

Advocates of GATT jurisdiction seek an evolutionary migration of the market from PTT/ITU control to market based competition conforming as closely as possible to the classic rules of free trade. This migration would have three features. First, GATT rules governing equipment would be tightened to govern procurement by government monopolies (like the PTTs) and the use of technical standards as nontariff barriers. Second, a GATT agreement on services would claim selective coverage over communications and information services among countries signing a services and communications sector code. It would cover enhanced services, while voice services would be beyond its scope. Third, since most countries would combine elements of monopoly and competition (if they adhered to the code at all), GATT would require rules to govern fair competition between the dominant telephone company and its competitors in selected markets. These rules would have the flavor of international agreements concerning the legitimate scope of domestic regulation.

The GATT alternative would leave most of the administrative and technical work concerning communications to the ITU. It would change the mix of institutional fora governing communications to devalue the political currency of the traditional telephone companies and would resolve the international coordination problem on terms familiar to many nontelephone companies.

The GATT ideal turns every good or service into a classical commodity market characterized by easy information, free access to many buyers and sellers, and open bidding. The heart of GATT is a small set of principles (reciprocity, nondiscrimination, transparency, and binding) to reduce the risks of disadvantageous agreements for governments and companies.

Reciprocity implicitly means that each country makes overall concessions of equivalent value to the concession of others, at least on a basis proportionate to their size. The principle of reciprocity has led to formulas to measure the value of each trade concession and to aggregate individual items into broad categories of commodities (such as transportation equipment) to balance concessions within each category. At the same time, the principle of nondiscrimination demands that trade concessions made to one country must be made to all countries. This reduces the possibility of coalitions sidestepping the practicalities of reciprocity. Negotiators must choose how much to move toward conditional reciprocity, a stricter standard for granting concessions.[31]

GATT also relies on principles of transparency and binding. Transparency obliges all nations to make trade restrictions self-evident, eliminating hidden barriers and hidden concessions in an effort to create conditions for free competition. Such rules reduce the costs of information for everyone involved. These conditions are binding, such that specific trade concessions may be withdrawn to a particular country if it violates an agreement. This stipulation provides credible and predictable retaliation for bad faith and limits the scope of retaliation to the narrow source of original offense.

Above all, the GATT effectively halts particular offenses. Even comparative newcomers to a market can identify problems and appeal quickly to trade bureaucracies at home. Unlike communications ministries or regulatory commissions, trade negotiators derive political rewards from successful, cross-cutting bargains.

The GATT nonetheless is not an ideal vehicle for resolving communications policy internationally. For example, to maintain cross-subsidies for smaller users, GATT negotiators have limited their efforts to defining agreements on value added and information services, largely ignoring basic voice services and underlying network facilities for the network. This approach parallels the division between monopoly basic and competitive enhanced services included in several stages of telephone deregulation in the United States.

Such a division, when transposed to international trade, makes it difficult to assure transparency and nondiscrimination in enhanced services.[32] First, there are always tactical difficulties when a monopolist faces competition in a few narrow market segments. A future GATT agreement would require that national telephone companies curtail cross-subsidies from monopoly to competitive markets, open procurement of goods and services from foreign competitors in these market segments, and offer foreign competitors terms for the use of the national communications infrastructure no less favorable than those enjoyed by the telephone company's own lines of business.

Second, it is difficult to distinguish permissible and impermissible competition, particularly when technology and customer demands are breaking down traditional market distinctions.[33] The 1988 United States-Canadian Free Trade Accord's treatment of telecommunications services set a poor precedent by simply accepting each country's regulatory distinctions about classifying various services.

GATT also has little experience with trade-related effects of technical standards and architecture of a complex network system. To date both bilateral and GATT negotiations have found it easiest to confront cases in which a specific technical standard served as an arbitrary discriminant against foreign telecommunications equipment. Essentially, for CPE the United States has persuaded many countries to switch to a simpler standard for judging the acceptability of any piece of CPE. The standard is essentially "no harm to the network"—that is, any design is acceptable if it neither harms its own network nor poses physical danger to the user. The United States has also won acceptance of "self-certification"—a company has a right to use any reputable commercial lab in its country to test and demonstrate equipment standards. Standards for network equipment, while presumably nondiscriminatory, are necessarily more complex than "no harm" because the equipment itself helps to run the network.

Despite progress on standards, trade negotiators have been relatively silent on the critical question of the effects of network design on meaningful competitive opportunities; this question will be central for the future of the international communications regime and is a major challenge for GATT. An important precedent on this issue was won in United States-Japanese bilateral talks when Japan agreed to open the standard-setting process to foreign companies.

Bilateral trade talks and GATT negotiations have reflected these problems when addressing the rights of large users to establish internal communications networks in foreign countries. For all practical purposes the United States has attempted to certify a minimum set of rights for these large users. These may range from the right to choose freely their CPE to rights involved in setting prices and types of local communications services available to corporate networks. For example, the United States argues that its firms have the right to secure leased circuits at flat monthly rates, a proposal often resisted by local telephone authorities who want them to use local data communications networks on a volume sensitive charge. These provisions make sure that foreign governments cannot use complex pricing or technical standards to forestall the new internal communications network of the large user. By the standards of international trade negotiations these are radical conceptual claims, no matter how carefully they are masked.

The right to foreign investment is similarly disguised by negotiators, but at the midterm review of the current GATT round the United States won consent to language endorsing a right to establish competitive market access and national treatment to approximate a right of foreign investment for enhanced service providers.[34] No matter how intrusive, these demands are sensible if the underlying network and basic services remain so monopolistic that only a firmly articulated right to do business assures meaningful competition in the limited segment open to free trade.

Thus, the GATT negotiations might extend to an unprecedented extent the range of international oversight of domestic regulations for communications. Once again, free international commerce in sophisticated services rests on assuring fair competition in the underlying domestic network. Nonetheless, even if GATT reaches a successful initial agreement, it may still stumble. More competition may lead communications service providers to offer more integrated global offerings than the GATT initially assures, which in turn might require a different form of bargaining policy.

At the same time, free trade negotiations concerning communications services significantly influence GATT negotiations concerning telecommunications equipment. What equations should be drawn between services and equipment?

To date American trade negotiators have treated services and equipment as complementary, assuming, for example, that IBM will use its own equipment in overseas computer communications networks, although not every company has the resources to do the same. However, no overall strategy links equipment and services in negotiations. In recent free trade agreement negotiations, American and Canadian participants considered telecommunications equipment and services in different working groups with little internal coordination within the delegations.

A workable GATT approach could be advantageous to the United States. The arena nicely represents the full diversity of interests at work in United States international policy, although small business may be underrepresented. The approval would discourage policies to use restricted competition in some services to gain special advantages in all other services and most equipment markets. It is also concerned about consumer interests. Nevertheless, the GATT can only succeed if the United States refrains from segregating its ITU and GATT strategies. Skeptics of GATT wonder if this is possible given GATT's limited expertise on telecommunications and the continued skepticism of developing countries concerning GATT services initiatives.

Mixed Bargaining under the GATT:
International Carriers

If GATT cannot provide effective market management or if dramatic shifts in trade balances for services occur, some fallback is likely. A GATT solution can provide its own guidelines for the fallback, blending features of bilateralism and multilateralism. Textile and automobile agreements, which feature multilateral and bilateral export restraints, respectively, are examples of this mixed bargaining.

Mixed bargaining for telecommunications would have three characteristics. First, it would organize equipment pacts with a more direct eye to strategic terms for services, similar to changes in the airplane industry. Second, it would deemphasize the rights of users in favor of fundamental measures to change the behavior of suppliers. Third, it would create tighter oversight and enforce equivalence in concessions, including the use of different bases to judge equivalence. It would not retreat behind protectionist walls because the interests of major firms are now global.

Can policymakers allow mixed bargaining to work efficiently under GATT codes? The emerging order for the international airline industry may suggest one way to do so.[35]

Imagine a world with tensions over true equivalence in competitive opportunities. At the same time, the leading telephone companies discover that common servicing of global customers through an IPCA hinders their individual interests in pricing and the design of marketing strategies.[36] Therefore, they would prefer to provide "end-to-end" service globally under their sole management control at their own financial risk. Moreover, by virtue of investing in many collective projects for the development of global infrastructure, some companies may acquire de facto rights to global facilities. (AT&T, for example, has invested so aggressively in global facilities that it has virtually created independent rights to facilities on a global basis. Some argue that AT&T is concealing a program similar to Cable and Wireless' announced intention to build a global fiber optic highway.[37]) Firms could acquire the global capacity for delivery of communications and information services under their own ownership, even if each individual facility in their network has an ownership shared with a number of different companies.

Even if firms preferred an integrated global service, they would still have to recruit customers and deliver services in several major countries without relying on the local telephone company as a partner. This poses enormous bargaining problems, particularly in establishing rights to do business. This challenge could lead governments to create a new framework governing market entry in the world communications market that would depart significantly from both the ITU and conventional GATT approaches. How can governments accomplish this? The global airline industry provides a model.

The airline industry is rapidly creating integrated global airlines. These global airlines often have local partners for particular segments of service, but each airline retains a distinct global identity and marketing philosophy. The carriers benefit from the ability to offer end-to-end service to minimize interconnection problems for passengers. They profit from the economies of their hub systems for the use of aircraft, and, most vitally, they benefit from integrated information systems to manage pricing, seating capacity, aircraft scheduling, and passenger booking. The analogies for communications include control over low-cost infrastructure, sophisticated tariffing and traffic management schemes, and proprietary software for service applications.[38]

The capacity to deliver services in the airline industry depends on swapping gateway rights between countries. Gateways constitute major nodes of international traffic which interconnect with local airline routes within a country. Countries bargain over the number of gateways available to foreign carriers. The foreign carrier may only take off and land at the gateways and must rely upon local airlines to feed traffic to other domestic markets. Rules govern the rights to pick-up traffic as well as delivering traffic. A central bargaining point in airline markets is matching the number of foreign carriers and gateways available overseas against the number of gateways and carriers permitted domestically.

In principle, there is no reason why the international communications market cannot be similarly organized. If companies want to be global carriers, governments could organize the market around gateway access. An international carrier could pick up and drop off traffic using its own facilities in any international gateway. It would rely upon the local telephone company to connect that traffic to the domestic market.

Governments could charge all international carriers, including its own national carriers serving that market, access fees to use the domestic network. International negotiations could determine access fees and gateway availability. Global customers would benefit from competition and flexibility, and governments would receive fees for the use of the national network by international carriers. Importantly, developing countries would be able to match policy instruments to their own goals by blending domestic monopoly for internal development with the equivalent to a global free trade zone for internationally oriented business.

Most major telephone companies deny any interest in global carriage. They argue against its duplication of facilities, characterizing such moves as fruitless attacks on the home base of fellow telephone companies. This view may underestimate the economic and political incentives for change. Some companies may well ponder the lessons of the airline industry: once rate-of-return regulation ended, airlines found out that highly flexible systems for managing their capacity were as vital as offering specialized services. Partnerships are less efficient than a unified management system.

The politics of these potential developments are intriguing. On the one hand, companies supplying services want expanded entry, and countries worry about genuine equivalence of concessions under traditional GATT bargaining formulae. Governments may therefore search for a new formula to measure equivalence while concurrently offering bilateral and multilateral bargaining; additionally, they seek to balance increased entry against continuing demands to protect the domestic marketplace. On the other hand, large equipment sellers may decide that integrating global competition in services would reduce protectionist strategies on equipment. In other words, a world of global service organizations is more cosmopolitan concerning equipment standards and sales.

Abstract political speculation already has real life exemplars. Cable and Wireless has shown that a determined foreign competitor can establish a competitive gateway in a foreign country. Britain's Cable and Wireless won the right to be a primary organizer of a new international long-distance company for Japan after a determined intervention by Prime Minister Margaret Thatcher. Similarly, a 1988 NEC discussion suggested a time line for liberalizing its telecommunications market.[39] After completion of liberalizing for competition in enhanced services and equipment, each country would accept foreign firm provision of basic international services. Today, foreign firms have a 20 percent stake in one major American common carrier.[40] There is de facto movement toward this approach in United States policy. It is promoting the entry of independent American satellite systems in the international market. In 1988 it temporarily withheld approval of an international resale license to a Cable and Wireless subsidiary in the United States. At issue was the granting of an American permit while British carriers continued to resist the entry of the new American satellite systems. The hesitation jogged the United Kingdom into accepting the American system.[41]

Thus, a new international telecommunications system would feature a GATT framework on services that established general principles governing competition in telecommunications. These principles would detail minimum obligations for all signatories to the sectoral code. They would also provide for a principle of elasticity that would allow interested countries to establish more rigorous competition.

The GATT framework would assure all countries the right to enter into the bargaining. (Even conditional Most Favored Nation status is better treatment of weaker countries than no guarantee at all.) In addition, bilateral bargaining on a market-by-market basis is often awkward because economic circumstances do not permit equivalent market benefits. Lodging negotiations within GATT could reduce this problem: first, if a country grants unreciprocated concessions bilaterally it could earn a "credit" to be applied against other service markets organized under the GATT; second, when senior trade officials meet at the end of a general GATT round, service concessions will be included even if services and goods are formally separated; third, oversight on trade-related aspects of communications services by trade ministries informally creates useful linkages because, as one veteran trade negotiator put it, "trade officials intuitively bargain by judging the overall state of the trading relationship, and they do this by counting all the items over which they have jurisdiction."[42]

What would such a system do about telecommunications equipment? The GATT could separate equipment issues from services, in all probability greatly strengthening free trade in equipment. An age of international communications carriers raises possibilities of network equipment politics resembling those in the aircraft industry. The United States could also propose a special GATT code on network equipment similar to the GATT aircraft code in its effort to curb government subsidies for exports and govern fair procurement practices.[43]

The code might contain additional requirements for countries adhering to the "carriers model."

Alternatives for United States Policy

The alternatives confronting the United States are particularly troubling because no single decisive agreement will reorient the world communications regime in the near future. Therefore, the sequence of choices is critical. Accordingly, recommendations for alternative policies fall into three groups.

(1) Create a strategy to favor an evolutionary migration of the core of the communications market from the market guidelines under the ITU to one under the GATT. This strategy must accommodate a dual regulatory structure without allowing the transition to more competition to stall.

(2) Reformulate the United States strategy for GATT so that it is not so narrowly tied to the "Computer Inquiry II" model for the world communications market. This requires a clear approach concerning network architecture, the scope and definition of services and equipment covered by the agreement, and relationships between domestic communications market structure and international obligations.

(3) Explore the notion of plurilateral negotiation to establish a "mixed bargain" under the GATT. The United States should consider a more formal framework for countries moving to competition in all phases of communications, featuring stricter reciprocity rules and closer links between liberalization of equipment and services.

Choosing Institutional Oversight

The long-standing world communications regime, anchored at the ITU, featured restricted market competition. Many countries would prefer to retain and modernize this system. The ITU scenarios of international corporate alliances and the grey market concede that free trade will play some role in the future communications market, primarily as limited special principles to cover the needs of the lowest denominator of international reform.

The United States national interest is to promote competition in the world communications market while preserving ITU leadership in designing the network of the future and respecting diverse government preferences about competition. Unless the United States encourages competition primarily by ad hoc bilateral agreements—which pose troubling questions about the precedent for managing the world economy and the consistency of the agreements—Washington has little choice but to position the GATT as an anchor for organizing fair competition in the market.

Its major problem is thus how to facilitate the coexistence and evolution of the ITU and GATT orders. To do this requires at least three steps. First, retain the ITU as a baseline for regulation. Monopoly is the established order of the international communications regime, and many countries want to retain it for all or some of their services. The United States should support a responsible rewriting of the ITU rules that meet these criteria. The rewriting should rationalize monopoly rules to emphasize greater efficiency for services supplied on monopolistic terms; it should accept these rules as guidelines for all services retained as monopolies, covering universal basic services provided jointly by common carriers or Recognized Private Operating Agencies on a monopoly basis. The terms for monopoly services should be defined to be compatible with services subject to liberalization in competition. Some form of exemption for countries wanting to arrange more bilateral competition is imperative.[44] The ITU should facilitate coordination on standards as long as it introduces reforms to accommodate the needs of competitive market architectures.

Second, support an evolutionary strategy to extend the mandate of GATT over equipment and services. The GATT requires expertise to extend its purview to this market, and international political backing is still limited. Working from its current areas of strength, it should extend its mandate by emphasizing liberalization of trade in equipment and enhanced services, following current policy. It should then define enhanced services to anticipate increasing overlap of basic with enhanced services, especially for larger users. This would permit coverage to expand over time by resolving the overlap in favor of competition among adherents to the GATT. Bilateral talks can help to promote competition in the underlying communications infrastructure, and additional offer bargaining incentives may encourage countries to liberalize.

Negotiating with an eye toward the integrated world economy should encourage all parties to emphasize the trade related effects of decisions concerning communications networks and regulations. Trade officials have slowly formulated a right to review items not covered by trade rules but directly impinging on traded goods and services. By vigorously pursuing "trade related effects," members can examine the process for deciding related issues. This could offer a basis for working with the ITU. Building on such a foundation, coordination between trade negotiators and the ITU needs firm support. The ITU should be the "hands on" organization governing communications; GATT rules should apply only to equipment and services as they become competitive and to trade related effects of monopoly services on equipment and competitive services.

As part of a broader GATT services agreement, a group of fifteen senior trade officials should meet monthly in Geneva to update the original agreement and discuss coordination with other international institutions. The group should have an express political mandate from member governments to review disputes concerning clashes of trade and communications rules that may hinder effective implementation of the trade rules.[45] Preparation for these meetings may also produce useful consultation between communications and trade officials at the national level.

The ITU should also expand official representation in the CCITT beyond members of government administrations and RPOAs. If CCITT delegations represented broader interests, international communications rules might be designed to be more responsive to the larger community of international suppliers and users of information and communications services.

Coordination is not a perfect solution to all telecommunications trade problems, even if GATT nominally has an upper hand in its area of competence. Dual ITU-GATT jurisdiction would entrench some inefficient economic practices in the global regulatory structure. If each organization has a mandate to protect its initial core constituency, some overprotection of basic services is inevitable, with some reverse discrimination in favor of enhanced service providers and large users. This bifurcated regulatory structure for services also assures that there will be no dominant approach to integrating equipment and services markets. Large global users will spawn some market niches; large public networks with more ambitious ideas about universal public service will spawn others, increasing the political viability of this outcome. Overall, a new communications regime will benefit from combining ITU technical expertise and concern for universal services with a GATT mandate to reintegrate the communications sector into a competitive market for the new information society.

Modifying the United States Strategy for GATT

If the United States promotes an evolutionary migration of the communications sector to the GATT, is its blueprint adequate? The United States strategy would promote the integration of telecommunications with other services and of services with goods. Successful rules for telecommunications are likely to lead the GATT into territory that could significantly alter traditional institutions of free trade. For example, reciprocity would be conditional, not unconditional. Trade rules would guarantee stronger rights of foreign investment and the rights of users in gaining access to national infrastructures influencing trade. More extensive review of domestic regulations by trade authorities would also result. This ambitious agenda promises more trade conflicts and more interdependence in national policies.

The danger for this strategy is that negotiators may be preoccupied with affirming continuity with the past. This is fine as a tactic but can hinder the formulation of strategy. The United States needs instead to rethink several of its policy positions. It needs a reformed approach to questions of technical standards and the design of networks, criteria for defining classes of services, formulae to evaluate equivalence of concessions, and incentives for opening competition in facilities.

The United States has used bilateral free trade negotiations with Canada and Israel, as well as numerous negotiations with Japan and Europe, to experiment with different organizing principles for the world's communications industry. This experience suggests the need for several measures.

The Right to Network Architecture. The question of standards is fundamental to communications, yet it is difficult to establish guidelines to design a technological network. To date both the GATT and bilateral trade negotiations have concentrated on equipment standards. However, nondiscrimination and openness in network equipment does not define an acceptable philosophy for the design of a network. This issue emerged in a recent dispute between the United

States and Japan about Japan's proposal to impose certain communications protocols on international VANs, a move the United States finds unacceptable for services designed for a limited group of users. The United States has also expressed alarm about South Korean regulations that might require open disclosure of proprietary network protocols.

To counter these problems the United States should consider support for a "right to network architecture." Such a right would oblige national network architectures to provide substantial latitude for interconnecting networks. Noncommon carriers run specialized networks, and they should not be expected to support the same approach to protocol problems as a general public network.

Clearly, this right is limited; engineering-specific technical interconnection are expensive. The rule could follow the pattern of United States negotiations for MCI and Sprint operating rights in other countries. Foreign telecommunications authorities may impose reasonable conditions about cost reimbursement if the interconnecting architecture requires extraordinary engineering. (Proprietary protocols need not be disclosed except to authorized mediators.) Contested decisions could be mediated using evidence from comparable engineering problems in telecommunications.

Minimum Definitions. Definitions of major types of communications and information services are particularly needed. Defining service classifications is an annoying business; in trade talks American and Canadian negotiators finessed the issues by letting each country define services in its own territory. For the long term this opens a door to trouble. It is far better and more efficient for negotiations to adopt a minimum list of services reserved from competition, a minimum list of services assured as acceptable for competition, and a commitment to periodic review of services on neither list. In this way countries could define services across all categories that are not bound to competition under the agreement, and each country could unilaterally remove services from this reserved list at a later date. A similar minimum list of services in each major category of service that must be subject to competition could be constructed, with some exceptions that could later be considered.[46] All other services would be regularly reexamined in working groups if they are not liberalized unilaterally. Contested definitions should be subject to standard mechanisms for resolving trade disputes.

Quantifying Equivalence of Concessions. Thus far, the United States has treated liberalization of communications services as a rulemaking exercise rather than as an elimination of barriers. Therefore, quantifying the equivalence of service concessions has not loomed large in trade talks. Although quantification should not delay negotiations, it is worthwhile to promote quantification of benefits. This would make it easier to swap service and equipment concessions and would allow each party to quantify offers of additional liberalizations. Quantified estimates might also allow communications concessions to be swapped against other types of services trades.

Competition for Facilities. Incentives for competition in communications facilities should be an intrinsic part of a GATT-oriented strategy. A minimum strategy for GATT requires additional support for international and domestic competition in facilities. Competition in facilities should motivate owners to provide competitive terms for access to those facilities. Absent competitive facilities, the GATT will have to extend burdensome restrictions and oversight to domestic regulation of communications services. The United States should therefore adopt a rule of thumb in telecommunications negotiations: in the absence of competitive facilities, the United States will insist on many controls over the conduct of telecommunications policy; as competition in facilities increases, it will selectively relax these safeguards.

It is much easier to run a free trade system if the major actors have a broader range of incentives toward procompetitive behavior than merely the formal rules of free trade. The goal is to provide safeguards if there is no competition in facilities and to reward facilities competition by reducing some trade safeguards.

A Broader Package of Measures

What should the United States plan to do if the GATT does not succeed in establishing a conventional multilateral package for telecommunications? Are bilateral and plurilateral talks among like-minded countries the only practical method to pursue change? Is there a way to provide for evolution to the most efficient form of mixed bargaining under the GATT? Our earlier discussion suggests some guidelines for policy reform.

(1) Provide an evolutionary clause in a GATT communications agreement. A GATT agreement on communications should cover enhanced services and equipment, but this may not be enough, politically or economically, to achieve long-term change. How could the GATT organize bargaining about underlying facilities and basic services? Rather than depending on pure ad hoc bilateralism, it might be better to provide a set of property rights to be bargained under the GATT. These property rights would take the form of gateway and carrier rights.

The GATT clause would permit interested parties to make special arrangements for basic services and facilities (as proposed at WATTC). It would permit the use of appropriate techniques to establish equivalent concessions in service and facilities rights. All interested members of the GATT who signed the communications agreement would be eligible to enter into this exchange of concessions. The clause would impose GATT requirements concerning transparency and binding on the supplementary accords. It would also allow for a "concessions link" between the supplementary accords and the broader communications/services agreement. This concessions link would permit, upon consent of all parties, crediting of concessions made in the supplementary accords against trade-offs made in the broader codes on communications.

(2) Encourage collective international ownership of gateways. Now that the Japanese government has opened its international carriers to significant (albeit minority) shares of foreign ownership, the United States could urge that all interested countries permit competition among international common carriers. It could also propose a distinction between a company's role as a common carrier and as an owner of an international gateway.

For example, suppose that MCI wants to be an international carrier to Japan under this new scheme. The United States would agree to choose it as a United States carrier and would bargain for its right to deliver a range of basic services to customers in certain Japanese gateway cities. MCI would be free to pick up and deliver traffic for its customers among those gateways in Japan (subject to some restrictions on becoming primarily a carrier of domestic traffic). Would MCI have to build all of its own facilities or simply lease them from local Japanese carriers?

Rather than accept this choice, the United States should urge that equity ownership shares in international carriers with widely diversified ownership not be counted against other MCI rights as a carrier. Thus, if MCI wanted to buy a share of the Cable & Wireless/Itoh venture, International Digital Communications (IDC), it could use its ownership role in IDC to assist in the provision of facilities for MCI's Japanese operations. MCI's ownership share in IDC would not count against the gateway rights it acquires as an independent entity.

The purpose of the consortium clause is to tap Japanese insight into the advantages of joint ownership for spreading risk and resolving bargaining problems among stakeholders with diverging interests. Minority ownership shares permit a foreign carrier to learn more effectively about local technologies and networking practices. At the same time, these shares allow all firms to spread risks on expensive facilities while competing on services. Instead of having to rely on a third party and local regulators to enforce its rights, a foreign carrier has some assurance of influence through its equity holding.

(3) Create special procurement obligations. Fostering international carriers may create a cosmopolitan market for both network and CPE equipment; nonetheless, carriers have national origins and identities. The GATT coverage of telecommunications equipment has been weak. The end of government ownership and monopolies will partially correct this situation in the future GATT negotiations, but it is not clear that the situation will be sufficiently corrected, especially on network equipment.

Creating a special class of international carriers opens the possibility of imposing special standards of scrutiny on procurement practices. In short, special privileges can incur special obligations. The United States can press for agreements to this effect at the GATT, and it can act unilaterally by imposing conditions on certification of foreign carriers in the United States market. It can also ensure that countries do not mask discriminatory purchasing under international consortium arrangements. For example, what response is appropriate if a European satellite consortium which exercises discriminatory purchasing practices wishes to enter the American market? Should the United States accept this practice simply because there is no single national owner of the consortium? One solution is to adopt a measure under consideration in the airline/aircraft market: create special legislation authorizing trade actions against international consortia.

Conclusion

In its telecommunications policy the United States will continue to encounter major diplomatic and economic policy problems. It must provide leadership in promoting international competition while co-operating on designing gateways linking the networks of the future.

The United States must also evaluate its telecommunications policy choices within a broader policy agenda. It is searching for a new formula to manage the world economy while its dominance over international politics and economics is declining. At the same time, managers of the world economy are confronting strategic choices independent of shifting power alignments. Fundamental trade policy must confront the role of the service sector of the economy in creating rules favoring increased competition and a single framework for commerce. Telecommunications is at the heart of this issue. Those who design the digital highways of the future can no longer ignore the mutual impact of technology and future international political economy.

The Third World and U.S. Telecommunications Policy

H. Kurt Hoffman and Michael G. Hobday

The effects of policy decisions and corporate actions in United States telecommunications, taken primarily in response to American domestic concerns, increasingly affect the international environment. This chain reaction is magnified when the United States government pursues national objectives within international fora concerned with regulating global flows of telecommunications-based services.

The interconnection between national policies and their international effects suggests that policy decisions relating to telecommunications should not be formulated without a clear understanding of their consequences. Not surprisingly, the United States telecommunications community is well aware of the impact of its policies on Japan and Western Europe. A less recognized dimension of these concerns is equally important to the United States policy—the impact of these on developing countries.

American public and private sector actors should give special attention to the effects of their actions on developing countries. First, these countries are growing in significance, both as markets and as competitors; therefore, what affects them affects the United States. Second, many developing countries lack both economic and industrial resilience and the self-balancing mixture of legislation, consumer protection, and functioning adjudication systems found in the developed countries; they are particularly vulnerable to the effects of decisions and events emanating from outside their national boundaries.

Third, telecommunications will provide the infrastructure to support the sustained growth and development of a wide range of information-intensive economic activities in the future. If telecommunications plays this historic role to maximum effect, all countries must help to provide the constituent parts of a single, integrated, worldwide network. As a leading global economic power, it is in the best interests of the United States to promote the full involvement of developing countries in global telecommunications developments and to minimize potential conflicts that may inhibit their international participation.

Few statistics convey the gap between developed and developing countries more clearly than those relating to telecommunications. Although there are now more than 600 million telephones in the world, two-thirds of the world's population have no access to telephones, with virtually all of them living in the Third World. With 70 percent of the world's population and 17 percent of its income, developing countries account for only 7 percent of the world's telephones.

Rural populations and those in the least developed countries fare the worst. In Africa, with a population of nearly 600 million (72 percent of whom live in rural areas), the telephone density averages seven per one thousand people, and in many cases there is no more than one telephone per thousand people. The social hardships imposed by these conditions are substantial; the economic costs are even greater. Studies carried out by the International Telecommunication Union (ITU), the World Bank (International Bank for Reconstruction and Development—IBRD), and others demonstrate a direct relationship between economic advance and the availability of basic telephone services.

For example, an ITU study in Kenya identified nine ways business firm efficiency could be improved with access to more extensive, reliable telecommunications services: through facilitating business expansion, sales price increases, improved purchasing decisions, reduced inventories, savings in vehicle use, reduction of down time, reduced distribution costs and lower managerial and labor costs. Cost benefit analyses carried out in the Philippines and Costa Rica, using samples of 200–300 small firms and measuring economic gains against telecommunications investment costs, established benefit-cost ratios of 25:1 and 48:1 respectively. Studies which examine the returns to investment in rural telecommunications show similar, and sometimes greater, ratios.[1] Lack of access to basic telecommunications infrastructure is one of the key constraints on economic development.

As a consequence of the impoverished state of much of the Third World's telecommunications, and the huge technological, industrial, and infrastructural gap between the developed and developing economies, there is a critical difference between the telecommunications policy agenda embraced by developing countries and that established in the United States and other industrialized countries.

Within the United States the basic telecommunications infrastructure has long been in place. Telecommunications services are an integral part of the productive effort in the economy, and there is a wide range of domestic enterprises able and willing to supply both services and equipment under competitive conditions. Given prior conditions that allow the operation of an efficient market, current United States policy discussions and actions assume that the social and economic benefits arising from telecommunications will best be attained by achieving the maximum possible degree of market freedom.

Thus, the scope and scale of regulation in the United States has been progressively reduced in the past decade, replaced by the introduction of market forces and by decoupling of prices from costs as a regulatory principle. This philosophy underlies moves to liberalize markets for equipment and service supply and also provides a rationale for United States policy in national and international institutions that govern standards and resource allocation.

With a few exceptions most developing countries lack a basic telecommunications infrastructure, a viable domestic equipment and service supply sector, and the conditions necessary for a properly functioning market. Consequently, telecommunications policy concerns and objectives in developing countries are primarily and explicitly developmental in character.

At their most basic these developmental concerns relate to the formidable task of building the basic telecommunications network and creating competent local suppliers to meet the social and economic needs of a growing economy. This is typically accomplished under state control and regulation and is usually undertaken as part of a broader, deliberate industrialization strategy—which may, of course, differ from country to country. As long as it is necessary to create basic network and service capacity, meeting developmental needs through the regulated expansion of the telecommunications sector will remain a paramount objective for most Third World countries.

The telecommunications development concerns of Third World countries sometimes conflict and sometimes mesh with the current American telecommunications policies. When conflict does arise, it is partly due to misunderstandings on all sides—misunderstandings that can be clarified and can lead to more effective, future collaboration. Phrased simply, issues of industrial development have conditioned developing country policies toward equipment supply and technology development in telecommunications. The regulatory focus of developed countries over the supply of telecommunications services contrasts directly with the efforts of developing countries to establish basic infrastructures.

Conflicts between regulatory and developmental concerns of industrialized and developing countries has led to many of the recent confrontations in international organization which address telecommunication issues. Policy change on all sides can, however, lead to fruitful interchange and future development in international telecommunications.

The Telecommunications Supply Sector

Technological change, primarily involving digital semiconductor technology, has led to massive upheaval in the international telecommunications supply market.[2] The transition from analog technology to microelectronic, digital systems has forced traditional equipment suppliers in the United States and Western Europe to restructure their operations in both industrialized and developing countries. All major suppliers now produce digital systems and have broadened their product ranges to include other elements of information technology.

This technological convergence is gradually leading to industrial convergence, blurring historically stable market boundaries between the telecommunications, computing, office equipment, and semiconductor industries. As a result, competition has intensified greatly among traditional suppliers, including market entry by large, vertically integrated information technology corporations from Japan, South Korea, and Taiwan determinedly challenging the established "electro-mechanical oligopoly" of Western firms.

In response to these dramatic changes government policies during the 1980s in industrialized economies have focused on ways to promote the competitive performance of indigenous equipment suppliers and to facilitate the speedy development and introduction of digital transmission and switching facilities. Such policies have two characteristics. First, there are massive, if sometimes well-disguised, programs of government support by all leading industrialized countries for research and development in the private sector in most segments of the complex of information technology industries, including telecommunications.[3]

The second, more widely discussed policy feature is the promotion of greater competitiveness in equipment supply and service markets; this includes breaking up the close and sometimes collusive relationships that existed between purchasing PTTs (Post, Telephone and Telegraph administrations) and equipment suppliers.[4] It has been assumed that opening these markets and relationships to increased competition will reduce costs and lead to greater investment in research and development and more rapid rates of innovation.

Given the importance of the telecommunications sector as the key infrastructural element in the emerging information economy and as a major segment of the burgeoning international market in information technology, the role of state policy in helping to promote and maintain the innovativeness and competitiveness of the sector is fundamental.[5] This is particularly so since both domestic competence and international competitiveness in the new information technology industries is viewed as a critical determinant of national economic well-being in the future.

In the United States the government is fulfilling this role by combining direct support for innovative effort and the legislated unleashing of market forces. Such policies assume the prior existence of a technologically competent domestic supply industry capable of responding to incentives, however they are offered. The industry was allowed to grow to technological maturity under extremely favorable conditions afforded by state protection of markets precisely because of its perceived importance to national economic interests.

There are similarities but more important differences between these features and conditions governing telecommunications equipment supply in developing countries. In developing countries the telecommunications system is a critical element of the economic infrastructure. Equally important, the new generation of digital technology will provide services and facilities central to the future competitiveness of firms in these economies.

Within this context the overarching policy objective of industrializing economies (like industrialized countries) is to ensure that communications capacity develops in line with domestic, economic, political, and social needs. Unlike Western economies, however, the domestic equipment industry of most developing countries, with some important exceptions, is still in its technological infancy. The creation of a domestic supply capacity—in line with their market size and technological and economic capabilities—is a defensible, if contentious a priori policy objective for developing countries. This objective is a source of conflict between the United States and developing countries, and yet also provides potential for long-term cooperation between them.

Telecommunications Investment in Developing Countries

Most Third World countries are currently installing and expanding their basic telecommunications infrastructures. The scale of investment involved suggests that, individually and collectively, developing countries face the task of managing projects of unprecedented proportions whose financial dimensions are large by any relative standard of industrial development. Together, the ten largest countries spent at least an estimated $9.5 billion on telecommunications equipment in 1987, expected to rise to $11.5 billion by 1990.

In each country these aggregate figures translate into massive expenditures of scarce resources. China, with the ninth largest equipment market in the world, invested $1.8 billion in the telecommunications sector in 1987 out of a total of $5 billion planned by 1990. India, the twelfth largest market, invested $1.5 billion in 1987; Mexico invested $950 million in 1987 out of a planned total of $6.5 billion by 1990; Brazil spent more than $900 million despite facing severe financial difficulties.

1987 expenditures in "second tier" countries such as Indonesia, Taiwan, and Argentina averaged $700 million each, and Venezuela registered $428 million in investment. Further down the economic scale, the national plan for Colombia calls for telecommunications investments at $300 million per annum over the medium term, slightly less than is expected by Thailand, also a medium-sized economy. Even large but very poor countries such as Pakistan ($320 million in 1987) and Bangladesh ($246 million) forecast total expenditures over the next five years of well over $1 billion each.[6]

While such figures do not approach, in aggregate terms, expenditures by developed countries, they are notable within the Third World context for three reasons. First, infrastructural investments on this scale were not conceivable in these countries as recently as twenty years ago. They undoubtedly compare on a relative basis with efforts by the advanced countries to develop railways, power, and communications sectors during their own periods of industrialization.

Second, given the present rate of investment, the bulk of the telecommunications infrastructure in developing countries, with the possible exception of Africa, will be in place twenty years from now. Telecommunications investment at the level now being undertaken will not be repeated. Once in place, the particular configuration of systems will determine the telecommunications trajectory of these economies for many decades.

Third, and of greater significance, infrastructural investments are occurring at a unique moment in technological history. Relatively low cost, robust and flexible digital systems offer developing countries the opportunity to "leapfrog" less efficient, more costly, earlier technology. Because these economies are still installing their basic network, they do not face onerous "economics of scrapping" decisions that confront many developed countries. In the long term this ability to leapfrog earlier technologies could provide important economic benefits to latecomer economies; it is the key reason why most observers argue that even the poorest countries should invest in digital as opposed to analog telecommunications systems.[7]

Accumulating Technological Capacity

Although the availability of a network has always played a key facilitating role in development, any indigenous technological capacities created with local participation in the design, production, installation, and maintenance of previous vintages of equipment were of relatively little use outside of the telecommunications sector. This is not the case with digital technology. Many skills involved in design and production of information technology telecommunications products and systems are generic and will be transferable across many sectors where information technology plays a major role.

The pervasive role of information technology in future industrial development in all countries means that any digital capacities created in the course of developing the telecommunications infrastructure will be widely applicable throughout the economy. This process is roughly analogous to the way that machine design and building skills which accumulated in capital goods industry were so crucial to early industrial development in advanced economies. This well-documented relationship in turn explains the widespread agreement over the need for developing countries to create a healthy capital goods sector.[8] By the same reasoning the wide range of capacities required to design, manufacture, install, and operate digital equipment can act as a "leading edge" in the accumulation of human resources and firm-specific skills on which the whole economy can subsequently draw in a future dominated by information technology.

The possibilities are bound up with the nature of digital technology.[9] Digital technology is intrinsically modular and horizontal: a system is comprised of a range of independent and compatible modules that form the building blocks of an expandable telecommunications network. The same logic holds in the manufacturing process, where microelectronic components constitute the building blocks of the product and increasingly resemble the final good itself.

This structure sharply contrasts with the vertically integrated production process in electro-mechanical technology, involving a large number of specialized components such as relays, screws, and connectors. Analog components were manufactured by the equipment suppliers themselves, a process which required specialized knowledge and thoroughgoing and large-scale fine engineering and electro-mechanical interfacing capacity in virtually all stages of production, installation, and maintenance.

Thus, the actual manufacture of Crossbar systems is far more complex than the production of digital systems, which resembles a simple assembly process with standard components available from outside semiconductor manufacturers. The software-intensive design stage is crucial in digital technology; although the skills involved are specialized, they are also generic, required in smaller numbers, and are easier and less costly to build up over time. These characteristics imply a far higher degree of technological and capital divisibility than was the case with earlier vintages.

Divisibility in turn implies more opportunities for smaller investments in specialized product areas—even in highly complex exchange systems—and means it is possible to master the design and production process by stages, gradually learning and accumulating skills to tackle more complex products and systems.

The divisibility of the technology itself as well as the design stage and production process makes for potentially lower barriers to entry by developing countries into less complex products such as peripherals (intelligent terminals, modem and codec equipment, key systems, mobile radio, and video display units) and some elements of transmission equipment, such as pulse code modulation (PCM) and time division multiplexing (TDM) equipment. Likewise, the modular nature of modern exchange software may provide opportunities for entry by more advanced developing countries into the design and production of smaller scale private and public exchanges. Brazil, for instance, has developed and produced not only simple digital equipment, but fairly complex small public exchange systems as well.

The prospects for particular developing countries successfully to enter telecommunications equipment production differ greatly, depending on market size, depth of economic, and technological development and government policies—the probability of Gabon engaging in its own system design or component production is clearly much less than possibilities open to Brazil, China, or Nigeria. Nonetheless, it is now much more feasible for developing countries gradually to "learn" their way up the chain of technological complexity with digital telecommunications technology than it was with earlier vintages. It is also likely (and indeed has happened) that many of the problems of "inappropriateness" that plague imported digital equipment used in developing countries—designed for the different technical conditions and operating environments found in developed countries—can be overcome.[10]

It is generally much easier for these countries to accumulate widely applicable information technology-related skills through "learning-by-doing" in telecommunications than in other segments of the information technology complex. Finally, the social and economic case for investing in telecommunications is widely accepted as valid for all developing countries and is being implemented by many on a large scale, with extensive international support. This is not true for other information technology industries, about which many legitimate questions have been raised concerning the need to establish these industries in developing countries.

This conjuncture of investment scale, technological evolution, and infrastructural development demonstrates powerfully that developing countries are in the midst of a period of historic importance.

Thus, for countries able to justify the effort on social and economic grounds, the process of building a digital telecommunications network could be a crucial cornerstone on which their technical progress and industrialization will depend.

Lessons from Newly Industrializing Countries

While it is critical to appreciate these dimensions of the telecommunications situation confronting developing countries, such understanding is frequently absent in United States policy addressing problems of the Third World. However, some governments in smaller newly industrializing countries and other larger state economies are indeed fully aware of the new and more dynamic role that investments in digital telecommunications can play in industrialization. These more advanced countries have been in a position to respond positively to these possibilities. Their strategies and successes suggest ways for developing countries to follow and indicate potential areas of conflict and cooperation with the United States.

Among the most notable successes have been Asian newly industrializing countries such as South Korea and Taiwan which, in line with their overall strategies, have pursued interventionist policies to support local equipment supply firms that promote their export orientation and international competitiveness. Some of these firms are now emerging as competitors to international telecommunications suppliers in particular segments of the market.[11]

Similarly, large, import-substituting countries such as China, India, Brazil, and Mexico, while not yet internationally competitive, have developed broad, indigenous technology development and supply capacity in the public and private sectors that increasingly incorporate products based on digital technology. Brazil's experience in developing and locally manufacturing 1000-line "tropicalized" exchanges is particularly interesting because it now plans to build on this capacity, gradually moving to larger public exchanges.[12]

Four points should be noted about the success of these countries in developing an indigenous telecommunications industry. First, analyses of these endeavors document a process of gradual learning.[13] Second, their telecommunications achievements parallel their considerable accomplishments in other technology intensive sectors in which they have also developed an export base and strong domestic supply.

As in telecommunications, these advances required the active involvement of local firms and research units in design and production, in turn supported by deliberate government intervention to facilitate research and development, technology transfer, and the development of local input supply.[14]

Third, the effective assimilation of imported technology and, in some cases, cooperation with foreign equipment suppliers played a significant role in capacity accumulation efforts. Finally, there is substantial debate and disagreement over short-term and long-term costs and benefits in relation to telecommunications and other sectors. Critics argue that equipment and technology developed under these policies could have been imported more cheaply and the benefits from its availability passed on more quickly to local users.[15] This argument is valid, but it is not universally applicable. It fails to recognize adequately the unique entry and learning possibilities inherent in digital telecommunications technology and the long-term benefits to these economies of acquiring indigenous capacities in information technology. Judging whether it is best to import on short-term comparative cost criteria or to invest in local learning and local development on long-term benefit criteria can only be taken on a case-by-case basis.

Foreign Equipment Suppliers and Government Support

Despite greater possibilities for local learning and local equipment supply, scale considerations and technical factors mean that market size and the existing technological and economic infrastructure are still extremely important development determinants. Most smaller countries, and indeed many larger economies, will remain dependent on outside suppliers for their equipment and technological requirements, to varying degrees depending on local circumstances. In all but a few cases this technological dependence will be coupled with a requirement for financial assistance to support investment.

However, such relationships need not be either as onerous on developing countries or as unprofitable to the equipment suppliers as is the case in some other sectors. Great technological strides have occurred within the PTTS of the advanced countries and within the research and development laboratories of the international equipment suppliers such as ITT, Siemens, and Ericsson. Consequently, access to the technology and knowledge accumulated by these firms is essential for the future development of telecommunications capacities in developing countries. More advanced countries have recognized this fact and have successfully sought to cooperate with foreign suppliers at the best possible terms.

Competitive conditions in world markets are in fact currently structured in favor of developing countries. Many large suppliers have based their expansion plans and justified heavy research and development commitments, particularly in digital exchanges, on the basis of capturing telecommunications equipment markets in developing countries. These markets interest equipment suppliers for two reasons. First, they are already fairly large in specific categories, in both relative and absolute terms. For example, the Latin American market for digital public switching currently accounts for 16.3 percent of world sales, compared with 27 percent for Europe and 28 percent for the United States. Second, rates of growth are generally more rapid than in advanced countries, particularly in areas like switching technology, where an explosive annual rate of growth of 25 percent through 1990 is predicted for developing countries.[16]

In contrast to the de facto markets in Japan, Europe, and the United States, developing country markets are uncommitted and relatively open to competitive bidding. Access to and success in these markets is crucial to international equipment supply firms; by the early 1980s they had collectively spent over $6 billion to develop sixteen major systems—all chasing annual uncommitted export markets of only $2–3 billion.

As a result, competition for market access has become increasingly fierce between established and new suppliers. Several large- and medium-sized developing countries have recognized the existence of this "buyers market" and utilized the monopsony purchasing power of their PTTs to encourage competition between suppliers not only on price, but also on criteria such as increased local research and development and manufacture of systems by subsidiaries of foreign firms —and in some regions large-scale technology transfer agreements and cooperation in joint ventures.[17] In addition, the supplier's home government is frequently brought in to sweeten the bid with offers of financial support and other assistance. Some firms and governments —such as those from the United States and United Kingdom—have resisted these pressures and lost contracts as a result.[18]

The trend toward greater competition between suppliers and the culmination of deals involving genuine technology transfer and government support is well established and widely documented. One of many examples is the struggle between ten major suppliers to win a recent Indian contract for switching systems. Eventually the French system won the order, but only after the French CIT-Alcatel agreed to transfer exchange technology; the French government was obliged to step in with an "aid for trade" cheap loan arrangement and support for a major training program involving French scientists. The French have employed this tactic vigorously to win contracts in Singapore, Chile, Argentina, Brazil, and Venezuela. They are now trying to win a contract to establish a 300,000 line digital exchange plant in China.[19]

Similar cases involve Sweden's Ericssons in Brazil, Venezuela, Ecuador, and Costa Rica; Cable & Wireless (United Kingdom) in China; Siemens (Federal Republic of Germany) in Taiwan and Indonesia. All feature the same elements of market access exchanged for financial support, technology transfer, and local production.[20]

A similar set of deals involving Japanese firms—which offer low price and favorable technology transfer terms to governments in Latin America and Asia—has proven particularly worrying to established suppliers because it marks a further breakdown of their long-standing traditional alliances with these governments. Firms such as NEC (now the third largest supplier of telecommunications equipment to developing countries), Fujitsu, and Oki have already employed these tactics to gain large shares of Third World regional markets and will undoubtedly continue this strategy in the future.[21]

Development Concerns

Several more advanced developing countries have been able to establish significant local supply capacities by exploiting their size, centralized negotiation and purchasing power authority, international market conditions, and the divisibility and learning possibilities inherent in digital telecommunications technology.

The design and implementation of these strategies have been driven by Third World developmental concerns. Such developmental rationales and the concomitant role of the state to advance these objectives will remain dominant determinants of policy for the foreseeable future—even though they are being forced by internal and external pressures to consider some regulatory reforms to allow more domestic private sector involvement in and competition for equipment supply.

Successful suppliers of telecommunications equipment, such as CIT-Alcatel, Ericsson, and NEC (and their home governments) have accepted NIC strategies as legitimate and have sought to gain market shares by working with these countries as partners in design, manufacture, technology transfer and network specification. Companies and governments which have not fully adopted this approach—preferring instead to view the NICs as traditional export markets—have done less well in securing business, and will find it even more difficult to succeed in the future as these countries grow in market size and technological sophistication.

Given the overall importance of the NICs and the larger economies in total Third World telecommunications markets, these issues should profoundly influence United States government telecommunication policy. However, the NIC experience is also likely to have implications for the telecommunications strategies and concerns of other, poorer, developing countries.

In the smaller, poorer countries of Asia, Africa, and the Caribbean, market size, local capacities, and purchasing power are all substantially lower than in larger economies. Their policy goals have been correspondingly less ambitious than those of the NICs. Nevertheless, these countries will eventually make sustained investments in their telecommunications infrastructure. Experience from other sectors where the poorer developing countries have followed the policy lead of the NICs suggests that these countries will be influenced by the "demonstration effect" of NIC success in telecommunications.

The confidence arising from this collective learning experience, combined with advisable regional collaboration between poorer countries, means that they will probably adopt a more aggressive approach to telecommunications equipment supply. In the near future these countries will, either individually or collectively, insist on contractual arrangements with foreign suppliers that include some form of technology transfer and local manufacture. United States government policy will need to consider carefully its responses to these new demands.

Domestic Regulation in a Developmental Context

Because of underinvestment in telecommunications, demand in developing countries enormously exceeds supply. The number of applicants for new lines usually far exceeds their availability, so that the waiting time for a new connection can reach up to ten years.

Existing services are massively overcommitted: business-hour traffic by subscribers overwhelms capacity on a daily basis. The resulting poor service means that call completion rates of below 50 percent for local, 30 percent for long distance, and 10 percent for international calls are common, while many hours can be spent waiting for overextended operators to connect calls outside the local network. Further evidence of underinvestment and poor maintenance comes from the frequent failure and long down time of inferior equipment and an extremely high incidence of faults on individual lines—three to six times a year in India compared to once in three years in the West.[22]

Even poorly operated PTTs generate substantial surpluses in local currencies, and rates of return to new investment, even in rural areas, are quite high. Consequently, observers informed by recent American and Western European experiences often seek to explain Third World telecommunications problems in the extent and nature of state involvement in the sector by citing four interrelated reasons.[23]

First, governments apparently fail to understand the crucial importance of investment in telecommunications to economic advance. This myopia is compounded by the misperception that telecommunications services only benefit a privileged minority and thus that expansion and improvement of the telecommunications system is a low priority.

Second, national PTTs are felt to be constrained by government interference in management and policy. As a result they lack managerial and administrative independence; senior management is frequently shifted in response to political change; investment authority is rooted in civil bureaucracies, which themselves face personnel and policy restrictions.

Third, PTTs commonly lack the financial independence needed to resolve the perennial problem of underinvestment. In the area of tariffs, for example, they are often not allowed a tariff structure that reflects costs, with pricing being largely dictated by conventional public utility financial criteria—that is, connection and service charges are alleged to be excessively low on economic grounds. This policy reduces domestic surpluses for reinvestment, even while governments are quite prepared to allow PTTs to make net contributions to their cash starved treasuries. In addition, while the foreign exchange cost of investment is high (50 to 60 percent of total costs), PTTs are barred from participating in capital markets and are thus forced to compete with other public enterprises for extremely limited capital resources. Finally, the management and organization of the PTTs themselves are often poor, resulting in high expansion and operating costs and efficiency problems in other areas such as maintenance and repair.

Another set of factors concerns the harmful effects of monopoly. Third World PTTs are thought to enjoy a degree of monopoly power at least as great as their counterparts in developed countries. Entry into the industry is strictly regulated to protect the PTT, and private by-pass arrangements are stringently opposed. Almost fully insulated from competition or public accountability, they have little incentive to improve or innovate and have ample opportunity for inefficiency. It is therefore not surprising that technological change and growing demands by large users for early access to new services raise serious questions about the ability of PTTs to cope with their environments.

Private and public authorities are thus calling for fundamental changes in the extent and nature of state involvement in the Third World telecommunications sector. Prospective reforms fall into three broad areas: opening the market for the provision and maintenance of equipment and services by domestic and foreign suppliers; recasting and reducing government control over PTTs, tariff structures, and investment capital so that PTTs can operate like commercial businesses; and loosening state ties to reform PTT structure, operations, and management, including privatization of some PTT functions.

This argument parallels those made in response to state management of developing country economies. The alleged success of deregulation in the United States, Western Europe, and Japan has given its proponents new energy.

Evidence suggests that Third World states and PTTs are beginning to respond to demands for change, and frustrated large users are attempting to set up bypass networks. Malaysia, for example, has established a private company (fully state owned) to handle operational functions. Telecommunications operations in Bombay and Delhi have been reorganized as an independent company able to raise funds in the local capital market, and Chile has privatized its main telephone company.[24] These governments are presumably exploring regulatory reform to respond to technological change, internal pressure for service improvement, external pressure from funding agencies, and the influence of well-publicized reforms in the West.

Despite such apparent shifts in regulatory environments, it is dangerous to generalize too quickly from a few examples. Because these changes occur under some circumstances in some countries, the same principles do not necessarily apply in all countries at all times: regulatory and structural reform in the direction of liberalization, privatization, and market forces is not automatically a "good thing" in developing countries simply because similar developments have been successful elsewhere. The context in which developing countries respond to pressures for liberalization and cope with radical technological change is very different from that faced by developed countries when they built up their networks. Pressures on PTTs to be competitive and responsive, particularly in profitable areas, were brought to bear upon developed countries after their networks were in place; developing countries have to face these powerfully "disintegrative" forces well before their networks and local supply industry have become fully established.[25] Thus, although problems faced by PTTs in developed and developing countries may appear similar, their causes are likely to be substantially different.

More specifically, public and private sector institutions in developing countries exhibit low levels of administrative, managerial, financial, and technological competence. One cannot therefore assume that, given the freedom to design and implement market-oriented reforms, such changes will solve the problems they face. Given the distortions in Third World markets, it cannot be assumed that market-oriented reforms, if introduced, will have the effects intended or address the equity and welfare concerns of a developing state. Changes are being introduced to create a more liberal regulatory environment and to release the allegedly restorative powers of market forces. These reforms are relatively recent and long-term impacts of these changes are still unknown.

Western Models and Their Problems

Recent regulatory reform in developed countries suggests that moves toward liberalization and greater reliance on market forces have not always (or yet) produced their intended results.

For example, liberalization in Western Europe and Japan have still left national PTTs with enormous power, capable of resisting further erosion of their powers. Moreover, despite public procompetitive policies, these governments are adept at using nontariff barriers to prevent or inhibit foreign competition in domestic markets.[26] This became clear when Cable and Wireless tried to gain a foothold in the Japanese telecommunications market through direct investment.[27] Cable and Wireless probably would have had just as much trouble gaining access to American, French, Dutch, or West German markets —or vice versa.[28]

Similarly, regulations of the West German Bundespost prevent subscribers to foreign information services from having direct access to international leased lines. Intermediate data processing must be undertaken in Germany before the information can be made available to subscribers over the local switched network. Such policies reinforce the Bundespost's monopoly, increase its revenues, and protect domestic data processing firms.[29]

Finally, British experience privatizing British Telecom demonstrates that such moves do not necessarily lead to predicted domestic social and economic benefits. In this case privatization appears thus far to have benefited only a narrow range of high-income consumers and users while costing the economy billions of dollars; it has led to deteriorating public service and has further undermined the international competitiveness of large segments of the British equipment supply industry.[30]

If such problems and unintended outcomes arise in a developed country with competent bureaucracies, working markets, and effective oversight, then what of developing countries? The net outcomes might be positive. But one could argue just as strongly, with considerable evidence from similar experiences in other sectors, that conditions which define the operating context in developing countries—inexperience and technological and managerial incompetence in the private sector, inequitable income distribution, corruption, a barely functioning market, lack of oversight capacities, and

PTT inefficiency—could result in a much worse situation for all concerned parties.

Examples from Developing Countries

In the Philippines, for example, telecommunications services are now largely provided by private firms under a United States privatization model. Growth has been insufficient to meet development needs, available poor and costly service is concentrated within a few urban areas, and corruption abounds—enough to prompt a comprehensive government review. Similarly, two private firms in Panama, allowed to offer international telecommunications services in competition with the public sector, are to be reabsorbed into the public sector because of poor performance and "irregularities."[31]

A solution often proposed to overcome revenue shortages caused by uneconomic tariff levels suggests that existing and new subscribers make a "capital" contribution through higher connection and monthly rental fees than are charged normally. When this proposal was explored in India, it transpired that to meet minimum revenue levels for planned investment purposes in the Seventh Investment Plan entirely from internal revenues, the annual bill to subscribers would more than double, from $320 to $750. How many Indians would be able to afford it? When applications charges of less than $1.00 were first tried, the waiting list was reduced by 100,000; when charges were increased from $80 to $400, the waiting list was reduced by 400,000. If subscribers were asked to make a capital contribution of $2400, the waiting list would probably disappear by eliminating all but the wealthiest fraction of city dwellers—hardly an equitable outcome.[32]

Market-oriented solutions locally to produce better and more equipment and services create other problems. Many proposals to increase the range of services (particularly new data services) by allowing private suppliers would require foreign firms to fulfill market demands. The mere availability of more services might be a positive development—yet it ignores likely negative impacts on local service providers and problems associated with data dependency, revenue generation, and predatory pricing.

In addition, not all users will equally be able to exploit competitively these new services. Many potential local users, particularly smaller, domestic firms, will lack the skills and fiscal requirements necessary to take advantage of the new services. Competing against wealthier foreign firms, they might be forced out of business, causing a net loss of employment and income to the economy—a phenomenon similar to changes in the tourist sector in many smaller Third World economies.[33]

Another dimension of this problem is exemplified by the role of the Caribbean and Asian economies in the booming American offshore data-processing business. Both foreign and domestic firms in these countries are setting up low-wage, labor-intensive facilities to "key-in" analog data provided by United States airline, credit card, publishing, and insurance firms, which is then shipped back through the digital telecommunications networks. United States firms certainly benefit from lower unit costs, although the original data-processing people often lose their jobs. Developing economies gain some employment and foreign exchange benefits, but they derive few benefits from "enclave" activities with few local linkages. These firms often require government subsidies to attract them in the first place and can, of course, close their operations without warning or regard to the local economy.

Governments and entrepreneurs justify these activities by their involvement with new technology—an entree into the information technology age. In fact, there is virtually no skill or technology transfer involved in these white collar sweatshops. As cost effective optical character recognition technology becomes available to United States firms, such operations have little long-term future.[34]

Certainly some countries are benefiting from being able to participate in the expansion of the international market for services from a domestic base—the rapid growth in software exports from India and Singapore are cases in point. However, these governments have already invested heavily in the prior creation of software capabilities. If this process is to occur where this prior investment has not taken place, then steps must also be taken to create local conditions that go well beyond relying on market forces in the telecommunications sector to bring about downstream linkages.[35]

Finally, it is necessary to distinguish among countries when discussing regulatory reform. Those developing countries best equipped to handle the pressures of regulatory reform and to capture its benefits will be more advanced. Their basic telecommunications needs are close to being met; they enjoy considerable local supply; they have competent managers in the public and private sector; and they have reasonably well developed absorptive capacity. Moreover, they harbor a belief that the public good and national economic welfare would increase if appropriate reforms were introduced.

However, as one moves down the line toward the poorer countries, these conditions are less likely to be met. The inequalities which distort the market will be greater, and possibilities grow that poorly planned regulatory reforms will lead to unexpected, unintended, and negative outcomes.

Direct United States Intervention in Overseas Regulatory Reform

The above discussion concerns issues raised by the growing but fairly diffuse "demonstration effect" pressures on developing countries to introduce regulatory reform. There are reasons to argue, however, that the United States government may be prepared to take more direct steps to influence regulatory regimes in other countries in service supply in telecommunications. The reasons for these interventions are not obscure. For United States producers of new telecommunications services access to these markets—as either local producers treated like national producers or as suppliers of imported products and services—is essential to take advantage of domestic production and foreign-trade multiplier effects of global demand for information technology products.

To help ensure this access the American government and particularly American courts have begun to extend or introduce novel interpretations of patent, copyright, investment, and trade laws in four areas: (1) the "national" treatment of foreign products, personnel, property holders, and enterprises; (2) "international reciprocity provisions" that may condition or directly conflict with the application of the principle of national treatment; (3) the "right of establishment" and of doing business in third countries; and (4) the protection of intellectual property rights of products or services originating outside of national borders.

These changes are taking place in various modalities relative to different aspects of the international flow and overseas production of information technology products and services. The thrust of such reforms is that United States firms should be afforded the same rights and privileges to establish production facilities and/or export goods and services overseas as foreign firms enjoy in the United States. If not, provisions included in national legislation grant to the president the power to impose penalties and trade sanctions on foreign governments.

The need to introduce new legislation or reinterpret old principles arises because of the unique character of knowledge-intensive information technology products and services and the equally knowledge-intensive nature of the underlying production processes. Among the more important features is the relative ease with which many of these products can be "illegally" copied and then sold, thus depriving the originators of revenue. By the mid-1990s United States revenue losses on third-party copyright infringement in relation to software "piracy" alone will probably be well over $1 billion and possibly as high as $6–8 billion.[36]

Among the legislation that incorporates these reciprocity and retaliation provisions are the United States Trade and Tariff Act of 1984 (Public Law 98-573), the Caribbean Basin Economic Recovery Act (Public Law 98-67), the 1984 Semiconductor Chip Act, the 1985 International Software Protection Act, the 1984 National Productivity and Innovation Act, and the 1980 and 1986 amendments of the 1976 Copyright Act. The relevant retaliatory provisions are bilateral; all concern the legal treatment of United States firms abroad and, in response, the treatment of foreign firms based in the United States. The United States fully intends to influence directly institutional reform in these areas at the multilateral and international level as well, through representations and proposals being made to General Agreement on Tariffs and Trade (GATT), World Intellectual Property Organization (WIPO), and the ITU on the treatment of intellectual property and international trade in services.

Perhaps the most illuminating legislation has been in the software copyright area. For nearly two hundred years the United States has refused to protect the intellectual property rights of knowledge produced abroad. This is enshrined in the "manufacturing clause" of the 1891 Chase International Copyright Act (designed to protect its then infant publishing industry). The United States therefore never joined the Berne International Copyright Convention, and it stands in direct conflict with the GATT on import restraints.

In the 1980s the United States finds itself in a position to capture nearly two thirds of the $50 billion annual global software market. Given the importance of establishing the legal originators of software, the United States has now taken up a strenuous "internationalist" stance concerning intellectual property. Reversing a long-standing policy, it now recognizes the property rights of foreign works and expects other countries to do the same. According to the 1985 Software Protection Act, if a country protects software for less than twenty-five years, the United States will suspend all protection for that nation's software.[37]

There is nothing new, of course, in efforts by a leading industrial country to protect its intellectual leadership through legislation (and coercion if need be) at the international level—the United Kingdom and other European countries exercised this power throughout the eighteenth and nineteenth centuries when they set out to establish the legitimacy of the Paris and Berne Conventions. Given the high stakes involved in the current struggle for technological hegemony with Japan and Western Europe (against whom most of the reciprocity provisions are directed) in the field of information technology, the new American policy is not unexpected and probably justified in particular circumstances involving advanced economy countries.

However, there is strong evidence that such measures are being brought to bear on developing countries in relation to "transgressions" they have committed in protecting or regulating foreign involvement in segments of their information technology industries. The United States government placed enormous legal and political pressure on Brazil and Mexico because of the restrictive policies these countries introduced on foreign access to segments of their computer market. Some developing countries have predictably amended their intellectual property laws in the shadow of retaliatory action threatened in the 1984 Trade and Tariff Act.[38]

If the United States is prepared to pursue open Third World computer and software markets with retaliatory threats, then logic suggests similar moves in telecommunications-related services. Great care should to be exercised in the unilateral extension of United States "rights" of reciprocity and retaliation in the information technology and telecommunications-related services sector to developing countries. Such retaliation does not pursue "rights" but exercises economic and political power by a stronger country over weaker ones—a situation to which the United States would not take kindly were roles reversed. Developing countries require special treatment because of their developmental concerns and conditions.

More pointedly, by using the threat of retaliation to force unequal competition between nascent Third World information technology service firms in their home markets with those from the industrialized countries, serious damage can be done to their long-term economic prospects. At the very least a sharp distinction should be drawn between those very few segments of advanced developing countries now competing as information technology equals with the industrialized countries and the large majority where this is not the case. The short-term commercial considerations of the world's wealthiest country must be balanced against long-term developmental concerns for the vast majority of developing countries.

Thus, developing countries are in a classic "second-best" situation because of major distortions to efficient market operation on the one hand and, on the other hand, because explicit action needs to be taken to meet the developmental imperative to create indigenous capacities for supply and the rapid diffusion of services to those most in need but least able to pay. For these reasons privatization and liberalization cannot provide blanket solutions to problems of service supply in developing countries. If they are introduced, such measures must be applied selectively and judiciously and must be accompanied by supportive measures and long-term development plans.

The opportunity costs are far too high to respond within the old monopolistic format to the challenges and possibilities posed by technological change and new telecommunication services. Developing countries, international agencies, and Western telecommunications actors must try to achieve complementarity between regulatory reform and developmental policy aims.

International Regulation and Administration

The principal arena for international telecommunications discussion, debate, and decision is the ITU. During the 1980s the ITU's main preoccupation has been to manage international dimensions of the transition from a stable era of international exchange based on conventional telecommunications to a period of rapid growth of services based on the convergence of digital telecommunications, computing, and media broadcast technologies.[39]

The same tensions which exist between regulatory and developmental concerns at the national level have permeated international telecommunications relations between advanced and developing countries. The ITU has therefore come under growing pressure from interests in developed countries to allow the new era to proceed unfettered by regulatory shackles. In turn the developing countries have been voicing collectively their growing concern over a set of what are essentially developmental issues—the widening gap in telecommunications between North and South, the need to redistribute investment resources to promote service developments, and their desire to achieve an equitable allocation of international telecommunications resources (including the radio frequency spectrum and the geostationary orbit) and equitable regulatory arrangements concerning transborder data flows (TBDF).

These struggles, in which the United States public and private sectors have been deeply involved, produce contentious and often acrimonious debate and have not settled many of the main issues. Grounds for compromise, however, do exist.

Structure and Focus of the ITU

The ITU, with the status of a specialized United Nations agency, is responsible for establishing interconnection standards and agreements on equipment, operating procedures, signaling, and routing between national networks and setting charges and accounting procedures. In addition, it regulates and distributes radio frequency for point to point and mass media communications; since the 1960s it has regulated the geostationary satellite orbit, a crucial part of the communications capacity of most countries.

Once the 162 member nations of the ITU agree upon a standard or a system of frequency distribution, the agreement is ratified in a binding treaty or regulation or accepted as a recommendation to be followed by all members. This regulatory authority is particularly important in relation to radio frequency spectrum and the geostationary orbit, which although a "natural resource" is limited and intrinsically international in character. Efficient use therefore depends on international agreement and regulation.

From 1865 to 1959 international agencies and committees established by industrializing countries to handle international telecommunications regulation did not have a specific mandate to address the problems of developing countries. Since 1959, and particularly since 1965, the ITU has increasingly adopted a developmental role toward the Third World.[40] This focus was underlined by the Maitland Commission, which highlighted the enormous inadequacies of telecommunications systems in the developing world. In 1986 the Centre for Telecommunications Development (CTD) was established to respond to requests for technical assistance and advisory services from developing countries.[41]

Regulation and Development at the ITU

Within the ITU three main organizations deal directly with standards and regulations: the Consultative Committee for Telegraph and Telephone (CCITT), the International Radio Consultative Committee (CCIR), responsible for all radio and broadcast matters, and the International Frequency Registration Board (IFRB). The detailed discussions and negotiations within these committees are critical in determining the final proposals that are put to member governments for agreement.[42] International telecommunications agreements are reached through large international conferences such as the World Administrative Radio Conference (WARC) and the World Administrative Telephone and Telegraph Conference (WATTC). These establish long-term rules for telecommunications operations. Tensions between telecommunications in trade and services (particularly with deregulation and privatization) and the need to control standards and provide for basic requirements of developing countries are manifest in the committees and conferences.[43]

The impact of technological advance, specialized uses for international networks, rapid diffusion of new services, and pressures for openness in international trade have all strained the ITU and its operating groups. New technologies such as fiber optics and cellular radio, and the rapid growth of enhanced services, have made the standard setting process complex and difficult.

At the same time the convergence of telecommunications broadcasting and computing technologies has produced large overlaps between the responsibilities of the CCITT, the CCIR, and the IFRB. New market entrants, supplying a wide range of information services for education, commerce, banking, and industry have emerged as autonomous service providers—outside the jurisdiction of the traditional PTT carriers and the ITU.

As a result of such changes, existing regulations dating from 1973 need to be fundamentally rewritten. Though the technical aspects are complex, the main issues facing the ITU are: whether the new international telecommunications services should be regulated at all and, if so, to what extent. The 1988 WATTC is a test case for the ITU to provide a broad regulatory framework for the 1990s and beyond.

Draft proposals for the WATTC extend ITU jurisdiction over new services and their providers and make compliance with CCITT recommendations mandatory. The United States, the United Kingdom, and the large International Telecommunications Users Group (INTUG), however, believe that the ITU should adopt minimal regulation, applied only to basic transmission and service provision. They argue that extending present regulations to "any entity" offering international services, including operators of private networks, will stifle deregulatory reforms and undermine current liberalized policies. INTUG and other opponents aver that compulsory standards and regulations would limit consumer choice, prevent competition, and restrain innovation—in effect, that they would "strangle the new information technology revolution at birth."[44]

Moreover, they argue that too many WATTC Preparatory Committee delegates are drawn from PTTs and thus do not fully appreciate the benefits that computing communications users derive from competitive, unregulated markets. This "cultural clash" between the liberalized computer/data communications community and the traditional, monopolized, and regulated PTT community underpins difficulties in reaching a compromise agreement to promote telecommunications services.[45]

The case for extending regulatory control to services and their providers rests on the need to consolidate the worldwide operation of one integrated, standardized service network and to ensure that individuals and countries have equitable access to both basic and enhanced services—a position largely endorsed by developing countries. Theodor Irmer, head of the CCITT, states the ITU position in fairly stark terms:

Will telecommunications services in future be traded like other commodities, at a marketplace available to those who can afford it? Or do we maintain the consensus as in the past that at least those services which are fundamentally needed by everybody will be offered worldwide, protected under ITU regulations? That is the burning issue at one of the most important and decisive conferences ever held by the ITU. . . . a compromise will demand a categorical departure from positions so far defended by opposing camps.[46]

Transborder Data Flows

One fundamental area of conflict concerns the regulation of transborder data flows—itself part of a contentious North-South debate over trade in services that will soon be formally tackled within the GATT.[47]

Modern telecommunications systems allow the unregulated transmission of machine readable data across national boundaries. On one hand, greater access by developing countries to data on scientific, medical, meteorological, technological, and financial data can significantly assist industrializing economies. In addition, equitable collaboration with foreign service suppliers can be a valuable mechanism by which developing countries could establish their own service infrastructure and create comparative advantage in some areas of service exports. On the other hand, the poorer economies are still highly dependent on developed countries for data processing and information services and see this dependence as a threat to their sovereignty in economic, political, technological, and cultural matters.

More specifically, they fear that control over TBDF by private sector entities, both large and small, in developed countries could limit the transfer of information to developing countries—either because access will be denied outright or because the terms of access will be too stringent and costly. Such limitations would seriously constrain the ability of these countries to participate in areas of production, distribution, and trade which depend upon TBDF. They also fear that valuable information can be transferred by multinational subsidiaries located within a developing country to the parent company at another location without the knowledge and control of the host government, resulting in commercial advantage to the foreign firm and lost revenue to the developing country. For example, firms might be able to place bids for mineral exploration rights based on knowledge unavailable to domestic companies or devise negotiating strategies based on insider knowledge.

United States policy discussions often dismiss these concerns. In fact, Third World fears are shared by Canada and Western Europe, who also worry that unregulated TBDF will allow United States multinational firms to achieve unhealthy dominance in the international data market, posing a serious threat to their own competitiveness and sovereignty.[48]

Some developing countries therefore strongly disapprove of moves to prevent the ITU from gaining jurisdiction over the regulation and content of TBDF. Needless to say, these opinions have been vociferously opposed by the United States. The stage is thus set for continuing contentious debates.

Conflict over the Geostationary Orbit

Advances in new technology have been at the center of conflict within WARC meetings. For many years developing countries have argued that the allocation of radio frequencies by the WARCs has been grossly unfair. In the 1979 WARC it was estimated that 70 percent of the world's population were confined to 10 percent of the world's radio frequencies. These alleged structural inequalities have led many developing country delegates to argue for a more equitable world information order—albeit without achieving any real measure of success.[49]

The WARC-ORB 88 (formally concerned with the use of the geostationary satellite orbit and the planning of space services) was established by the ITU explicitly to ensure equitable access to the geostationary orbit for all countries. Developing countries want to gain a guaranteed orbital slot in relatively unused frequency bands and improved procedures for satellite coordination in heavily used frequency bands. If guaranteed slots are not secured, they fear they will be denied access to the geostationary orbit (or be forced to pay excessively high entry fees) solely because they are not yet ready or able to utilize them, because they lack domestic demand, or are constrained by economics and technology.[50]

This planned approach to allocating satellite services has been directly challenged by the United States National Telecommunications and Information Administration (NTIA). Its opposition rests partly on demand considerations: guaranteed slots for developing countries unable to use them would deny access to interests in developed countries ready and able to now exploit them commercially. It also opposes guaranteed access because it seems to confer property and/or permanent rights on outer space, radio frequencies, and the orbital arc, all specifically proscribed in the Outer Space Treaty and in ITU Conventions and Final Acts. The director of NTIA, for example, has stated that the United States requires a flexible, market-driven approach for allocating satellite orbital slots.[51]

If the ITU and developing countries do not give way to demands by developed countries for flexibility and minimal regulation in this and other areas of conflict, the latter groups will also refuse to compromise, thus throwing the whole system of international telecommunications regulation into chaos.[52]

Compromises

These damaging conflicts arise at the international level because each side believes its position to be unimpeachable. In fact, there are large areas of complementarity between them, if each side recognizes the validity of the other's position.

The ITU and the developing countries should recognize that massive increases in redistributed revenue, required to meet their basic infrastructural needs, can only come from international sources and can best be generated within a rapidly growing international economy. The global diffusion of telecommunications services and resources is critical to stimulating global growth. Deregulation and relatively free exchange within the industrialized countries is the best way to achieve this and thus create the conditions for resource transfer.

Developed countries, and particularly the United States, should at the same time recognize the legitimacy of Third World fears that the single-minded pursuit of total deregulation and an unrestrained market, free for all, without allowance for telecommunications resource transfers, could increase the gap between North and South at an extraordinary pace, effectively eliminating whole segments of the Third World from participating in the most dynamic sectors of the future global economy. This cost is unacceptably high.

Instead, the United States government should look for innovation and compromise in international bodies. It will need to contain pressures for complete deregulation and open access while also using its considerable powers to convince the recalcitrant ITU regulatory faction and developing countries that both sets of objectives can be partly achieved. Global deregulation can be combined with national control and structured technical and financial assistance.

Conclusion

The developmental concerns of the Third World are historically, economically, and technologically legitimate. The rapid expansion of their telecommunications network is a key determinant of economic growth, but this expansion needs to be carried out in a planned and equitable manner that also allows for the creation of indigenous technological capacities.

The structure and management of the telecommunications network reflects many of the problems characteristic of less developed countries—underinvestment, limited availability, and poor service; inadequate and often myopic management; excessive regulation and state interference; and the biased allocation of resources toward high-income urban groups, away from subsistence-income rural populations. These difficulties are compounded by the unique pressures, opportunities, and dangers caused by technological change and the ongoing revolution in international telecommunications and by the accompanying explosion in transnational flows of information and services.

Broad challenges face developing countries. To start they must take steps to transform telecommunications and their main service providers into dynamic, efficient engines of development at three levels. Rapid expansion of the basic infrastructure is needed, with due weight to rural requirements as well as the telecommunications needs of the commercial sector. This will require major reform of PTTs to make them more efficient, competitive, and innovative; it will also require the recasting of state involvement, particularly in the financial services sector.

Development implies greater integration with the world economy and inevitably greater dependence on developed economies. Not only technology but also investment requirements are far beyond the capacity of most developing countries, and external resources are essential. If these countries want to capture benefits from the world information economy, they will have to ensure that conditions exist to stimulate global exchange and economic growth. This means facilitating the relatively rapid and free diffusion of new services. At the same time, they need to reach a mutually advantageous accommodation with international firms concerning their domestic operations and international exchange of services.

Making progress toward these goals does not demand that developing countries privatize, break up their monopolies, allow foreign competition, or cede national sovereignty to outside entities in matters of regulation and information flow. In some cases, however, liberalization may bring benefits. The more advanced developing countries, for their part, must realize that they could benefit from a relaxation of the more restrictive elements of their regulatory regime. This is particularly true where the pursuit of exports is an objective and where steps must now be taken to ensure the international competitiveness of domestic producers in an environment attractive to foreign firms.

Nevertheless, some regions of the developing world do not yet have sufficiently sophisticated economies to take advantage of liberalization policies to stimulate performance. Such policies require a minimum degree of indigenous, dynamic technological and industrial capabilities, coupled with stable institutions that can define the "rules of the game" and allow the advantages of liberalization to be captured by the whole economy. Unless these minimum conditions exist, market-oriented solutions could further reduce public accountability and ultimately transfer income to the most favored groups in the economy.

The challenge for developing countries is to formulate policies that address both their equity concerns and the need for efficiency and innovation in the domestic context. They must also balance independence and interdependence in their relations with the global economy. These are difficult accommodations to achieve.[53]

Given a willingness on the part of developing countries to tackle these problems, there is great room for both the public and private sectors in advanced economy countries to cooperate in solving the telecommunications problems besetting the Third World and to resolve the conflicts that divide North and South in this field.

Capacity Accumulation and Domestic Reform

In the long-term, developing countries will benefit if they can use large-scale investments in telecommunications to build their domestic technological capacities. This is a process that can—indeed must—involve foreign suppliers. Suppliers need to receive a minimal rate of return, for example, if full cooperation is to be achieved. At the same time, suppliers must recognize that the best way to establish profitable, long-term business arrangements in developing countries is to help them to meet their development objectives.

The United States government can educate American telecommunications companies to understand that there is good business to be done with developing countries and that to succeed they must accept development "ground rules."[54] The government can play its part in these arrangements by providing the same kind of financial support and guarantees that American competitors receive to secure access to third markets. This can greatly enlarge the pool of investment resources on which the Third World could draw.

Different country conditions require modulated policy instruments. The dynamic capacities of the NICs are such that preferential technology transfer and financial support are not vital. United States companies will not be able to transit business in these countries unless they are prepared to make available core technology—a commercial decision, not a political one.

There is much more to be done in relation to the larger economies like India and China. Because of their size and broad requirements, they need access to foreign knowledge on a large scale, including support for training and local research and development in the design and manufacture of central exchanges, transmission, and peripheral equipment. The returns may be long-term, but foreign firms who cooperate in technology transfer now will be well placed to reap future benefits.

For smaller, "second tier" economies such as Thailand and Indonesia, the needs are similar but not as extensive. These countries want to build their software and hardware design capabilities to modify imported technology to suit local conditions. They do not yet need a central exchange capability, but they do need external support to carry out a limited amount of manufacturing and technical change in peripherals and transmission equipment.

Finally, for the much larger group of poorer, smaller economies, choices are more difficult. Training in planning, installation, and maintenance is necessary, as is manufacturing support. Undoubtedly the greatest contribution the United States could make to capability development in these countries would be to support regional approaches to design and manufacture, backed by financial and technical assistance.

The direct involvement of foreign governments in domestic regulatory reform must necessarily be limited. Logic and compromise suggest that the United States first needs to accept the legitimacy of Third World developmental concerns in its domestic telecommunications sectors. This implies endorsing and respecting the concept of national sovereignty over domestic regulation. In practical terms this means that in the majority of developing countries the United States does not impose reciprocity conditions in the area of service supply and production. Correspondingly, blanket deregulation and privatization is not a universal solution to the problems of telecommunications in developing societies. Rather, it is possible for United States development agencies to work with developing countries and other groups to design innovative investment financing to reduce the pressure on PTTs to increase connection and rental fees in order to generate surpluses.[55]

The United States can at the same time support domestic development projects of the ITU and the CTD both by making more funds available and by seconding technical and training staff to its projects. If an appropriate mechanism can be found, bilateral training schemes can supplement multilateral programs to train engineers and technicians in such areas as maintenance, installation, network expansion, and modification. Bilateral training programs could also introduce planners to the general importance of expanding basic telecommunications and the particular conditions needed to ensure dynamism and innovation in the supply of the new technology and services. The experience of developed countries with deregulation and reform, while not an irrefutable model, can nonetheless be instructive.

International Leadership

A pluralist approach may help resolve the contentious issues now separating North and South in telecommunications. Regulation of the basic international infrastructure, with major commitments from the North to support a planned expansion of telecommunications in the South and to ensure adequate access to international resources in the future, is one side of the equation. This approach could help allay the legitimate fears of developing countries that their interests are being sacrificed in the headlong pursuit of unilateral deregulation.

Quid pro quo, developing countries should recognize that substantial deregulation of international service flow could stimulate global economic growth. This, in turn, could help to improve their telecommunications networks, mobilize new technologies in development efforts, and enhance the broader expansion process. This means applying market allocation principles to new service regulation within an international framework.

On the specific question of access to the geostationary orbit, both sides should consider favorably proposals for fixed-term leasing of guaranteed orbit spectrum assignments by developing countries to carriers in developed countries. This arrangement would secure future access to the geostationary orbit for developing countries, generate income from assets they cannot now exploit, and help firms in developed countries secure commercial opportunities.[56]

In all of these cases, and particularly in relation to regulating international trade in services, all sides must help depoliticize negotiations. Pragmatism rather than polemics should be the guideline.[57] Furthermore, the United States should make clear its intention to work within the framework of the ITU to find solutions to problems. As part of these efforts, it should take steps to ensure much more effective participation of developing countries in the deliberations of the CCITT and CCIR — with financial assistance, training, and information to participants in developing and developed countries.

At this critical juncture in the creation of new international telecommunications structures, primary efforts should be devoted to expansion, innovation, and participation by all parties. A "positive-sum" strategy will not only redound beneficially to American political and economic interests in the Third World and in telecommunications, but will also help to ensure that the global telecommunications system plays its full role in growth of the global economy.

New Communications Technologies, Banking, and Finance

Anthony Saunders

Over the last decade the influence of new communications technologies on banking and finance has been dramatic. In particular, advances in telecommunications technology, and associated advances in computer technology, have changed these industries from total reliance on paper transactions, products, and services to domination by electronic methods of transfer and services. The effects of the change from paper to electronic banking and finance have important public policy implications regarding the efficiency of the payments system, the stability of the payments system, and the competitive structure of the domestic and international financial services industries. In this essay these policy issues will be addressed, including an examination of the effects of new communications technologies on the efficiency and stability of the payments system and the concomitant effects on the competitive structure of both the domestic and international financial services industries.

Efficiency and Stability of the Payments System

The efficiency and stability of the financial system and, in particular, the banking system is a major public policy concern. Specifically, if the payments system fails to work efficiently and/or the public loses confidence in the system, then major economic dislocations and externalities can arise. Indeed, this "specialness" aspect to banking via the payments mechanism is the raison d'être for regulation by such bodies as the Federal Reserve and the Federal Deposit Insurance Corporation (FDIC).[1]

Financial theory argues that a payments system emerges as the natural (optimal) cost-minimizing arrangement given legal, regulatory,

Table 1 Volume and Value Composition of U.S. Payments, 1983

Type of Payment Instrument	Volume Composition (percentage)	Value Composition (percentage)	Average Dollar Value per Transaction
Nonelectronic	99.50	21.50	247
Cash	70.41	1.54	25
Checks	25.14	19.80	910
Credit Cards	3.13	.11	42
Money Orders	.47	.03	67
Travelers' Checks	.50	.02	35
Electronic	.35	78.50	258,993
ACH	.25	.39	1,800
ATM	.05	.00	70
POS	.01	.00	30
Wire Transfers	.04	78.11	2,500,000

Source: David B. Humphrey, "Payments System Risk, Market Failure, and Public Policy," *The Payments Revolution: The Emerging Public Policy Issues*, ed. Elinor Solomon (Boston: Kluwer-Nijhoff Publishing, 1987), 84.

and institutional structures and that banks and other financial services firms are the major agents in effecting transactions among wealthholders.[2] Thus, in recent years we have seen the emergence of a payments system based on electronic means of transfer from a system based largely on cash and checks. Table 1 shows the most recently available compositional breakdown, in terms of both volume and value, of United States payments.

As can be seen in terms of volume, nonelectronic methods—cash, checks, credit cards, money orders, and travelers checks—were used in 99.5 percent of transactions; however, in terms of dollar value they accounted for only 21.5 percent of transactions. By comparison, electronic methods of payment—automated clearing houses, automated teller machines, point of sale terminals, and wire transfer systems—accounted for only .35 percent in volume, but 78.5 percent in value. Wire transfer systems accounted for 78.11 percent of all dollar transactions, measured in value.

The two wire systems that dominated the payments system are Fedwire and CHIPS (Clearing Houses Interbank Payments System).[3] Fedwire is a wire-transfer-telecommunications network linking over 7000 domestic banks with the Federal Reserve System. This system

Table 2 Ratio of Fedwire and CHIPS Dollar Payments to
GNP and Bank Reserves

	Fedwire and CHIPS ($)	
	GNP	Reserves
1970	16	2
1980	48	17
1983	65	38
1985	66	42

Source: David B. Humphrey, "Future Directions in Payment Risk Reduction," *Journal
of Cash Management*, 1988.

is used to make deposit and loan payments among banks, to transfer
book-entry securities among banks, and by banks acting as payment
agents on behalf of large corporate customers including other financial
service firms. CHIPS is operated by the New York Clearinghouse Association and is therefore a private network. At the core of the system
are 140 member banks who act as correspondent banks for a larger
number of domestic and international banks in clearing mostly international related payments (foreign exchange, euro-dollar loans,
certificates of deposit).

Together, these two wire transfer networks have been growing at
around 25 percent per annum. Indeed, at the end of 1986 the value of
payments sent over these two networks exceeded $1 trillion a day.[4]
By comparison $150 billion was being made as payment by check,
$11 billion by cash, and $3 billion through automated clearinghouses,
which are designed to electronically transfer payroll and undertake
other retail transactions among banks.

Another way to see the tremendous growth in these payment
networks is to compare their dollar payment values to gross national product (GNP) and to bank reserves (R). This is shown in table
2.

Thus the value of wire transfers has increased more than four times
relative to GNP and more than twenty-one times relative to bank reserves over the 1970–85 period. The important question is: why such
a phenomenal rate of growth? There are at least three explanations.
The first is the development and growth of new financial instruments;
the second is growing use of book entry securities; the third is the

cost subsidy element implicit in the current pricing of wire-transfer services.

New Financial Instruments

Since the 1970s and the increase in volatility of financial markets, a whole spectrum of derivative securities have emerged in the guise of financial futures, options, and swaps.[5] These instruments have been designed for hedging and arbitrage purposes for large institutional investors, both corporate and financial; that is, they are used largely for financial rather than real goods (production) related transactions. Aligned with the growth of these new instruments has been growth of exchanges on which these instruments are traded, including the New York Futures Exchange and the International Money Market in Chicago. As with all financial contracts, settlement needs to be effected in a timely and orderly manner and the chosen mechanism for such settlements has been the wire transfer systems. Thus, when a problem occurred on Fedwire on 19 October 1987 (Black Monday), when Fedwire went "down" in Chicago for a couple of hours, a major dislocation to the settlement-payments process took place with potentially disastrous consequences.

Book-Entry Securities

Virtually all government bonds, notes, and bills are now issued in book entry/computerized form rather than in paper certificate form. As a result, these securities can be transferred directly among Fedwire participants in the same manner as regular payment transactions. The growth of securities wire-transfers has in turn been fueled by the enormous growth in the budget deficit and the need to finance that deficit through new issues of treasury debt. As a result, at the end of 1986 over $250 billion in wire-transfer transactions were related to government securities transactions. It might also be noted that mortgage backed securities as well as corporate bonds now have the potential to be issued in book-entry form, and there is every likelihood that in the near future book-entry transfers of these securities will add to the total volume of transfers on the wire networks.

Figure 1 Daylight Overdrafts on Fedwire

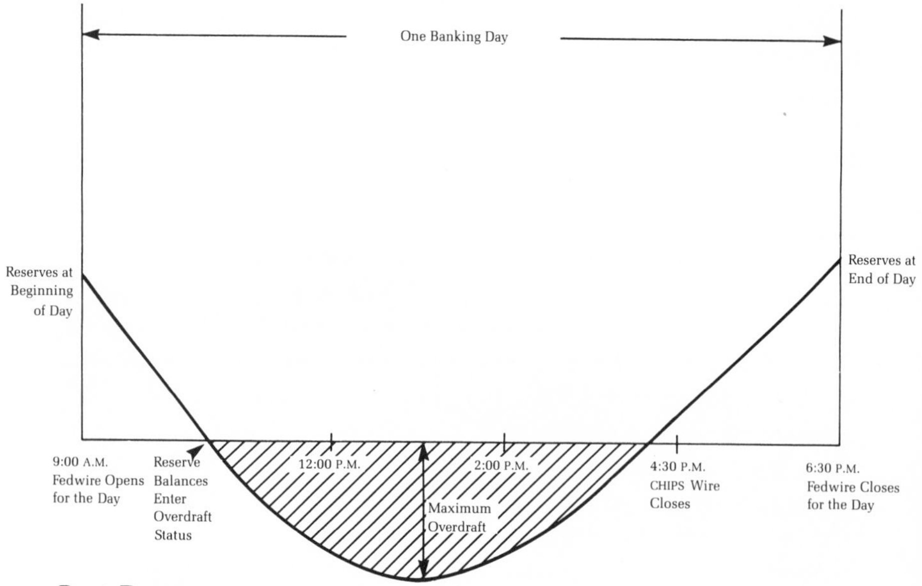

Cost Reasons

There are two cost reasons underlying the growing volume of wire transfers. The first has been the efforts of the Federal Reserve (the Fed) since 1980 to cut down on check float. This reduces the relative attractiveness of a check-based payments system to a wire transfer system. The second, and probably the most fundamental, has been the failure to charge system users (either the banks or indirectly their large corporate customers) for "daylight overdrafts" run on the wire transfer systems. At first sight the problem of daylight overdrafts might seem somewhat arcane. However, the centrality of wire transfers to the payments system as a whole, and the fact that daylight overdrafts pose a potential threat to the stability of the financial system, means that the size of these overdrafts, and the need for their control, is one of the major issues in financial market and economic regulation today.

To understand daylight overdrafts figure 1 shows a "typical" daily pattern of net wire payment transfers (debits minus credits) of a representative large money center bank using Fedwire.

Under the Federal Reserve Act banks must maintain cash reserves on deposit at the Fed. In addition, these reserve accounts are used to settle banks' net wire transactions that have occurred during the day.

For Fedwire (as well as CHIPS) settlement occurs at the end of the banking day by the Federal Reserve adjusting each member bank's accounts to reflect that bank's net debit (credit) position with other banks. Under current regulations the end-of-day reserve position of member banks cannot be negative. However, what is true at the end of the day is not true during the day—the Fed allows banks to run daylight overdrafts (or negative within-day balances in their reserve account). These negative reserve balances arise under current payment practice because large banks (and their customers) tend to repay overnight (Federal fund) loans and make interest payments at the beginning of the banking day and to borrow funds back at the end of the day. For periods during the day (as shown by the cross-hatched area in figure 1) banks run a daylight overdraft on their reserve account at the Fed.

In effect, the Fed is "lending" banks' within-day reserves. There are two other important institutional aspects to this process. First, the Federal Reserve does not charge banks any explicit interest rate or fee for these daylight overdraft loans. There is thus no incentive for banks or their large corporate customers to economize on these transactions. Daylight Fedwire transfer overdrafts are effectively a "free-good" and are therefore oversupplied. Second, the Federal Reserve (under Regulation J) guarantees payments finality for every wire transfer. Therefore if the representative bank in figure 1 was to fail at 12:00 P.M., then the Federal Reserve would be liable for all of the transactions made by that bank, and there is no risk that any receiving bank (or its customers) will be left short of funds at the end of the day. Essentially, the Federal Reserve bears the total "credit risk" of bank failures by granting free overdrafts without charging a concomitant fee.

On CHIPS net payment flows often take on a similar daily pattern as in figure 1 except that, as a pure net settlement system, the beginning of day position must be zero for all banks. As on Fedwire, big banks will run a daylight overdraft (be a net debtor) that is often larger and more pronounced early in the morning than on Fedwire. Again, large banks will seek to borrow funds (be a net creditor) in the afternoon to cover net debit positions made earlier in the day. While CHIPS does not charge banks explicit fees for running daylight overdrafts (similar to Fedwire), the resolution of a bank failing to settle at the end of the day is treated very differently than on Fedwire. On Fedwire all payments are in "good funds"; that is, the Federal Reserve guarantees the finality of any wire transfer at the time it is made prior to actual failure. By contrast, on CHIPS, since it is a private network, all within-day transfers are "provisional" and only become final on settlement among CHIPS members at the end of the day. In this case, if a bank with a "daylight overdraft" were to fail at 12:00 P.M., CHIPS would resolve this by "unwinding" all of the failing bank's transactions with the N−1 remaining banks. This individual bank failure could therefore result in a systemic crisis in the banking and financial system.

In particular, a bank that would have been in a net creditor position at the end of the banking day had the failing bank settled, may after the bank's failure and CHIPS unwinding all transactions, find that it is a significant net debtor. Conceivably, its net debtor position may be so bad that it cannot settle its transactions with the N−2 remaining banks, and all its transactions will have to be unwound. Such a process would have to continue until all banks could settle their transactions. While no settlement failure has yet occurred on CHIPS, any such failure could be potentially disastrous with financial ramifications far exceeding the October 1987 stock market crash.[6]

For example, Humphrey simulated the effects of a single large CHIPS settlement failure on a random day in January 1983.[7] The settling participant selected had a net credit position of $321 million for the day. (This failure was viewed as being a least worst situation since realistically only net debtors are likely to default.) After deleting the transactions of this bank with all other banks and reestimating the transaction creditor-debtor matrix, he found that twenty-four banks had settlement obligations increased by more than the amount of their capital and ended up in a net debtor position. Of these, eight had been in a net creditor position prior to the removal of transactions with the nonsettling participant. It was then assumed that all banks whose net debtor positions deteriorated by an amount equal to or exceeding their capital were also unable to settle. Another revised transactions matrix had to be constructed. This process was continued until no participant failed following a transactions matrix revision. It was found that six such iterations were required and that fifty banks "failed." These fifty banks accounted for 39 percent of the total dollar value of messages sent for that day.

Policy Solutions to Daylight Overdraft Risk

If daylight overdraft risk poses one of the major threats to the payments system and financial market stability, what are the policy alternatives? Various possibilities have been suggested. The first possibility would be to prevent or prohibit daylight overdrafts altogether. The Fed now has the technical and communications ability to monitor bank reserve positions on a real-time basis over the day. It could thus refuse to effect a debit (payment) transaction if a bank had at some point in the day "no reserves" left in its account at the Fed. This type of policy has recently been instituted on the Swiss national bank wire system. Unfortunately, such a policy may induce gridlock in the payments system and may seriously inhibit its efficiency. Specifically, while daylight overdrafts have potential social costs (in terms of systemic failure risk), they may also have considerable potential benefits since they may allow a more optimal form of daily transactions settlement than if they were prohibited. Indeed, one may readily conceive that the real goods sector and commerce might be seriously affected by such prohibition—since a significant volume of wire transfers are commercially related and undertaken by banks on behalf of their corporate customers.

The second alternative would be to impose maximum limits or caps on the volume of daylight overdrafts. This policy, in effect, is currently being used to limit the credit exposure of the Fed on Fedwire and the systemic risk on CHIPS. Since October 1984 CHIPS has required each receiving bank to impose bilateral credit caps on all other banks from whom it receives payment messages (that is, to whom it advances within-day overdrafts or loans). This is bolstered at the aggregate level by a systemwide cap—no bank can have outstanding a net debit balance (overdraft) exceeding 5 percent of the sum of its bilateral credit ceilings. On Fedwire each bank faces a daylight overdraft cap as a proportion equity capital. A bank's equity capital is seen as an insurance fund that protects depositors and indirectly the Federal Reserve (and the FDIC) against exposure on the wire transfer systems. Under the scheme implemented in March 1986 each bank is meant to evaluate itself in terms of its creditworthiness, its payment system operational procedures, and its general credit policies as a bank that is of the highest standing, above average standing, or otherwise ranked. These caps are shown in table 3. As can be seen, there is a daily

Table 3 Cross-System Debit Caps on Fedwire and CHIPS

	Net Debit Cap	
Cap Class	Two-Week Avg. Plus	Single Day
27 March 1986 through 13 January 1988		
High	2.0	3.0
Above Average	1.5	2.5
Average	1.0	1.5
Limited*	0.5	0.5
No Cap	0.0	0.0
14 January 1988 through 18 May 1988		
High	1.70	2.55
Above Average	1.275	2.125
Average	0.85	1.275
Limited*	0.425	0.425
No Cap	0.0	0.0
19 May 1988 and After		
High	1.50	2.25
Above Average	1.125	1.575
Average	0.75	1.125
Limited*	0.375	0.275
No Cap	0.0	0.0

Source: *Federal Register* 52, no. 151 (6 August 1987).
*The Limited Cap remained in effect until 1 January 1989.

cross-system cap as a maximum ratio of a bank's capital as well as two-week average cap. Moreover, these caps were lowered by some 25 percent between March 1986 and May 1988.

In terms of a pricing scheme these caps imply zero fees for overdrafts up to a bank's cap and then an infinite price at the cap. It is far from clear that this is the most efficient pricing scheme. From a public policy perspective those banks and their corporate customers who most use the wire-transfer networks and therefore daylight overdrafts should presumably bear most of the cost. The easiest way to do this would be to allow overdrafts on Fedwire and CHIPS, but charge an explicit fee or interest rate on these overdrafts to reflect the credit/ systemic risks involved. The most often quoted fee is that of a 1 percent per annum interest charge on the maximum daylight overdraft balance.[8] The 1 percent per annum charge reflects the current interest rate charge on within-day loans by banks to securities houses to finance the latter's inventories of new issues of equity and debt.

By charging an explicit fee not only will those banks that most use overdrafts pay more (in dollar terms), but they will also face stronger incentives than under the current "free good" system to cut down the level of overdrafts they run. As noted earlier a large bulk of wire transfers are financial transactions that are often reversed later in the day. For example, large banks typically repay overnight (Fed fund) borrowings early in the morning and borrow those funds back (often from the same bank) later on in the day. Given the ongoing and repeated nature of these interbank transactions, there is no obvious reason for this institutional arrangement.

With a direct fee or interest rate charged on daylight overdrafts, banks would have an added incentive to replace many daily transactions, such as those on the Fed funds market, with longer-term funding and transactional arrangements. This would also apply for procedures relating to interest payments and securities settlements. In many cases these longer-term contractual relationships could be implemented without adversely impacting the efficiency of the payment system. Indeed, since a large volume of daylight overdrafts involves potential social costs, these costs may be reduced without adversely affecting the social benefits of a payments system based on wire-transfers.

A final alternative would be to moderate or even eliminate explicit caps and, like the Fed on Fedwire, to guarantee payments finality on CHIPS—thereby eliminating systemic risk. In return banks might be required to hold, with the Federal Reserve and CHIPS, special reserve or escrow accounts that could be used as collateral should any member fail to settle at the end of the day. For example, were a bank to fail to settle on Fedwire, the Federal Reserve would guarantee all payments made by that bank (as currently) but would then seek compensation by extracting funds from the escrow/special reserve accounts of surviving banks. A similar process could take place on CHIPS. Since, in effect, the good banks are bailing out the bad banks, the good banks have an incentive to impose "overdraft discipline" on perceived bad banks through bilateral and multilateral credit limits and ceilings.

Either the fee scheme or the collateralized (escrow) account scheme is superior to the current system of self-imposed (regulated) cap limits. More important than the design of the scheme to control daylight overdraft risk is the equity of treatment across both wire networks. If the Federal Reserve were to charge either explicit fees/caps for overdrafts on Fedwire but no such fees/caps were imposed on private wire transfer networks such as CHIPS, then one would expect to see a major switch of wire transactions away from the public sector network to private networks. This would lead to a dramatic increase in the level of payments system risk in the financial system. However, if payment finality were guaranteed on CHIPS (for example, via collateralized escrow accounts), then one might witness greater private-sector involvement in the payments system. This may not be bad. In the long run it might have the effect of inducing greater public versus private sector competition for the provision of payment system services, as well as inducing greater technical and telecommunications innovation in funds transfers as a natural outcome of this process. A wire transfer system that charged explicit fees for overdrafts, that guaranteed payments finality, and that allowed both private and public sectors to compete for shares might well offer an optimal social welfare arrangement for the provision of payment services.

Finally, these potential policy solutions to the daylight overdraft problem are basically reactive. That is, they are ways of ameliorating or mitigating the potential risk explosive. By comparison wire transfer and other telecommunication developments are primarily technology driven and may have forecastable effects. Were there greater involvement of the expert telecommunications community in the development of public policy relating to the payments system (and other financial service issues as well), potential problems might be identified earlier. There is a positive role to be played by telecommunication experts in determining optimal bank regulatory policy in a highly complex and sophisticated world where financial experts/economists may have limited experience or understanding of the true nature of the real technology involved.

Domestic Competition

Historically, the twentieth-century financial system in the United States has been segmented along fairly rigid service or product lines. Conventional wisdom notes that there has been a traditional separation of commercial banking from commerce, commercial banking from investment banking, and insurance from banking. This conventional wisdom has support in the 1933 Glass-Steagall Act, which separates commercial banking from investment banking, and in the Bank Holding Company Act and its 1956 and 1970 amendments, which separate commercial banking from commerce.

Despite these laws, the forces of financial and technological innovation have increasingly challenged the boundaries separating these industries or sectors. It is due largely to developments in computers and telecommunications that we now talk of "financial service firms" rather than commercial banks, investment banks, or insurance companies.

The seeds for this dramatic change lay in the economic environment facing commercial banks in the late 1960s and early 1970s and their responses to that environment. At a time when investment banking was largely paper based and back-office driven, the traditional area of commercial bank profitability—commercial lending funded by cheap core deposits—eroded. Large banks responded in two ways to this challenge. The first was to expand into new activities permitted under the Bank Holding Company Act (such as leasing and data processing) that, while not traditional "banking" activities, were nevertheless "closely related to banking." The second was to expand their investment in new computer and communications technologies such as the automated teller machine (ATM) and cash management hardware and software, in order to offer a new range of services to their corporate and retail customers. Indeed, Salomon Brothers has estimated that the nation's forty largest bankholding companies increased their data processing and telecommunications budgets at a rate of 25 percent per annum in the 1980s.[9] Perhaps the premier (bank) user of computers and telecommunications budgets as a strategic implement to its competitive strategy has been Citicorp. In 1973 Citicorp, in association with Transaction Technology Inc. (TTI), was instrumental in developing the ATM, which now covers the United States and most of the world. Citicorp's customers alone have access to over 11,000 ATMs in forty-five different states, as well as access to facilities in Puerto Rico, Hong Kong, and Europe via owned and leased telephone line agreements. Since 1973 Citicorp has actively sought to develop a domestic and communications network that links in real time each major branch bank and subsidiary throughout the world.

As a result, Citicorp now has a round-the-clock communications capability that directly links 140 cities in eighty-five different countries with a number of earth stations connecting branches directly to its own communications satellite. It also operates a proprietary message and data network by means of leased domestic and international telephone lines which allows it to control its telecommunications costs.

This competitive edge in technology and communications, aligned with shrinking profitability in traditional banking, resulted in banks challenging the traditional barriers among financial service firms as well as being in the forefront of developing fee-related services and products (off-balance sheet banking). The barrier to come under greatest threat has been that between commercial and investment banking. Until the abolition of fixed commissions in May 1975, investment banks and brokers had shown little interest in investing heavily in new technologies. Using this reluctance to their advantage, commercial banks began to offer open- and closed-end mutual funds, discount brokerage type and other investment services, and commercial paper underwriting as well as mortgaged-backed bond underwriting services. While some legal challenges by the securities industry inhibited commercial bank progress, a consensus now appears to be forming that the social welfare benefits of eliminating Glass-Steagall type barriers far outweigh its social costs. The major area of potential social benefit would emanate from greater price competition in the provision of investment banking products as well as allowing greater access by smaller banks to the nation's capital markets.[10] The major potential social cost arises from conflicts of interest that may arise when a bank offers both commercial bank and investment bank type products.[11] In March 1988 a Congressional moratorium on the Bank Holding Company's new securities activities expired. This allows banks now to enter securities activities at the discretion of the Federal Reserve.

While technology has allowed, and indeed has helped erode regulatory barriers between commercial banking and investment banking, technological considerations have made regulators more determined than ever to keep the separation between banking and commerce intact.[12] Their major concern relates to commercial firms gaining access to the payments system via the acquisition of commercial banks and then undertaking actions that increase instability and risk to the payments system. The underlying argument takes the following form: a large commercial undertaking acquires a small bank which is reluctant to impose appropriate credit controls on its corporate parent; as a result, and acting on behalf of the parent, it transmits an excessive volume of payment messages across the wire networks. If the corporation gets into trouble, the affiliated bank will be unable to settle its net position with other banks on Fedwire or CHIPS. To avoid outright default and systemic effects, the Fed or the FDIC will lend funds to the bank either through the discount window or directly to keep the bank in business. These loans implicitly will support the failing commercial firm via its banking affiliate. As a result, the federal safety net is extended to commercial firms, a result Congress did not intend in establishing the Federal Reserve and the FDIC.

Some observers have argued that this concern can be directly addressed by modest changes in regulations, without requiring blanket prohibitions on commercial firm acquisition of full service banks (under the Bank Holding Company Act) or on limited service, or "nonbank" banks, as under the recent 1987 Competitive Equality Banking Act.[13] Specifically, by imposing restrictions or "firewalls" on interaffiliate funds wire transfers (that is, among firms and their bank affiliates) and with punitive financial and even criminal penalties on managers and stockholders if these restrictions are breached, adequate protection to the payment system can be maintained. It is hard to believe that this small potential social cost outweighs the potential social benefits of allowing commercial firms to achieve greater integration of their operational activities with their financial activities. Such integrations have the potential for achieving far-reaching economies of scope in information, telecommunications, and resource utilization.[14] In addition, important social and private benefits may exist through greater exploitation of potential economies of scale and by eliminating barriers in the market for corporate control, which ultimately disciplines managers and forces them to undertake decisions in the stockholders' best interests.[15]

Finally, while wholesale payments/wire system concerns have created stiff resolve on the part of regulators to restrict the growth of limited service (nonbank) banks, at the retail payments level there has been an increasing trend toward bank-commercial firm joint ventures in the form of point of sale (POS) terminals and debit cards (Publix supermarkets, J.C. Penny, Mobil Oil). A retail customer can now buy goods by automatically debiting his bank account and crediting the commercial firms through a POS terminal rather than using cash, check, or credit cards. The commercial firm gains payments immediacy, the customer economizes on cash balances, and the bank gains a fee for providing this service.[16]

Not only are technological and communications advances eroding industry barriers, but they are generating a new array of on-and-off-balance sheet products for banks and other financial service firms. Perhaps the most discussed (but not necessarily the most important) are cash management services provided by banks. The need for cash management services arose partly in response to greater interest rate and exchange rate volatility in the United States in the 1970s, as well as in response to interstate banking limitations. While corporations could generate cash revenues anywhere in the United States, banks were locationally constrained by branching restrictions imposed under the 1927 McFadden Act. Thus, corporations needed efficient transfer and communications systems to consolidate, centralize, and optimize their working capital at just a few locations. To ease this process banks developed hardware and software cash management products, including controlled disbursement accounts, account reconciliation, wholesale lockbox, remote terminal access, and treasury workstations. Interestingly, the 1980s have witnessed the gradual erosion of barriers to interstate banking and along with it the demand for cash management related products. The greatest force for erosion has been the creation of regional banking pacts among states, allowing reciprocal rights of entry across state lines for banks in pact member states. It is currently proposed that those states (more than forty) with regional banking pacts will have to evoke nationwide trigger clauses in 1991. Such a move is likely to further national consolidation in the banking industry, thereby reducing the demand for cash management services —although banks will require enhanced communications networks efficiently to manage nationwide branching-ATM systems.

More important quantitatively has been the development of new fee-based off-balance sheet services and products, many heavily reliant on new financial and computer technologies. The amalgam of a bank's off-balance sheet activities is often called the "invisible" bank, which often exceeds the assets of the visible bank.[17]

For example, Citicorp's foreign currency commitments (mostly forward exchange contracts) amounted to $200 billion in September 1986. These alone were much larger than the whole of its on-balance sheet assets for that year. (Further, the bulk of the cash payments relating to these foreign exchange contracts are transferred over the CHIPS wire network.) A large component of these off-balance sheet products take the form of insurance or contingent guarantee contracts (letters of credit and stand-by contracts), in many cases originated by customers using computer terminals and transmitted via wire networks/telephone lines to servicing banks. Under such contingent contracts a bank guarantees the (contractual) performance of a customer and, for a fee, substitutes its own credit standing for that of the customer's.

However, this is only a partial picture of the size and scope of "the invisible bank"; it does not incorporate the trend toward bank's selling and securitizing their loan portfolios. Again, advances in technology and communications have enabled banks to originate, package, and remove from the balance-sheet all types of loans (real estate, small business, receivables, credit card/credit loans) rather than holding them to maturity as under the traditional asset-transformation mode of bank intermediation. This securitization, aligned with the growing dominance of off-balance sheet products, has transformed banks into organizations that act more like brokers who originate and then sell assets for a fee, than asset transformers.

This change in mode of behavior is not without risk to the financial and banking system. Each off-balance sheet activity involves some form of credit or interest risk exposure. Letters of credit and standby letters of credit, for example, are contingent liabilities that directly expose a bank to credit risk. Any losses on off-balance sheet business have to be written off against on-balance sheet capital. The rapid growth and proliferation of off-balance sheet activities, fueled by technological advances, has caused great concern among regulators — especially in light of the inadequacy of some banks' capital reserves.[18] Currently, the Federal Reserve, in conjunction with the Bank of Japan, the Bank of England, and other OECD countries has proposed implementing a uniform capital ratio on banks that is related to the riskiness of both their on- and off-balance sheet activities.[19]

While securities activities and off-balance sheet activities are changing the competitive structure of the banking and financial system, innovations in home-banking may change significantly the future structure of the financial services industry. Home-banking has yet to live up to its potential. Demographics suggest that increasingly the

American work force is choosing to work, at least part-time, from home; moreover, the fastest growing sector of United States business is small business. These factors are likely to create a huge demand for remote (off-site) access to bank accounts, bill paying, securities transactions, insurance, and pension plans. A number of banks have already invested significant resources in home-banking projects, generally involving a home-based personal computer linked to a bank's central computer via a telephone modem and telephone lines. If demographic projections are correct, there is likely to be increasing demand to conduct personal banking and financial service transactions without setting foot inside a bank. Of course, the rate of growth of home-banking will depend on the rate of growth of home-banking products, the rate of acquisition of personal computers, and the relative cost advantages larger banks and financial firms have in supplying such services over smaller firms. Nevertheless, home-banking has one real practical disadvantage—it cannot give the customer immediate access to cash. This limitation, along with the proliferation of local ATMs, mitigates the growth of home-banking.

What about the role of small banks? These banks are faced with two competitive strategies. The first is to become specialist "retail" banks providing a qualitatively "better" set of financial services to individual customers than do larger banks. The second is to offer a full range of retail and wholesale services to their customers by franchising products produced by the large banks and/or leasing time on large banks' private networks and computers. The ability of small banks to offer a full range of services at competitive prices depends on whether economics of scale exists in the provision of bank services. To date there appear to be no major economics of scale in banking.[20] This suggests that smaller banks can compete with larger banks on a relatively equal cost basis, given current technological-telecommunications infrastructures. Emerging telecommunication systems—ISDN, virtual networks—may well reduce the need for large banks to maintain conventional private networks and may enhance any potential degree of economies of scale in banking.

The ability (and strategy) of small banks offering a full range of services has potential social costs because their local deposit bases are smaller and because of their concomitant need to grow in order to offer a full range of services. In recent years many smaller banks have used the wire-transfer systems to tap the national deposit market.

The ease with which this has been accomplished has been increased by the proliferation of deposit or money brokers who seek to arbitrage the $100,000 deposit insurance ceiling. Money brokers break up large deposits into smaller lots, which are then placed with different small banks by wire transfer. Each smaller package will now be fully covered by deposit insurance, whereas if the funds had been deposited with one bank, only a small portion of the total amount would have been covered. The bank gains from this process by increasing its deposit base, the depositor by gaining greater insurance coverage and generally higher interest rates on deposits, and the broker by charging a fee to the bank. This system imposes clear risks: since the bank has to pay higher interest plus fees for these deposits, it has the incentive to invest the funds in riskier loans. A large number of small bank failures in "small banking" states such as Kansas and Missouri have been attributed by regulators to such brokering and associated managerial incentives to increase risk-taking. Perhaps the best example of the potential danger of such strategies was the failure of the Penn Square bank in 1982, and its effects on larger banks such as Continental Illinois.[21]

Various steps have been taken to contain the activities of deposit brokers, including civil and criminal litigation using Racketeer-Influenced and Corrupt Organizations (RICO: Title Nine of the Organized Crime Control Act of 1970) laws—accusing brokers of "causing" bank failures by breaching interstate wire transfer and other communication laws. In addition, attempts have been made to limit the deposit insurance coverage of brokered funds. Nevertheless, the fault appears to be more with small bank mismanagement and perverse risk-taking incentives under the current deposit insurance system. Arguably, money brokers are simply using the telecommunications networks to effect a more efficient working of the national deposit market.

International Competitive Considerations

Financial service products, unlike the manufacture of real goods, need efficient delivery systems within a targeted market. Unlike a Japanese car manufacturer who can exploit significant production and operational benefits in Japan by building cars and shipping the finished product to the United States for sale, financial services generally need to be both produced and sold in a targeted market.

Given the technological and communications advancements of American banking and financial service firms, and the fact that foreign financial service firms do not nearly have the same technological infrastructure or expertise, it seems paradoxical that United States banks' share of world banking assets is declining.[22] For example, twenty years ago seven of the world's ten largest banks were United States banks. By comparison, in 1987 only two United States banking companies (Citicorp and Bank of America) were ranked among the world's twenty-five largest. Currently, fourteen of the top twenty-five are Japanese (including the world's four largest), four are French, three are British, and two are German.

The explanation for this demise is clear: for American banks to sell financial products and services abroad they need ease of entry to the foreign market and efficient and low cost delivery mechanisms for the services they seek to sell. Even if United States banks have enormous cost advantages in producing and innovating financial services in the domestic market, these cannot be readily turned into a profit overseas if there are significant regulatory barriers to market entry and/or the delivery systems for these services are inefficient and costly.

Whereas the United States offers a fairly level playing field (or so-called national treatment) for potential foreign entrants, American banks entering overseas markets often encounter a wide array of product line, size, branching, and other discriminatory regulations that puts them at a comparative disadvantage relative to the local banks.[23] However, this is only a partial explanation; two of the United States' major competitor countries, Japan and Great Britain, now have regulations on foreign banks that are at least as liberal as those imposed on foreign banks here. Japan even offers American bank holding companies more than national treatment in two areas by allowing them to establish limited securities affiliates and trust banking affiliates, activities prohibited to the large domestic Japanese city banks. Despite this, in 1986 total foreign bank assets amounted to only 3 percent of total bank assets in Japan compared to a 19 percent asset share of foreign banks in the United States (9 percent of which is Japanese).

An important reason for the low share of American banks in overseas markets may lie in the inability of these banks to translate fully their domestic technological/communications advantages and infrastructures into foreign competitive advantages. While the United States has been a major pioneer of ATMs—products that should be popular in overseas markets—overseas, these systems are often in a transient stage. For example, ATMs in Germany have grown very slowly, largely because of prohibitive charges imposed by the Bundespost for the use and leasing of domestic telephone lines. In countries where telecommunications are public utilities and there are pervasive restrictions on private (proprietary) communication networks, it is very difficult for American banks to translate domestic comparative advantages in financial service innovations into overseas sales and revenues.

Another good example is cash management services. American banks are at the forefront in developing cash management products and communication systems to allow domestic corporations to overcome problems posed by prohibitions on interstate banking and financial market price volatility in managing their working capital. Yet the demand in Europe and elsewhere for such services has been small, partly because there are no restrictions on interstate banking similar to those existing in the United States; more important, the appropriate communications infrastructures do not exist or are prohibitively costly to install.[24] Finally, in Japan, where no large wholesale payment interbank wire transfer system like Fedwire exists, money markets remain comparatively underdeveloped and the competitive advantage of United States banks is curtailed. The Fed funds and repurchase agreement markets—collateralized Fed funds backed by exchange of book-entry securities—form a major component of United States banks' asset-liability management strategies and expertise. In the absence of such a communications network this expertise cannot be easily translated by American banks into a competitive advantage in Japan.[25]

In addition to explicit barriers to entry or telecommunication access, there are secondary reasons for the difficulty American banks encounter in transferring their technological advantages abroad. The first are socioeconomic or implicit barriers to trade: United States banks have developed considerable expertise in the retail mortgage market, including "securitizing" packages of mortgages in the form of Government National Mortgage Association (GNMA) pass-throughs and collateralized mortgage obligations. However, cultural differences in countries such as Japan dictate that retail mortgages be self-financed or financed by loans from local, nonbank money lenders. This has rendered an entire area of American financial services and technology nontransferable. Second, the McFadden Act and its restrictions on interstate banking have arguably diverted considerable American bank efforts toward overcoming local and domestic entry barriers at the expense of international expansion. In effect, the McFadden Act may well have worked to blunt the international competitive edge of United States banks.

The ability of American banks to profit internationally from new services and products they have innovated domestically depends crucially on an efficient delivery network overseas. To the extent that communications technology in many countries is old or inefficient, that the price of gaining access is prohibitively high, and that private networks are restricted, American banks will be unable to exploit fully their technological advantages over foreign providers of financial services. United States banks will be unable to overcome the disadvantages due to explicit regulatory barriers, socioeconomic implicit barriers, and the dead-weight burdens of the McFadden Act and the Bank Holding Company Act. It is therefore just as important for Congress to develop a long-term international communications policy to encourage other countries to lower the cost of access to domestic communications systems (or to allow the development of private/proprietary "competing" systems), as it is for them to push countries into lowering regulatory barriers on foreign bank entry into their markets. Freedom of entry by itself may be a rather empty prize without an accompanying communications policy to help lower the cost of United States financial firm access to overseas communications networks. Ease of local communication system access must be viewed as an important part of the U.S. Trade Representative's agenda in the Uruguay Round of the General Agreement on Tariffs and Trade (GATT) negotiations, which now addresses nontariff barriers to trade in services.

Other Issues

The growth and improvement of banking technology and telecommunications raises other important issues.

Crime. The replacement of check-based (paper) exchange by wire transfer has raised new problems regarding theft and white collar crime. Because huge sums are transferred across the wire networks each day, and a few bank employees must have specialized knowledge of PINs and other entry codes, the incentives for white collar criminals appear to have increased. For example, at the First National Bank of Chicago, low-level computer operatives reportedly attempted to divert wire transfers. In the future greater bank and regulatory resources will have to be spent on surveillance and employee monitoring, as well as developing fail-safe and unbreakable entry codes to wire transfer accounts.

Regulatory Avoidance. The improvement of telecommunications networks also enhances the power of bankers vis-à-vis regulators, effectively aiding regulatory avoidance. For example, each state imposes usury ceilings on banks. These ceilings place caps and controls on fees and interest rates that bankers can charge on credit cards and mortgages. Because credit card operations are heavily communications based and do not need to be located directly in the customer's market, the two states that now dominate the credit card market are South Dakota and Delaware—two states that are among the most liberal regarding credit card fee and interest rate regulations.[26] A further example of regulatory avoidance was the "last minute" international wire transfers by large money center banks in anticipation of President Jimmy Carter's freeze on Iranian assets. The growth of telecommunications networks and improvements in technology change, perhaps irrevocably, the balance of power between large multinational financial institutions and governments—both local and national—in favor of the private institutions.

Tax Avoidance. The development of international wire networks as well as international banking networks has enabled banks rapidly to shift funds and profits through "internal pricing" mechanisms to minimize their overall United States tax burden by maximizing their foreign tax credits. Prior to 1986, many large New York banks were paying almost no United States corporate taxes, despite large reported profits, by arbitrating across different tax regimes. This raised considerable public policy problems and was a major reason underlying the 1986 tax reforms. These reforms imposed a minimum corporate tax rate of 20 percent and limited the ability of American banks to use foreign tax credits to offset their domestic tax burden.

As a result, the ability of United States banks to avoid taxes has been significantly curtailed.

Conclusions

The influence of the new communications technologies on banking and finance has been profound. First, the effect on the payments system and the movement away from a paper-based transactional system to one based predominantly on electronic wire transfers has brought social benefits: lowering the cost of economic transactions, while raising the potential for significant social costs (and financial system failure) unless the problem of daylight overdrafts is satisfactorily addressed. Second, the effect on the competitive structure of the domestic financial sector has been to help erode traditional barriers among financial service firms, as well as between financial service firms and commercial firms. In addition, the mode of financial intermediation has changed with securitization and off-balance sheet activities inducing banks to act more like "brokers" than traditional asset transformers.

Third, these technologies have had serious effects on the international competitive position of United States banks. While new technologies have induced greater domestic service and product innovations, efficient delivery systems need to be in place overseas to be able to market these services. Such delivery systems are strongly communications dependent. Foreign banks coming to the United States usually have access to a more efficient, lower-cost communications technology for financial services delivery than do American banks abroad. The problems and costs that American banks and other financial firms confront in overseas communications systems present a potential economic barrier to entry that may more than offset any liberalization of regulatory barriers.

To further the market posture of United States banks and firms, policies limiting the risk of daylight overdraft on wire transfer systems should be uniform across such systems and be based on risk-exposure of each individual bank using fees rather than volume caps. Since wire transfer systems and other telecommunications systems are technology driven, telecommunication professionals should have a greater say in establishing optimal regulatory policies; they may have better insights into the technological causes of risks on these systems than financial and economic experts. More specifically, future GATT negotiations on the international trade in financial services should focus more on the role of telecommunications barriers as a restraint on free-trade than more traditional forms of explicit entry barriers such as restrictions on direct investment and branching.

Appendix: Compatibility Standards and Telecommunications Policy

Thomas G. Krattenmaker

It is commonplace to observe that telecommunications cannot take place without some coordination of technologies. Radio reception depends not only on proximate stations employing different frequencies but also on radio receivers that can tune to, and discriminate among, the same frequencies on which stations broadcast. Two people can converse over telephones only if both possess phones that can plug into a network interconnecting them. Compatibility standards underlie every telecommunications system and market.

How and when to establish standards for coordinating telecommunications equipment and methods, therefore, have always been central problems of telecommunications regulation. These problems have become both more urgent and more complex in the past decade, principally for four reasons.

First, technology—and, therefore, opportunities for uncoordinated, nonstandardized systems—has grown rapidly. The videocassette recorder, stereophonic AM radio and television, cellular radio telephones, high definition television, and broadcast satellites have all entered the U.S. telecommunications marketplace since 1970. Without some degree of standardized format and compatible technology, none of these goods could survive in that marketplace.

Second, policymakers have increasingly emphasized competition as a method for establishing prices for telecommunications services as well as the amount and types of those services offered. In a general way this development enhances the role of standardization, because the absence of standards can blunt the forces of competition by fragmenting markets and creating entry barriers. For example, should high definition television (HDTV) be offered by three firms, each employing different transmission systems and requiring different types of receiving sets, those firms are less likely to compete with each other for viewers on a daily basis. Further, their presence can serve as an entry barrier to a fourth firm employing yet another HDTV technology.

More specifically, the decision to end AT&T's monopolies over terminal, equipment, and long distance services has removed AT&T as the single American standards setter for attachments (including telephone devices and interconnection switches) to the still-monopolized local phone company exchanges. Consequently, regulators have been required to monitor the ways in which local telephone networks are designed to assure that competition and entry in these services remain free, as present policy goals dictate.

Third, telecommunications increasingly flow across geopolitical borders. Standards, and the procedures for implementing them, consequently have increasingly become international issues.

Broadcast satellites do not respect national boundaries. Firms want their computers in one country to be able to interface over telephone lines with their computers in other countries. Because different nation-states may wish to foster different industries (for example, Western Europe and Japan differ on the preferred system for transmitting HDTV signals) or because they may prefer different regulatory philosophies (most Western European countries are comfortable with a single, state-owned telephone service and so are unlikely to see the utility for international open architectured networks), conflict resolution over standards within a domestic economy may produce results wholly inadequate within the global telecommunications markets.

Fourth, theoretical and empirical research during the past decade has greatly increased our understanding of the nature of compatibility standards, the factors that bring them into being, and the conditions under which they are likely to prove efficient. Not surprisingly, this burst of intellectual energy has made the regulators' task more, not less, daunting and complex.

At this stage, then, two things are clear. First, a key to issues in any thoughtful appraisal of telecommunications policy is how, what, and when compatibility standards should exist. Second, that issue is both more urgent and more complex today than it appeared a decade ago because of technological growth, the increased reliance on competition as a disciplining force in U.S. telecommunications policy, the rapid internationalization of telecommunications markets, and our increased understanding of the economic factors that shape the development of compatibility standards.

This essay seeks to summarize some of those economic factors and to provide a checklist of issues that the informed, conscientious regulator should consider in determining the United States government's role in fashioning, furthering, or frustrating emerging compatibility standards. At this stage of our knowledge no more can be done. There is no rabbit in this hat. A priori analysis, at present, cannot predict confidently when unregulated market forces will produce efficient, timely compatibility standards or, conversely, when public control or oversight of standards, or the processes for establishing them, will improve the market's results.

Determinants of Voluntary and Efficient Compatibility Standards

We can identify four key determinants of whether and when voluntary action by firms is likely to produce an efficient compatibility standard. These determinants are: (1) the extent to which adoption of a standard enhances demand for a firm's service, (2) the extent to which a firm is committed to a particular standard, (3) the availability of information to a firm about the technology relevant to the standards and about the preferences of its rivals and customers, and (4) the extent to which all firms or countries will gain from increased demand, are bound by similar technology commitments, and have similar information about technology and preferences. For the sake of convenience, these determinants are illustrated in the context of a single compatibility issue: what standard to employ for HDTV transmission.

Will it enhance consumer demand? To a firm the principal advantage of an efficient compatibility standard is that it will enhance consumer demand for the service. A standard may produce this result by lowering costs (and hence prices, thus increasing sales), by making the service more valuable to those already employing it, or by making the service accessible to more consumers. Without a standard HDTV transmission system, consumers may value HDTV less because subscription gives access to only one firm's fare. Other consumers may lack access to the technology employed by the firm, or the firm may, accidentally or purposefully, employ a more expensive technology.

In such a case, adoption of a single, more efficient system can increase consumer demand for HDTV. The extent to which that demand will increase is a major factor in determining the value of a standard and, consequently the likelihood that it will be adopted.

Is the standard already preferred for extrinsic reasons? Where any one of several standards may have approximately equal value in enhancing demand, a firm is likely to prefer the standard to which it is most committed. A firm may be committed to one standard because it has invested heavily in that process, because the firm has a patent or other exclusive right to the process, or because adoption of the standard for one use may aid the firm in other endeavors. Thus, for example, a firm that owns a patent on hardware essential to a particular type of HDTV transmission process likely will prefer adoption of that process as a global standard.

Is information widely available? The role of information about the technology is fairly obvious. A firm must know that an HDTV transmission process is available and how it can enhance consumer demand before the firm is likely to advocate its use. Information about rival firms and customer preferences is also important. If these groups prefer a different standard, the firm is less likely to be able to advocate successfully its own first choice. If the firm is confused about these preferences, then it has less incentive to adopt a standard because it is less certain about its payoff.

Do firms (and countries) have similar views? The situation becomes more complex when we consider that several firms may confront the same issue or issues but with different expectations as to one standard's payoff, technology, or attractiveness to others or with different commitments to the technology.

Two extreme cases illustrate how differences or similarities among firms can affect the determination of a standard. As a first case, assume four firms are contemplating entry into HDTV transmission and must choose between two processes. If each knows that process A is clearly superior to process B (both in enhancing demand and reducing costs) and each knows that the others know this and none has an investment in or patent on either process, then each can be expected voluntarily to adopt process A, so long as the cost of implementing process A does not exceed the value of the enhanced demand it will generate. In this case, then, an unregulated marketplace should yield an efficient outcome.

Even in this fairly extreme case, regulatory intervention might be useful if either of two conditions is met. First, to each firm the cost of designing and implementing process A may exceed its expected share of the returns from enhanced demand. Government might reduce each firm's costs by, for example, providing certain design or testing facilities for all, thus spreading the costs over four firms. Second, if entry barriers into HDTV transmission exist, competition among the four firms might not be sufficiently robust to prevent one of them from seeking to differentiate its product by adopting process B. In such a case a mandatory uniform standard might be appropriate if it is quite clear that process A is substantially more efficient that process B.

At the opposite extreme assume a hundred firms are considering ten HDTV processes. Each may gain so little from a universal standard that none will bear the costs of searching through all of them and installing one. Further, each may fear that many of its rivals may evaluate the technology differently or may prefer a standard in which they have invested. If the firms are regulated in different countries, they may further fear that some firms will be constrained by regulation from making certain choices. In this case it is quite likely that no HDTV standard (and, hence, no HDTV market) will emerge even if, to an objective observer, it appears that one standard is superior to the others and that its implementation would stimulate demand substantially in excess of its costs.

Regulation might provide a preferable outcome in the second case. But regulators are mortal, too. Knowing they might choose an imperfect standard, regulators must choose among various strategies. These include: picking one compatibility standard; narrowing the field by rejecting some standards; facilitating information exchange (as by conducting comparative experiments on different processes); and negotiating with other regulators. The utility of each strategy will vary with the particular, detailed facts of the case.

Lessons for the Regulator/Legislator

We can derive two principal lessons concerning compatibility choices. First, the thoughtful, conscientious regulator cannot assume a priori that voluntary, unregulated markets will or will not compel firms universally to adopt efficient compatibility standards when these are available. Rather, markets sometimes will and sometimes will not generate such results.

Second, the principal determinants of when compatibility standards will voluntarily emerge—and, hence, the major question on which a regulator must be informed—are the degree to which adoption of the standard will enhance demand, the extent to which certain firms are already committed to certain standards, the adequacy and penetration of knowledge about the technology, industrial rivals and potential customers, and the nature of expectations among competitors, customers and regulators. Answers to these questions can help to determine whether regulation or legislation can facilitate the adoption of efficient compatibility standards and, if so, how that intervention might best be structured.

Conclusions

Compatibility standards have always been a key issue for telecommunications policy. They are now more central to a wise policy and more complex than ever before.

The appropriate role for the regulator or legislator in compatibility issues will vary from case to case. Sometimes the issue is best resolved in the marketplace; other times government should set the standard; in yet other cases regulators can usefully contribute by facilitating the process without dominating it—for example, by providing an information clearinghouse.

Our knowledge has not yet advanced to the stage where clearly correct answers to the appropriate role of regulation or legislations appear. The recording industry existed for years with discs available at 33, 45, and 78 RPM. The Federal Communications Commission is widely thought to have acted correctly when it overturned its previous decision to adopt a CBS technology for color television transmission and instead directed the industry to adopt the RCA techniques. In its Computer II decision, the FCC decided to settle for a role as an information facilitator: it required that telephone companies which owned subsidiaries that sold equipment must provide to independent suppliers the same technical network design information they gave to their subsidiaries. All that is certain is that, for the foreseeable future, compatibility standards issues will loom very large on the telecommunications regulation agenda and that informed analysis will follow the paths traced above.

Notes

||||||||||||||||||||||||||||||||||||||||||||||||||||||||||||||||||||||||||||||||||||||||||||||||||||||||||||||||||||||||||||||||||||||||||||||||||||||||||||||||||

Data Wars

1 United States House of Representatives, *The Computer and Invasion of Privacy*, Hearings before the Special Subcommittee on Invasion of Privacy of the Committee on Government Operations, House of Representatives, 89th Cong., 2nd Sess. (Washington, D.C.: Government Printing Office [GPO], 1966), 6.

2 See David Flaherty, *Privacy and Government Data Banks* (London: Mansell, 1979).

3 Pub. Law 91-508, Sec. 604(e).

4 United States Department of Health, Education and Welfare, Secretary's Advisory Committee on Automated Personal Data Systems, *Records, Computers and Rights of Citizens* (Washington, D.C.: GPO, 1973).

5 Priscilla Regan, "From Paper Dossiers to Electronic Dossiers: Gaps in the Privacy Act of 1974," *Office: Technology and People* 3 (1988): 279–296.

6 James Rule, Douglas McAdam, Linda Stearns, and David Uglow, *The Politics of Privacy* (New York: Elsevier, 1980), 97.

7 Privacy Protection Study Commission, *Personal Privacy in an Information Society* (Washington, D.C.: GPO, 1977), 14–15.

8 Ibid., 107

9 See Janlori Goldman, testimony on behalf of the American Civil Liberties Union on S. 496, the Computer Matching and Privacy Protection Act of 1987, before the Subcommittee on Government Information, Justice and Agriculture, House Government Operations Committee, 23 June 1987.

10 Regan, "Paper Dossiers to Electronic Dossiers," 288.

11 Rule et al., *The Politics of Privacy*, 143.

12 Privacy Protection Study Commission, *Personal Privacy*, 362–391.

13 United States Courts, Administrative Office, *Report of the Director on Applications for Delay of Notice and Customer Challenges under Provisions of the Right to Financial Privacy Act of 1978* (1986), 2.

14 Steve Connor, "The Invisible Border Guard," *New Scientist* (5 January 1984): 13.

The Right to Know

1 In this essay *public information* is defined as federal government information which is either disseminated by federal agencies or which must
be disclosed under the laws of the United States. Thus, it does not include government created or collected information which is exempt from
disclosure under the Freedom of Information Act, such as classifed national security information or personally identifiable information which
would violate individual privacy. Citizen access to electronic public information under state law is beyond the scope of this essay. Throughout
this essay public access to electronic public information should be understood to broadly include access to public information available through
online databases, tape, floppy diskette, CD-ROM, or other electronic storage
mediums.

2 U.S. Congress, Office of Technology Assessment, *Federal Government Information Technology: Management, Security, and Congressional Oversight* (Washington, D.C.: GPO, 1986), 28.

3 Information USA, *The Federal Database Finder: A Directory of Free and
Fee-Based Databases & Files Available from the Federal Government*, 2nd.
ed. (Maryland: Information USA, 1987), 1; OTA, *Federal Government Information Technology*, 143–146.

4 Information USA, *The Federal Database Finder*, 1–3. In fiscal year 1985
there were 1,022 agreements by federal agencies for use of sixteen major
commercial on-line retrieval systems. The most used services were Dialog, BRS, Lexis/Nexis, Orbit, and Westlaw. Alan F. Westin, *Reference Point
Prospectus* (unpublished September 1987).

5 U.S. Congress, House, Committee on Government Operations, *Electronic
Collection and Dissemination of Information By Federal Agencies: A Policy Overview*, Report. no. 99-560, 99th Cong., 2nd sess., 1986 (Washington, D.C.: GPO, 1986).

6 OTA, *Federal Government Information Technology*, 142–143.

7 U.S. Congress, *Electronic Collection and Dissemination*, 47–52.

8 Congress passed legislation to authorize EDGAR and establish system requirements and reporting procedures. Public Law 100-181, Sec. 101 (1987)
(adding Sec. 35A to the Security and Exchange Act of 1934). See U.S.
Congress, House, Committee on Energy and Commerce, *Securities and
Exchange Commission Authorization Act of 1987*, House Rep. 100-296,
100th Cong., 1st Sess. (Washington, D.C.: GPO, 1987).

9 See the floor statement of Rep. Glenn English, chairman of the House
Subcommittee on Information of the House Government Operations Committee during debate on H.R. 2600, 133 *Congressional Record*, H7415 (10
September 1987) (daily ed.).

10 United States Securities and Exchange Commission, SEC *Request for Proposals For an Operational Edgar System*, Solicitation no. SEC HQ1-86-
R-0637 (Washington, D.C.: SEC, 7 May 1986) C-110-C-112.

11 U.S. Congress, *House Report on Electronic Collection and Dissemina*

tion, 62.

12 Peter Hernon and Charles R. McClure, *Federal Information Policies in the 1980s: Conflicts and Issues* (New Jersey: Ablex Publishing, 1987), 179–183.

13 U.S. Congress, *House Report on Electronic Collection and Dissemination*, 13–15, 62–64. Information USA, *The Federal Database Finder*, passim.

14 OTA, *Federal Government Information Technology*, 152–153; the average cost of government information databases provided through DIALOG by the private sector is $93.26 while databases provided directly to DIALOG by the collecting agencies costs $45.70 per connect hour. Statement of Dr. Harold B. Shill, chair Legislation Assembly American Library Association, *Hearings on Federal Information Policy* before the Subcommittee on Science, Research, and Technology of the House Committee on Science, Space, and Technology, 14 July 1987.

15 Support for the "public's right to know" is a widely shared principal. In reality access rights have not been won easily. The Freedom of Information Act was passed in 1966 but was undermined by agency interpretations. The 1974 Amendments required an override of a veto by President Gerald Ford to enact into law. The Reagan administration has devoted considerable time and effort to scale back citizen access rights under the FOIA. Peter Hernon and Charles R. McClure, *Federal Information Policies*, 52–66; Allan Adler, ed., *Litigation under the Federal Freedom of Information Act and Privacy Act*, 13th ed. (American Civil Liberties Union Foundation, 1988), 4–6; Eve Pell, *The Big Chill* (Boston: Beacon Press, 1984), 45–58.

16 5 U.S.C. Sec. 552 (1982). The act was partly amended in 1986 as part of the Anti-Drug Abuse Act of 1986. Freedom of Information Act of 1986, Pub. L. no. 99-570, Title I, Subtitle N, Sec. 1801–1804, U.S. Code Cong. & Ad. News (100 stat.) (amending 5 U.S.C. Sec. 552); Senate Report no. 93-854, 93rd Cong., 2nd Sess. 12 (1974).

17 44 U.S.C. Sections 3501–3520 (Supp. 1986); 44 U.S.C. Sec. 3501 (Supp. 1986).

18 Ibid.

19 44 U.S.C. Sec. 3504 (Supp. 1986); Office of Management and Budget, *Management of Federal Information Resources: Circular No. A-130*, 50 *Federal Register* 52730–52738 (24 December 1985).

20 OMB, *Circular A-130*, 52736. Circular A-130 has been used by the Reagan administration to justify severe cutbacks in the availability of public information. See Donna Demac, "Keeping the Citizens Uninformed," in *Government Information: An Endangered Resource of the Electronic Age* (Special Libraries Association, 1986), 25–41; John Shattuck and Muriel Morisey, "The Dangers of Information Control," *Technology Review* (April 1986): 70–72; OMB Watch, *Paperwork Reduction: The Quick Fix of 1986* (OMB Watch, November 1986); American Library Association, *Less Access to Less Information by and about the U.S. Government: A 1981–1987*

Chronology (ALA 1988). Thus, one is tempted to argue that its restrictive policies on electronic data dissemination are cut from the same cloth. Unfortunately, here the administration is simply carrying out the dictates of current law. Citizens have not demanded nor won rights of access to electronic data.

21 OMB, *Circular A-130*, Sec. 6(f), 52735 and Sec. 7(g), 52736.

22 See Yeager v. Drug Enforcement Administration, 678 F.2d 315 (D.C. Cir. 1982); SDC Development Corp. v. Mathews, 542 F.2d 1116 (9th Cir. 1976); Dismukes v. Interior, 603 F. Supp. 760 (D.D.C. 1984).

23 42 U.S.C. 11023 (j) (Supp. 1988).

24 OMB, *Circular A-130*, 52547 (Appendix IV).

25 Ibid., 52736.

26 Peter Hernon and Charles R. McClure, *Federal Information Policies*, 164–194; American Library Association, *Less to Less Information by and about the U.S. Government: A 1981–1987 Chronology* (ALA Washington Office, February 1988), passim.

27 OMB, *Circular A-130*, 52748.

28 Ibid.

29 Ibid., 52748. (emp. sup.)

30 5 U.S.C. 552 (b) sets out nine exemptions for matters such as classified national security information, trade secrets, and personal information which would violate personal privacy. If the government contends and the courts agree that information sought under the FOIA is within one of these exemptions, the information is not disclosed. See Allan Adler, ed., *Litigation under the Freedom of Information Act*, passim.

31 New communications and computer technologies were so identified in a seminal book on the need to rationalize the new technologies with First Amendment values. Ithiel de Sola Pool, *Technologies of Freedom* (Massachusetts: Belknap Press, 1983). See also Alan F. Westin, "The Technology of Secrecy," in *None of Your Business*, ed. Steven Gillers and Norman Dorsen (New York: Viking Press, 1974).

32 Westin, "The Technology of Secrecy," 305.

33 Ibid., 311.

34 Ibid., 312.

35 Ibid., 312.

36 Ibid., 317.

37 Ibid., 319–320.

38 See also Alan F. Westin, "Computers and the Public's Right to Know," in *Advances in Computers Volume, 17* (New York: Academic Press, 1978).

39 Plaintiffs' Memorandum in Opposition to Defendant's Renewed Motion to Dismiss and Motion for a Protective Order and in Support of Plaintiffs' Motion for Partial Summary Judgment, Public Citizen et al. v. Occupational Safety and Health Administration (Civil Action no. 86-0705, U.S.D.C. District of Columbia), 2 February 1988.

40 Public Citizen cites proposed Department of Labor regulations, 29 C.F.R. Sec. 70.5 which state that "Nothing in [the FOIA] requires any agency or

component to create a new record, either manually from preexisting files or through creation of a computer program, in order to fill a request for records." Ibid., 3, 9, 16.

41 Ibid., 24. Unfortunately, this is not likely to be resolved by the courts since OSHA, under the pressure of litigation, has now discovered that the data can be accessed without reprogramming.

42 *National Security Archive Request under the Freedom of Information Act to John E. Carter Chief of FOI and Privacy Acts Office of Administrative Services United States Department of Energy* (24 September 1987); letter from Bonnie C. Carroll, deputy assistant manager for Information Services Department of Energy, to Quinlan Shea, Jr., National Security Archive (22 October 1987).

43 *Decision and Order of the Department of Energy Appeal by Petitioner National Security Archive* (Case no. KFA-0158) (18 December 1987). The Department of Energy asked the Office of Hearings and Appeals to reconsider its decision to require reprogramming on the grounds of cost and time. *Memorandum To George B. Breznay Director Office of Hearing and Appeals Regarding Freedom of Information Act Appeal Filed by the National Security Archive* (Case no. KFA-0146. 19 January 1988). The office reaffirmed its decision. *Decision and Order of the Department of Energy Motion for Clarification* (Case Number KFA-0158, 26 May 1988).

44 Letter from David Burnham to Donald K. Ross, director, Rockefeller Family Fund (29 July 1987).

45 Even though computerized information has no copyright, citizens have been denied requests for the electronic version of public data. SDC Corporation v. Mathews, 542 F.2d 1116 (9th Cir. 1976) (electronic tapes containing database of biomedical literature are not agency records for FOIA purposes and are not available pursuant to an FOIA request). See also Clark v. United States Department of the Treasury and W. M. Gregg (Civil Action no. 84-1873, U.S.D.C. Eastern D. Penn., 1986) (denial of computer data on treasury bonds even though plaintiff prepared to pay programming costs to extract data); letter from Rep. Glen English to Honorable C. William Verity, secretary of commerce (19 February 1988) (requesting explanation why citizen was denied a copy of an on-line database available free from the government); *Appeal to Administrator Animal and Plant Health Inspection Service by Public Citizen on behalf of Hillel Grey* (15 June 1988) (FOIA appeal based on agency refusal to provide revised computer tapes similar to those which plaintiff had previously obtained from USDA because USDA had now decided these were not agency records under FOIA or would place an unreasonable burden on the agency to produce them in computerized rather than published form).

46 See, for example, Long v. IRS, 596 F.2d 362 (9th Cir. 1979), cert. denied, 446 U.S. 917 (1980).

47 Letter from David Burnham to Donald K. Ross, director, Rockefeller Family Fund (29 July 1987).

48 Long v. IRS, 825 F.2d 225 (9th Cir. 1987).

49 Jerry J. Berman, "National Security vs. Access to Computer Databases: A New Threat to Freedom of Information," *Software Law Journal* (Winter 1987).

50 Statement of Donald Latham, assistant secretary of defense, *Computer Security Policy: Hearings on NSDD 145 before the Subcomm. on Transportation, Aviation and Materials of the House Comm. on Science and Technology*, 99th Cong. lst Sess. (1985).

51 Michael Schrage, "U.S. Seeking to Limit Access of Soviets to Computer Data," *Washington Post*, 27 May 1986, p. A18, col. 3.

52 National Telecommunications and Information Security Policy no. 2, *National Policy on Protection of Sensitive but Unclassified Information in Federal Government Telecommunications and Automated Information Systems* (29 October 1986).

53 Berman, *National Security vs. Access to Computer Databases*, 9.

54 Public Law 100-235 (1988) (The Computer Security Act of 1987).

55 U.S. House, *Report On Electronic Collection and Dissemination*, 27–36.

56 Berman, *National Security vs. Access to Computer Databases*, 11; U.S. House, *Report On Electronic Collection and Dissemination*, 27–36.

57 For example, by one estimate only 1 percent of all voluntary organizations were users of on-line information services in 1985. Alan F. Westin, *Reference Point Prospectus* (unpublished, September 1987), 27.

58 Public Law 99-499 (1986).

59 42 U.S.C. Sections 1101–11050 (Supp.1988).

60 Environmental Protection Agency, "EPA Announces New Toxic Chemical Reporting Requirements," *Press Release* (8 February 1988)

61 42 U.S.C. 110239(j) (Supp. 1988).

62 U.S. Congress, House, *Conference Report Superfund Amendments and Reauthorization Act of 1986*, 99th Cong. 2nd Sess., Rept. 99-962 (3 October 1986), 299.

63 "The Revolution Ahead: Public Information on Toxic Emissions—CMSA talks with EPA's Charles Elkins," *Chemical Times and Trends* (January 1988): 18, 22.

64 Ibid., 22–23.

65 Under the FOIA, 5 U.S.C. 552(a)(6)(A)(i), agencies must reply within ten working days, but some agencies take longer and others have significant backlogs. Allan Adler, *Litigation under the Federal Freedom of Information Act*, 12–13; Charles Elkins, "Risk Communication: Getting Ready for 'Right to Know' *EPA Journal* (November 1987). Elkins gives this example to demonstrate some concerns that the data could cause public alarm and be misleading because the chemical releases in the example may not be unreasonable or cause harm since there is no necessary direct correlation between emission levels and exposure levels. Nevertheless, it is a nice illustration of electronic information and computer analyses.

66 Chemical firms are planning just such use of EPA toxic release data. "Pollution: Trying to Put the Best Face on Bad News: Manufacturers Struggle to Cope with a New Disclosure Law," *Business Week* (18 July

1988): 76–77.

67 Environmental Protection Agency, *Overview of Requirements for the Toxic Chemical Release Inventory (TRI)* (prepared by CRS Systems, 6 November 1987); Environmental Protection Agency, *Public Report for Options to Make the Toxic Release Inventory (TRI) Data Base Accessible to the Public* (prepared by CRS Systems, 4 March 1988); 53 *Federal Register* 7567 (9 March 1988) announcing public hearing on TRI. Database public report on 30 March 1988 at EPA.

68 U.S. House, *Report On Electronic Collection and Dissemination*, 18–23.

69 Ibid. See also Robert Gellman, "Federal Information Practices," in Special Libraries Association, *Government Information: An Endangered Resource of the Electronic Age* (Special Libraries Association 1986), 22. "You have to be aggressive in guarding your own interest. You should insist on getting involved in the planning. You have to identify your own needs and how these new electronic systems will affect your operations." Founding organizations of the Working Group include the Advocacy Institute, Citizens Clearinghouse for Hazardous Wastes, Environmental Policy Institute, National Center for Policy Alternatives, National Wildlife Federation, OMB Watch, Public Citizen, and U.S. Public Interest Research Group. The Environmental Defense Fund, Natural Resources Defense Council, and Environmental Action Foundation have also joined.

70 The technical assistance arrangement was worked out with the Public Interest Computer Association and the ACLU Project on Information Technology. See letter from Carol Dansereau, Environmental Action Foundation, to Jerry Berman, ACLU and Denise Vesuvio, PICA, On Behalf of the Community Right-to-Know Working Group, 22 April 1988.

71 Environmental Protection Agency, *Public Report For Options to Make the Toxic Release Inventory (TRI) Data Base Accessible to the Public* (prepared by CRS Systems, 4 March 1988).

72 Ibid., Executive Summary, 2.

73 Ibid., Executive Summary, 4.

74 Ibid., Executive Summary, 4–5.

75 Environmental Protection Agency, EPA/NLM *Interagency Agreement: Toxic Release Inventory Public Database* (Draft 2, 20 June 1988).

76 EPA, *Draft EPA/NLM Interagency Agreement*, 10.

77 EPA, *Public Report*, Exhibit 3-2, chapters 3, 7.

78 The EPA rationale for choosing Tier A may indeed prove more costly. While at one point the *Public Report* makes the assumption that user demand is a function of "price," at other points the *Public Report* suggests that user demand will increase if it is more user-friendly. For example, in weighing fee waiver costs to the government, the Public Report states that those costs will "increase by tier, because usage is expected to increase with improved capabilities." Ibid., chapters 2, 4. In fact, in estimating costs, the EPA did not take into consideration "usage increases which may result as the result of an expanded user community." Ibid., chapters 2, 6. It is therefore possible that by implementing a user-friendly system, system

costs to the government could decrease.

79 42 U.S.C. Section 11023 states that the database must be "accessible by computer telecommunications . . . to any person on a cost reimbursable basis." "Any person" must mean that Congress had some kind of user-friendly system in mind. Certainly Congress knows that most citizens cannot use basic computer data and search and retrieval software or statistical software to sort and index data. Nor is it reasonable to assume that Congress added the database requirement so that citizens could "dial up" and access only reports prepared by EPA. The statute states that the database must be accessible by "any person" and not "any person who is a sophisticated computer user." EPA's interpretation of basic requirement of the law appears contrary to congressional intent.

80 Charles Elkins, "Risk Communication: Getting Ready for 'Right to Know,' " EPA *Journal* (November 1987).

81 See Public Interest Computer Association and American Civil Liberties Union, *Initial Outline Toxic Release Inventory Database Interagency Agreement* (Washington, D.C.: Public Interest Computer Association, 26 April 1988). The document identifies the range of issues that must be resolved and specified in the interagency agreement between EPA and NLM. EPA and NLM have both expressed the view that this document of system requirements is an excellent basis for serious negotiations. The Environmental Working Group and Chemical Manufacturers have also concurred in this judgement; see also Environmental Protection Agency, *Public Online Access to TRI Data: Discussion of Fee Waiver Criteria* (prepared by Putnam, Hayes & Bartlett, Washington, D.C.) 3 March 1988.

82 According to one study, revenues for on-line data bases amounted to $3.65 billion in 1984 and recent estimates indicate that revenues are growing at an annual rate of 15 percent. See Berman, *National Security vs. Access to Computer Databases*, note 1, p. 1; OTA, *Federal Government Information Technology*, 142.

83 U.S. Congress, *House Report on Electronic Collection and Dissemination*, passim.

84 EPA, *Public Report*, chapters 2, 4, 5.

85 Ibid., chapters 3, 8–11.

86 EPA, *Public Report*, chapters 3, 19.

87 Ibid., chapters 3, 22.

88 Ibid., chapters 4, 6.

89 Ibid., chapters 3, 11, and Executive Summary, 3.

90 Mary Gardner Jones and Nancy Chasen, *The Potential of Telecommunications for Nonprofit Organizations* (Washington, D.C.: Consumer Interest Research Institute, 1987). On May 11 the Public Interest Computer Association sponsored a meeting of TCN, BITNET, PEACENET, and other nonprofit on-line providers to discuss how to increase service to the nonprofit community. *Memorandum to Participants of the Online Providers Meeting from Denise A. Vesuvio, Director, Public Interest Computer Association* (Washington, D.C.: PICA, 11 May 1988).

91 Reference Point proposes to establish an on-line electronic clearinghouse for nonprofit organizations which would provide electronic directories of members; store and disseminate member documents, reports, and alerts; and provide "gateways" to on-line government and commercial databases. It is in the developmental stages. See Alan F. Westin, *Reference Point: A National Computerized Database, Communications Network, and Historical Archive for the Non Profit Sector and the Active Citizenry* (Prof. Alan F. Westin, 1100 Trafalgar St., Teaneck, N.J., 07666).

92 See Opinion, United States of America v. Western Electric et al., Civil Action no.82-0192, slip op. (D.D.C. 7 March 1988).

93 See Frances Seghers, "The $3 Billion Question: Whose Info Is It, Anyway?" *Business Week* (4 July 1988): 106–107.

94 U.S. Congress, House, Hearings before a Subcommittee of the Committee on Government Operations, *Electronic Collection and Dissemination of Information by Federal Agencies*, 99th Cong. 1st Sess., 29 April, 26 June and 18 October 1985 (Washington, D.C.: GPO, 1986).

95 5 U.S.C. Secs. 552a(1) and (2), (1982).

96 See Association of Research Libraries, *Technology and U.S. Government Information Policies: Catalysts for New Partnerships* (ARL, October 1987). The Joint Committee on Printing is circulating a new plan for electronic pilot projects for public comment. See letter from Rep. Frank Annunzio, chairman, and Wendell H. Ford, vice chairman, to Members of the Information Community (July 13, 1988) (attaching *Dissemination of Information in Electronic Format to Federal Depository Libraries: Proposed Project Descriptions June 1988*). The private sector must understand the need to provide electronic databases and products through libraries, and the library community has to understand the issues posed by electronic pilots. Since access to electronic information is often the same as disseminating information, a line needs to be drawn to protect electronic publishers from having the libraries become tax-supported publishers of information. While government documents are public and may be copied on a copy machine, this is not the equivalent of electronic "downloading" of data. For example, would a library which has created a database of government documents with an intricate menu system take kindly to a "borrower" asking, not to search the system, but obtain a "copy" of the database so that he or she can mount it on a computer and dispense the information free of charge to anyone who dials up the bulletin board?

97 Statement of Glenn English, *Congressional Record* (10 September 1987), H7415.

Copyright Law and Policy

1 U. S. Constitution, Art. I, Sec. 8, cl. 8.

2 *The Federalist*, no. 43, at 267 (New York: H. Lodge, 1888).

3 Twentieth Century Music Corp. v. Aiken, 422 U.S. 151, 156 (1975).

4 For the argument that mechanisms other than property rights can enable producers to successfully appropriate the value of their works, see S. Breyer, "The Uneasy Case for Copyright," *Harvard Law Review* 84 (1970): 281. See also B. Tyerman, "The Economic Rationale for Copyright Protection for Published Books: A Reply to Professor Breyer," *U.C.L.A. Law Review* 18 (1971): 1100.

5 See generally K. Arrow, "Economic Welfare and the Allocation of Resources for Inventions," in *The Rate and Direction of Inventive Activity*, National Bureau of Economic Research (1960).

6 R. Cooter and T. Ulen, *Law and Economics* 135 (1988).

7 See E. Mansfield, "Size of Firm, Market Structure, and Innovation," *Journal of Political Economy* 71 (1963): 556; J. Markham, "Market Structure, Business Conduct and Innovation," *American Economic Review* 55 (1965): 323.

8 Act of 12 December 1980, Public Law no. 96-517, Secs. 10, 94 Stat. 3015, 3028 (codified at 17 U.S.C. 101, 117 [1982]); National Commission on New Technological Uses of Copyrighted Works, *Final Report* (1978).

9 Public Law no. 98-620, 98 Stat. 3335, 3347–3356 (1984) (to be codified at 17 U.S.C. 901–914).

10 See G. Cary, "Copyright Registration and Computer Programs," *Bulletin of the Copyright Society of the U.S.A.* 11 (1964): 362.

11 See Bleistein v. Donaldson Lithographing Co., 188 U.S. 239, 251 (1903).

12 See, for example, Reiss v. National Quotation Bureau, 276 F. 717 (S.D.N.Y. 1921); Eckes v. Card Prices Update, 736 F.2d 859 (2d Cir. 1984); Apple Computer v. Franklin Computer Corp., 714 F. 2d 1240 (3rd Cir. 1983), cert. dismissed, 464 U.S. 1033 (1984).

13 See generally P. Goldstein, "Infringement of Copyright in Computer Programs," *Univeristy of Pittsburgh Law Review* 47 (1986): 1119.

14 See Whelan Associates v. Jaslow Dental Laboratory, 797 F. 2d 1222 (3rd Cir. 1986), cert. denied, 107 S. Ct. 877 (1987).

15 See generally Paul Goldstein, "Infringement of Copyright in Computer Programs," *University of Pittsburgh Law Review* 47 (1986): 1122–1123.

16 H.R. Rep. no. 781, 98th Cong., 2nd Sess. (1984), 22.

17 Ibid., 3.

18 Ibid., 8.

19 National Commission on New Technological Uses of Copyrighted Works, *Final Report* (1978).

20 17 U.S.C. Secs. 106–118.

21 Cable Television Report and Order, *Federal Register* 37 (1972), 3252–3277.

22 17 U.S.C. 111(c)(1).

23 Report and Order in Docket no. 20487, 57 F.C.C. 2d 625 (1975).

24 Ibid.

25 Century Communications Corp. v. Federal Communications Commission, 835 F.2d 292 (D.C. Cir. 1987); Quincy Cable TV v. Federal Communications Commission, 768 F.2d 1434 (D.C. Cir. 1985), cert. denied, 476 U.S. 1169 (1986).

26 United States v. ASCAP, 1950–1951 Trade Cas. (C.C.H.) Paragraph 62,595, pt. IX.

27 See Buffalo Broadcasting Co. v. American Society of Composers, Authors, and Publishers, 744 F.2d 917 (2d Cir. 1984), cert. denied, 469 U.S. 1211 (1985).

28 Senate Committee on the Judiciary, Report on the Berne Convention Implementation Act of 1988, 100th Cong. 2d Sess. (1988); House Committee on the Judiciary, Report on the Berne Convention Implementation Act of 1988, 100th Cong. 2d Sess. (1988).

29 See House Committee on the Judiciary, Report on the Berne Convention Implementation Act of 1988, 100th Cong., 2d Sess. 10 (1988).

30 See, for example, California Civil Code Sec. 987 (West 1986); *Louisiana Revised Statutes Annotated* Secs. 2151–2156 (West 1987); N.Y. Arts and Cultural Affairs Law, Sec. 14.03 (McKinney 1986).

31 17 U.S.C. 109 (1982).

32 Sony Corp. of America v. Universal City Studios, 464 U.S. 417 (1984).

33 See Fortnightly Corp. v. United Artists Television, 392 U.S. 390 (1968); Teleprompter Corp. v. Columbia Broadcasting System, 415 U.S. 394 (1974).

34 See Williams & Wilkins Co. v. United States, 487 F.2d 1345 (Ct. Cl. 1973) aff'd by an equally divided court, 420 U.S. 376 (1975) (per curiam) (photocopying); Sony Corp. of America v. Universal City Studios, 464 U.S. 417 (1984) (videotaping).

35 National Commission on New Technological Uses of Copyrighted Works, *Final Report* (1978); U.S. Congress, Office of Technology Assessment, *Intellectual Property Rights in an Age of Electronics and Information* (1986).

Civil Remote Sensing

1 More generally, "remote sensing" refers to the gathering of information about an object without being in physical contact with the sensed object. Aerial photography, for example, is one form of remote sensing. In this paper, however, the term is reserved for the gathering of information by orbiting satellites.

2 A brochure entitled "Surveillance" is now being distributed by the French headquarters of SPOT image. The prospectus offers the services of the satellites for gathering information about the location and use of targets deep within the territory of other nations. It also shows how SPOT images can be used to construct accurate maps and digital terrain models to assist the customer in avoiding the antiaircraft missiles defending the targets selected for action.

3 Walter A. McDougall, *The Heavens and the Earth* (New York: Basic Books, 1985), 221.

4 The Delta booster, workhorse of the U.S. satellite program right up to the present, is a direct descendent of the Thor missiles first launched in the late 1950s. The Delta 180 and Delta 181 missions flown by the Strategic Defense Initiative program were carried into space by Deltas equipped

with solid-propellant strap-on rockets.

5 McDougall, 224.

6 Ted Greenwood, "Reconnaissance and Arms Control," *Scientific American* (February 1973). Reprinted in *Arms Control: Readings from Scientific American* (San Francisco: W.H. Freeman, 1973), 223.

7 The Morison pictures have been reprinted in many places. Perhaps the most generally accessible copies are in William E. Burrows, *Deep Black: Space Espionage and National Security* (New York: Random House, 1986), 166–67 and 330. As of this writing (May 1988), Morison is free pending the outcome of his appeal of his espionage conviction.

8 The U.S.-Soviet "duopoly" on military satellite imagery may have ended on 9 September 1982 when, according to Burrows (ibid., 274), the Chinese launched their first reconnaissance satellite.

9 The figure of merit normally used for remote sensing satellites is, technically speaking, not strictly the resolution of the pictures but rather the instantaneous field of view (IFOV) on the ground of the smallest element of the sensing instrument. Because most modern satellites use digital electronic cameras, this is equivalent to one picture element (or "pixel"), the smallest area which is individually reproduced. High resolution images on television are often decomposed into pixels for graphic effect, as when a picture of Abraham Lincoln dissolves into an array of squares in which, barely, the face of the president is recognizable.

10 David Julyan, executive vice president, SICORP, interview with author, 6 May 1988.

11 Telex messages from Dr. V. Piskulin, director general of Soyuzkarta to the author. The Carnegie Endowment's Project on Commercial Observation Satellites has now purchased two images from Soyuzkarta. One is of the United States; the other is of the Federal Republic of Germany. There was some question among knowledgeable observers in the United States and Sweden as to whether Soyuzkarta would sell so-called third-country imagery. We believe that they will, so long as the third country is not a member of the Socialist bloc. Both images are of high quality; the one of Germany is clearly better than could have been obtained using the SPOT panchromatic sensor.

12 This restrictive policy was, apparently, part of President Carter's classified space policy. Although Carter and Reagan administration officials have privately confirmed the existence of this prohibition to the author, no public statement has confirmed its existence.

13 The Land Remote Sensing Commercialization Act of 1985, Public Law 99-62 (HR 2800) signed by President Reagan on 11 July 1985.

14 Public Law 99-177, signed by President Reagan on 12 December 1985 and colloquially known as the Gramm-Rudman-Hollings legislation.

15 "Landsat Commercialization Stumbles Again," *Science* 235 (9 January 1987): 155.

16 Briefing given by KRS executives to the Carnegie Endowment project on commercial observation satellites, February 1988.

17 See the author's article, "Photos From Space: Why Restrictions Won't Work," *Technology Review* (May/June 1988): 47; the Office of Technology Assessment's 1987 report *Newsgathering from Space*; and Peter Glaser and Mark Brender, "The First Amendment in Space," *Issues in Science and Technology* (Summer 1986).

18 Ibid.

19 Based on discussions with marketing officials of EOSAT, September–November 1988.

20 David Julyan, speech given at National Military Intelligence Association Meeting on Multi-Spectral Sensing, White Oak, Md, August 1987, and private communications since then.

21 According to M. Courtois and G. Weill: "These follow-on satellites may include significant capability upgrades, enhanced application capabilities (spectral bands), and increased cost effectiveness." "The SPOT Satellite System," *Monitoring Earth's Ocean, Land and Atmosphere from Space — Sensors, Systems and Applications*, ed. A. Schnapf, vol. 97, *Progress in Astronautics and Aeronautics* (New York: American Institute of Aeronautics and Astronautics, 1985).

22 Private communication.

23 SPOT image of Kharg Island acquired 21 March 1986 showing damaged oil storage tanks and leaking tanker.

24 Study done by Dr. Richard Fleeter of Defense Systems Inc. and briefing papers based thereon given to the author by Dr. Fleeter. Dr. Fleeter has several years of experience designing and building lightweight, low-cost satellites.

25 The author believes that the Soviet images at 5–6 meter resolution are not available in either a practical or a timely way. Because the pictures are taken on photographic film and then physically returned to earth, each frame represents the expenditure of a scarce resource. As yet there is no indication that the Soviets will acquire individual images at the request of a customer.

26 Dow Chemical Co. v. United States, 476 U.S. 227 (1936).

27 Ibid., 238.

28 Several treaties are referred to by their colloquial names in this paper. Those agreements are: "Treaty Between the United States of America and the Union of Soviet Socialist Republics on the Limitation of the Anti-Ballistic Missile Systems," signed 26 May 1972 ("ABM Treaty"); "Interim Agreement Between the United States of America and the Union of Soviet Socialist Republics on Certain Measures with Respect to the Limitation of Strategic Offensive Arms," signed 26 May 1972 (called "SALT I" or "the Interim Agreement"); Treaty Between the United States of America and the Union of Soviet Socialist Republics on the Limitation of Strategic Offensive Arms" signed 18 June 1979 ("SALT II"); and the "Treaty Between the United States of America and the Union of Soviet Socialist Republics on the Elimination of Their Intermediate-Range and Shorter-Range Missiles" signed 8 December 1987 ("INF Treaty"). Full texts of these

agreements are available from the United States Arms Control and Disarmament Agency.

29 Burrows, 166–67 and 330. Photographs leaked by S. L. Morison to *Janes' Defence Weekly*.

30 Bhupendra Jasani and Christer Larsson, "Remote Sensing, Arms Control and Crisis Observation," *International Journal of Imaging and Remote Sensing* 1, no. 1 (1987): 31–41.

31 Final Document of the Stockholm Conference on Confidence and Security-Building Measures and Disarmament in Europe, signed 19 September 1986.

32 See the SPOT image of the Nikolaev Shipyard published in the 1988 edition of *Soviet Military Power* and see as well Thomas Ries and Johnny Skorve, *Investigating Kola: A study of Military Bases Using Satellite Photography* (London: Brassey's Defence Publishers, 1987). The book by Ries and Skorve demonstrates the utility of even LANDSAT pictures in locating, measuring, and identifying military installations and naval vessels. It is a classic.

33 Provided to the author by Space Media Network.

34 U.S. Department of Defense, *Soviet Military Power: An Assessment of the Threat* (Washington, D.C.: Department of Defense, 1988).

35 Based on conversations held in November 1987 with officials of SPOT, Space Media Network, and the Swedish Foreign Ministry.

36 Robert F. Kennedy, *Thirteen Days: A Memoir of the Cuban Missile Crisis* (New York: Signet Books, 1969), 30.

37 Maj. Gen. Jack Thomas (USAF, Ret), former head of Air Force Intelligence spoke on remote sensing and national security at the March 1988 meeting of the American Physical Society in New Orleans, La. In his talk General Thomas suggested that it was time to return to an era in which responsible journalists did not publish what their government found objectionable.

38 This story was broadcast by ABC on its evening news program, 2 April 1987. The picture was printed by *Defense News* in its 6 April 1987 edition, p. 1.

New Communications Technologies and Services

1 Topics explicitly not covered in this paper include: (1) technology or industrial policy issues (e.g., should R&D tax credits be extended?), (2) international trade policy issues, and (3) military developments or military applications of communications technology, except as they affect civilian policies.

2 For a good discussion of both "hard" and "soft" technologies and their network implications, see Richard Vickers and Toomas Vilmansen, "The Evolution of Telecommunications Technology," *IEEE Communications Magazine* 25, no. 7 (July 1987) 6–18.

3 I. E. Sutherland, C. A. Mead, and T. E. Everhart, *Basic Limitations in Microcircuit Technology* (Santa Monica: Rand Corporation, R-1956-

ARPA, November 1976).

4 Kenneth J. Macleish, "Mapping the Integration of Artificial Intelligence into Telecommunications," *IEEE Journal on Selected Areas in Communications* 6, no. 5 (June 1988): 892–898.

5 The technical literature on ISDN is already enormous and growing rapidly. For introductory technical discussions, see the "Special Issue on Integrated Services Digital Network," *IEEE Communications Magazine* 24, no. 3 (March 1966), and Manu Malek, "Integrated Voice and Data Communications Overview," *IEEE Communications Magazine* 26, no. 6 (June 1988): 5–15.

6 Kenneth L. Phillips, "ISDN's Built-In Problems," *Telecommunications* (October 1987): 55–58.

7 Steven E. Minzer, "Toward an International Broadband ISDN Standard," *Telecommunications* (October 1987): 94–106; Richard J. Solomon, "Broadband ISDN," *International Networks* (September 1987). As a first step toward the broadband ISDN concept, the U.S. telephone industry has adopted a Synchronous Optical Network (SONET) standard of 155.52 Mbps.

8 For example, a single CD-ROM can store the equivalent of a year of the *Los Angeles Times*.

9 H. C. Willard, "High Technology Improves Cable Economics" (Portsmouth: General Electric Company, Consumer Electronics Business Operations, October 1984).

10 Peter W. Huber, *The Geodesic Network: 1987 Report on Competition in the Telephone Industry* (Washington, D.C.: U.S. Department of Justice, Antitrust Division, January 1987), 1.3.

11 Data on cable and VCR growth are from *Cable TV Investor* and *The VCR Letter* (Carmel: Paul Kagan Associates, 1988).

12 Citizen band (CB) radio seems a striking counterexample. It was adopted largely by middle- and lower-middle-class consumers in the early 1970s, but never achieved true mass market acceptance.

13 Michael J. Marcus, "Technical Deregulation: A Trend in U.S. Telecommunications Policy," *IEEE Communications Magazine* 25, no. 1 (January 1987) 66–68.

14 47 U.S.C. 151, *et seq*. State regulatory authorities, of course, must also approve telco investments in their jurisdictions.

15 William C. Jakes, Jr., "New Techniques for Mobile Radio," *Bell Laboratories Record* (December 1970), 327–330.

16 See Charles Jackson's essay in Volume One.

17 See Kenneth Gordon and Alex D. Felker, *A Framework for a Decentralized Radio Service* (Washington, D.C.: Federal Communications Commission, Office of Plans and Policy Working Paper, October 1983). Similar recommendations for the U.K. are contained in CSP, International, *Deregulation of the Radio Spectrum in the UK* (London: HMSO, March 1987).

18 Stanley M. Besen and Garth Saloner, "Compatibility Standards and the Market for Telecommunications Services" (Santa Monica: Rand Corporation, P-7393, February 1988); John Carey, "The Downside of Deregulation:

A Case Study of U.S. Teletext," *Electronic Publishing Revue* 6, no. 1 (1986), 37–40.

19 Eric C. Jensen, "An Electronic Soapbox: Computer Bulletin Boards and the First Amendment," *Federal Communication Law Journal* 39, no. 3 (October 1987): 217–258.

20 See Roger Noll's essay in Volume One.

21 For two excellent recent discussions of alternative HDTV systems, see "Special Issue on High Definition Television," *IEEE Transactions on Broadcasting* BC-33 (December 1987); and "Special Issue on Advanced Television Systems," *IEEE Transactions on Consumer Electronics* 34 (February 1988).

22 Other ATV systems have been proposed by MIT, AT&T Bell Laboratories, CBS, Hitachi, Matsushita, and Scientific Atlanta, among others. Eureka, a European consortium, is developing its own HDTV production system and transmission system that will not be compatible with any of systems listed in table 2.

23 The degree to which any of these systems will degrade the picture shown on standard NTSC receivers is still very much in question.

24 The Faroudja system will be field tested on two California cable networks beginning in the fall of 1988.

25 Local UHF channel assignments have been widely separated so that television receivers could tune to one UHF channel without interference from another. The channel spacing rules are known as the UHF "taboos." Technical improvements in TV tuners now could permit eliminating many of these taboos. See Gary S. Kalagian, Robert P. Eckert, and William A. Daniel, *Advanced Technology UHF Receiver Study, Part 2, Effect on UHF Television Allotments* (Washington, D.C.: Federal Communication Commission, FCC/OST R-84-1, March 1984).

26 William E. Glenn and Karen G. Glenn, "Let's Not Lose Another Market to Japan," *New York Times*, 6 March 1988.

27 W. Russell Neuman, "The Mass Audience Looks at HDTV: An Early Experiment," paper presented at the Annual Convention of the National Association of Broadcasters, Las Vegas, Nevada (11 April 1988), 11.

28 Federal Communications Commission, *Interim Report of the FCC Advisory Committee on Advanced Television Service* (Washington, D.C., 16 June 1988.)

29 Michael J. Marcus, personal communication.

30 Federal Communications Commission, *Tentative Decision and Further Notice of Inquiry*, MM Docket no. 87-268 (Washington, D.C., 1 September 1988).

31 Federal Communications Commission, *Notice of Inquiry*, MM Docket no. 87-268 (Washington, D.C., 20 August 1987).

32 Technically, an "open architecture" smart television receiver requires a standard interface between the signal decoders and the picture display. Different decoders might be needed to process different ATV signals distributed over different media, but the display (the most expensive part of

the TV receiver) would be able to accept any decoded signal. See William F. Schneider, "HDTV Technology: Advanced Television Systems and Public Policy Options," *Telecommunications* (November 1987): 37–42; Indra Paul, "Advanced Television System Model," Bell Communications Research (6 June 1988), paper submitted to the Systems Subcommittee of the FCC Advisory Committee on Advanced Television Service.

33 Several recent issues of the *IEEE Journal on Selected Areas in Communications* provide further technical background on fiber optic and broadband network development. See *Special Issue on Fiber Optics for Local Communications*, SAC-3, no. 6 (November 1985); *Broadband Communications Systems*, SAC-4, no. 4 (July 1986); *Special Issue on Fiber Optic Systems for Terrestrial Applications*, SAC-4, no. 9 (December 1986); *Switching Systems for Broadband Networks*, SAC-5, no. 8 (October 1987); *Fiber Optic Local and Metropolitan Area Networks*, 6, no. 6 (July 1988); *Photonic Switching*, 6, no. 7 (August 1988).

34 Walter S. Baer, "Telephone and Cable Companies: Rivals or Partners in Video Distribution?" *Telecommunications Policy* 8, no. 4 (December 1984), 271–289; Tom Valovic, "The Rewiring of America: Scenarios for Local-Loop Distribution," *Telecommunications* (January 1988), 30–36.

35 M. Gawdun, "Lightwave Systems in the Subscriber Loop," *Telecommunications* (May 1987): 65.

36 Thus telco implementation of ISDN services to both homes and businesses has assumed copper wire local loops. Of course, fiber optic networks with data rates greater than those shown in table 3 could offer faster response times for information retrieval, facsimile, and other services, but whether consumer demand would justify the higher cost remains questionable.

37 R. K. Snelling and J. Chernak, "The Revolution in the Loop Network: The Evolving Broadband Technology," *Proceedings ISSLS 1986* (September 1986), 210–215; R. K. Snelling and K. W. Kaplan, "All Fiber Networks —A Reality by 1988–89," *Conference Record, ICC 1987* (June 1987), 44.1–44.1.5; Scott Ticer, "Jeno Paulucci's Dream: Bring Fiber Optics Home," *Business Week* (21 September 1987): 34–35.

38 George P. Lynch, "Illinois Bell Studies Local Loop Fiber," *Telephony* (10 August 1987): 62; Howard Rausch, "Telephone System in the Year 2000," *Lightwave* (August 1988): 17–18. Future cost comparisons are difficult because they depend so crucially on such assumptions as future copper and fiber costs, maintenance costs, and household densities. For a good illustration of how sensitive the results are to these assumptions, see Myron Keller, "Economic Considerations of Fiber in the Loop Plant" (St. Louis: Southwestern Bell, February 1988).

39 Marvin Sirbu, Frank Ferrante, and David Reed, "An Engineering and Policy Analysis of Fiber Introduction into the Residential Subscriber Loop" (Pittsburgh: Department of Engineering and Public Policy, Carnegie Mellon University, May 1988), 21–22.

40 Progress in fast packet switching techniques looks promising, but broad-

band digital switches that are cost competitive for residential services may be a decade away. See "Switching Systems for Broadband Networks," especially D. R. Spears, "Broadband ISDN Switching Capabilities from a Services Perspective," 1222–1230; and P. E. White, J. Y. Hui, M. Decima, and R. Yatsubashi, "Guest Editorial—Switching for Broadband Communications," 1217–1221; and S. Cheng and L. Wu, "Reconfigure in a Flash," *Telephony* (May 18, 1987): 76.

41 An interim step could be a hybrid system delivering digital voice and data, along with analog video. See M. F. Mesiya, "Implementation of a Broadband Integrated Services Hybrid Network," *IEEE Communications Magazine* (January 1988): 34–45; Fred Dawson, "Three RBOCs Set Local Loop Tests of New Technology," *Lightwave* (August 1988): 1, 6.

42 C. N. Judice, E. J. Addeo, M. I. Eiger, and H. L. Lemberg, "Video on Demand: A Wideband Service or Myth?" *Conference Record ICC 86* (June 1986), 1735–1739.

43 A. Michael Noll, "Videotex: Anatomy of a Failure," *Information and Management* 9 (1985), 99–109.

44 Fred Dawson, "Seeing Fiber Optics in a New Light: Cable's Mindset Beginning to Change," *Cablevision* (12 October 1987): 48.

45 "Cable Wrestles with Possible Pactel Entry into Business," *Broadcasting* (4 July 1988): 32–34.

46 FCC, *In re General Telephone Co. of California*, Memo Opinion, W-P-C-D 5927, 12 April 1988.

47 "GTE Details Fiber Plans for Cerritos," *Broadcasting* (27 June 1988): 66–68.

48 Large business customers have competitive alternatives to local exchange carrier (LEC) services, but "[r]esidential and small business users still have few practical alternatives to LEC lines for short-haul transmission." Peter Huber, *The Geodesic Network*, 2.23. Cable systems, in particular, do not have the two-way switched facilities in place to compete with the telcos for residential and small business telephone service.

49 FCC, CC Docket 87-266, *Further Notice of Inquiry and Notice of Proposed Rulemaking in the Matter of Telephone Company-Cable Cross-Ownership Rule*, Sec. 63.54-63.58, adopted 20 July 1988. See also "FCC Wants to Loosen Cable-Telco Prohibitions," *Broadcasting* (25 July 1988) 31–32.

50 U.S. Department of Commerce, National Telecommunication and Information Administration, *Video Program Distribution and Cable Television: Current Policy Issues and Recommendations* (Washington, D.C.: NTIA Report 88-233, June 1988).

51 Clay T. Whitehead, chairman, *Report to the President* (Washington, D.C.: Cabinet Committee on Cable Communications, Office of Telecommunications Policy, 1974). See also Ithiel de Sola Pool, *Technologies of Freedom* (Cambridge: Harvard University Press, 1983), 151–188.

Federal Policies for Telecommunications Research and Development

The author is grateful to Kenneth Flamm and Frederick Weingarten for unusually helpful comments.

1 National Science Board, *Science and Engineering Indicators—1987* (Washington, D.C.: National Science Board, 1987), 313.

2 The information in the remainder of this paragraph is from *Science and Engineering Indicators—1987*, 235–237, 265.

3 Gerald W. Brock, *The Telecommunications Industry* (Cambridge: Harvard University Press, 1981).

4 An implicit assumption behind this reasoning is that U.S. firms are disadvantaged if they have to buy technology from foreign sources. This could result from restrictive trade policies, but probably the more important reason is the subtle effects of understanding the technology better when it is developed domestically, e.g., from know-how and sophistication within the domestic workforce. Office of Technology Assessment, *Information Technology R&D: Critical Trends and Issues*, OTA-CIT-268 (Washington, D.C.: GPO, 1985).

5 Molly K. Macauley, ed., *Economics and Technology in U.S. Space Policy* (Washington, D.C.: Resources for the Future, 1987).

6 Linda R. Cohen and Roger G. Noll, "The Political Economy of NASA's Applications Technology Satellite Program," in Space Applications Board, *Proceedings of a Symposium on Space Communications Research and Development* (Washington, D.C.: National Research Council, 1988).

7 Roger G. Noll, Merton J. Peck, and John J. McGowan, *Economic Aspects of Television Regulation* (Washington, D.C.: Brookings Institution, 1974).

8 OTA, *Information Technology R&D*.

9 Space Applications Board, *Proceedings of a Symposium*.

10 A. Michael Noll, "Bell System R&D Activities: The Impact of Divestiture," *Telecommunications Policy* (June 1987): 161–178.

11 This section draws heavily from joint work by the author and Roger Noll. Linda R. Cohen and Roger G. Noll, *The Technology Pork Barrel*, forthcoming from the Brookings Institution.

12 Barry R. Weingast, Kenneth A. Shepsle, and Christopher Johnson, "The Political Economy of Benefits and Costs," *Journal of Political Economy* 89 (1981): 642–664.

13 A large literature exists on retrospective voting. See, for example, Morris P. Fiorina, *Retrospective Voting in American National Elections* (New Haven: Yale University Press, 1981); Anthony Downs, *An Economic Theory of Democracy* (New York: Harper and Row, 1957). For specific applications to legislative incentives, see Cohen and Noll, *Technology Pork Barrel*.

14 George J. Stigler, "The Theory of Economic Regulation," *Bell Journal of Economics* 2 (1971): 3–21; Sam Peltzman, "Toward a More General Theory of Regulation," *Journal of Law and Economics* 19 (1976): 211–240.

15 Mancur Olson, *The Logic of Collective Action* (Cambridge, Harvard Uni-

versity Press, 1965).

16 Richard Fenno, *Homestyle* (Boston: Little, Brown, 1978).

17 This discussion is drawn from chapter six in Cohen and Noll, *Technology Pork Barrel.*

18 See ibid., chapter 10.

19 Banks, "The Space Shuttle," in Cohen and Noll, *Technology Pork Barrel.*

20 See also Nancy L. Rose, "The Government's Role in the Commercialization of New Technologies," in *Economics and Technology: U.S. Space Policy.*

21 A variant of this conclusion is that programs may be organized to enhance political benefits, by distributing pork barrel benefits to enhance political support. See R. Douglas Arnold, *Congress and the Bureaucracy* (New Haven: Yale University Press, 1979).

22 This is only one aspect of the licensing story. See Cohen and Noll, *Technology Pork Barrel,* for details.

23 William J. Niskanen, Jr., *Bureaucracy and Representative Government* (Chicago: Aldine-Atherton, 1971).

24 OTA, *Information Technology R&D.*

25 Brock, *Telecommunications Industry,* 92.

26 National Academy of Engineering, *The Technological Dimensions of International Competitiveness* (Washington, D.C.: National Academy of Engineering, 1988).

27 Space Applications Board, *Proceedings of a Symposium.*

Telecommunications and Foreign Economic Policy

1 The relative importance of goods and services is at the heart of the debate provoked by Stephen Cohen and John Zysman, *Manufacturing Matters* (New York: Basic Books, 1987).

2 Most categorizations of the services are deficient, but we shall use familiar distinctions here among basic (voice, telephone, and telex), value-added (including items like protocol conversion and packet switching), and information (for example, remote computer services) services. Value added networks (VANs) and information services are also called enhanced services. In addition, we distinguish between all services and the infrastructure facilities—the physical plant—that make them possible.

3 The Huber report suggested that data transmission is about 8 percent of the total communications transmission services market. This $8 billion market in 1985 was mostly in private networks, not networks provided either by common carriers or the major private value added networks (such as Tymnet). The growth rate of many enhanced services (such as electronic data interchange to provide common billing, order, and inventory systems electronically for suppliers and buyers) is from 35 to 50 percent per year. For example, electronic mail is estimated to grow from $200 million in 1984 to about $2 billion by 1990. In addition, the market for information services, the pure content carried by communications sys-

tems, was zooming. Electronic data bases revenues were about $3 billion in 1987, triple the level of 1982. The "900" and "976" numbers offering various services (e.g., sports scores) are already about a $1 billion market. See Peter W. Huber, *The Geodesic Network — 1987 Report on Competition in the Telephone Industry* (Washington, D.C.: U.S. Justice Department, Antitrust Division, January 1987), pp. 5-1 (and footnote 1 on that page), 7-1, 8-2, and 11-4.

4 See Leland Johnson's essay in Volume One.

5 Centrex services and the PBX are rivals, but services and equipment can also be complementary. The $900 million per year market in the United States for alarm monitoring services has proven a complement to additional services and equipment for the individual premise that run over $2 billion per year. Huber Report, pp. 13-2 and 13-3.

6 For example, AT&T long sold itself as the agent for assuring universal services at a low cost to households in the United States. It only ran into trouble when its opponents argued convincingly that AT&T might not provide the lowest cost services for the people who voted most (upper-middle-income and upper-income households) and for important parts of the economy (the users in the Fortune 500).

7 See Anthony Saunders's essay in this volume.

8 The typical rationale for the monopoly was twofold. The PTTs argued that there were either economies of scale in the production of the equipment or control over the equipment was necessary for maintaining consistent technical standards and high quality of service. Few countries ever sanctioned a single national monopoly on these supplies. But most countries assigned a monopoly either to a handful of national companies or a few national companies and one foreign firm (which undertook extensive obligations for local production, as in the case of ITT in European countries or Northern Telecom in the United States).

9 The FCC's abortive attempts to monitor the purchase of foreign equipment by the RBOCs should remind us that the United States is not exempt from this game.

10 The United States, Japan, and the U.K. have 177 million of the world's 341.2 million access lines for communications. They constitute the majority of the world's equipment and domestic services markets. They only are a miniority in the international basic services market, but they dominate the traffic of the major transoceanic routes. Calculated by author from confidential corporate planning documents of an international communications firm and Malcolm Kitchen, David Lewin, and Hans Schoof, *Telecommunications: the Opportunities of Competition* (Princeton: Ovum Ltd., 1987).

11 The most visible case of this development is the current dispute before the FCC concerning the AT&T Tariff 15 that is initially being offered for services to General Electric and Dupont. FCC, Docket 88-741.

12 The RBOCs seek permission to offer completely integrated voice and advanced information services. Their critics charge that this will simply

replicate the monopoly power that AT&T once enjoyed. The supporters of the RBOCS argue that it is impossible to take advantage of economies of scale and scope in the local provision of enhanced services unless they have the freedom to enter all these deals. The supporters also suggest that there is enough competition for the most lucrative parts of the market in the private business sector to impose competitive discipline on the RBOCS. RBOCS are free to manufacture equipment or provide services outside the United States and Carribean region. There is more controversy on whether they can provide protocol conversion and electronic messaging as a gateway service between the United States and other countries.

13 I thank Professor William Davidson of the University of Southern California for sharing unpublished research on this point with me.

14 This campaign has its roots as much in politics as technological efficiency. In particular, it caters to regional development outside of Tokyo, especially small business development, by keeping prices down and extending fiber optic services via the public carriers.

15 Certainly, despite the NTT procurement agreement with the U.S. concerning its purchasing policies, there is ample reason to wonder why the Japanese selected Northern Telecom of Canada over AT&T in 1985 for its new central office switch system (a $250 million deal over five years that might lead to later add-ons). NTT chose a smaller switch for the rural market in this decision—a technology that would not have so thoroughly opened up the heart of its network design to foreign scrutiny as would the purchase of AT&T's flagship switch (the ESS-5). Perhaps the most interesting wrinkle to Japanese policy is the tax subsidy to the new common carriers for purchasing foreign network equipment. This permits Japan to increase imports on a national basis while reducing the pressure on NTT to become more reliant on foreign suppliers.

16 The United States convinced several countries to certify equipment as long as they met the much less restrictive standard of "no harm to the network." It also advanced the principle of "self-certification" by the supplier rather than relying on a few national testing establishments. It also obtained a pledge from some countries to set tariffs for leased circuits on terms compatible with the needs of U.S. users and enhanced service suppliers. Jonathan Aronson and Peter F. Cowhey, "Bilateral Telecommunications Negotiations," paper prepared for the International Institute of Communications, 1987.

17 U.S. commercial interests have varying interests about the route for change. AT&T is most comfortable with stressing reform of ITU regulations. Both AT&T and the RBOCS give higher priority to bilateral talks than to the GATT, but all have supported the GATT services initiative. (In truth, some RBOCS view all multilateral commercial frameworks as relatively unimportant in a rapidly changing world.) The computer industry strongly supports the GATT, but sometimes splits because of feuds between IBM and its rivals on computer communications architectures. Most companies want to assure open architectures written on a collective basis in order to negate IBM's

advantage of a large installed base. Large users and specialized service providers are the most hawkish critics of the ITU and the most sympathetic to the GATT supplemented by bilateral negotiations.

18 MPT subsequently offered to have the United States and Japan jointly design a supplementary standard to the X.75 in order to satisfy both parties. U.S. firms responded that the problem was insisting on a single interconnect protocol rather than allowing flexibility in business arrangements among buyers and sellers.

19 For example, West Germany announced significant libealization of its rules for enhanced services and CPE. This included a promise that pricing would fit the needs of U.S. VANs.

20 OECD, Directorate for Science, Technology and Industry, Working Party on Telecommunications and Information Services Policy, "Trade in Telecommunication Network-Based Services, Note by the Secretariat," DSTI/ICCP/TISP/88.2, 30 May 1988.

21 The traditional ITU system illustrates how rules governing international coordination reinforced the choice of dominant national bureaucracies and commercial interests. Most PTTs of industrial nations had similar political and economic constraints at home. They sought roughly the same degree of profit maximizing in international services for the purposes of subsidizing domestic operations. Moreover, their monopoly over representation of national interests in international fora excluded newcomers with different preferences, which in turn encouraged trust among the PTTs.

Moreover, rules constructed under the auspices of the ITU reduced bargaining and information costs. There were, for example, general outlines of the formulas to govern pricing and the relationships between countries in negotiating international prices for telephone calls. There were common technical standards and detailed discussions about the ideal architecture for telephone networks. There were also rules prohibiting cheating on international agreements. For example, rules about the routing of traffic and pricing of international phone calls effectively meant that one country could not attempt an end-run around the jurisdiction of another country in regard to the pricing and routing of international phone calls.

22 The ITU Plenipotentiary Conference of 1982 authorized the WATTC to "establish, to the extent necessary" a new set of rules. Robert Bruce has argued that the coverage of new services could have been done by bilateral discussions under Article 31 of the Convention or through CCITT recommendations. Robert R. Bruce, Jeffrey P. Cunard, and Mark D. Director, "WATTC and the Future of the ITU; Realism about the Limits of Regulation" International Institute of Communications, 1987.

23 Bruce et al., "WATTC," 29.

24 See, for example, Article 1.6 of the CCITT/WATTC draft regulations.

25 P. Michael Nugent, "WATTC-88: Global Harmonization, or Entirely New International Law," *Telematics* 5, no. 2 (February 1988): 1–6.

26 IPCA are a very special form of traditional joint ventures. A joint venture

takes place when firms from two or more countries join together to provide any form of production or distribution or collective task such as research. Joint ventures are the stuff of everyday international commercial life. IPCA imply something much more ambitious.

27 Sir Eric Sharpe, the chairman of Cable and Wireless, one of their competitors, has written: "AT&T is the dominant supplier of internatioal cable facilities and, with British Telecom and Japan's KDD, is endeavoring to control access to these facilities." "Technical Superabundance and Scarcity of Customer Choices: The Need for Global Alternatives," *Promothee*, no. 7 (July 1988): 13.

28 All quotations are from *Telecommunications Reports*, 25 April 1988, 31.

29 The proposals to allow countries to create an alternative framework for competitive services among consenting parties showed up in a proposed new Article 9 to the draft regulations. The early progress of the WATTC meeting is reported in *Telecommunications Reports* (5 December 1988): 36–37.

30 To be fair the opposite could happen. Boeing Computer Services just entered the equipment market for the first time by offering a specialized terminal of its own design that complements its service offerings.

31 Gil Winham, *International Trade and Tokyo Round Negotiations* (Princeton: Princeton University Press, 1986). John MacMillan, "International Trade Negotiations: A Game-Theoretic View," paper prepared for the Ford Foundation.

32 OECD, *Trade in Telecommunications Network-Based Services*, 2–4.

33 Several factors work against the old division. For example, there is a very thin line indeed between a wide-area network, encompassing voice and data, and local communications services. Moreover, users are going to demand an end to artificial distinctions between free trade arrangements for data and international regulation through the ITU of voice when those users want integrated voice and data services. Because this will be an explosively growing part of the most profitable part of the market, it is unlikely that any regulatory framework could continue over time that did not provide for a common set of rules governing this segment. Canada has recognized this dilemma in a preliminary manner. It has ruled that mixed voice and data services may be provided by competitive value added carriers if the primary purpose of the service is not simply to bypass the public voice telephone services. And, paradoxically, many users want to segregate data from voice because data services remain far more critical to them. You can always replace a telephone call, but a disruption of a computer network can often be disastrous. Telephone companies are talking about marrying voice and data in such a way as to make designs for the primacy of data in jeopardy. Unless there is a strong GATT, it will be difficult to challenge efforts by phone companies to migrate data services into mixed voice and data as a general principle of the evolution of network architecture.

34 The United States argues in trade talks that a right to a commercial pres-

ence is not the same as foreign investment. It is a functional right to compete, not an ownership right. This distinction represents a fairly radical idea for how to organize social control. It is akin to those in the Law of the Sea negotiations who said that the jurisdictional range of a state over its offshore area depended on the function. Some functions were said to deserve large geographic jurisdictions without implying sovereign ownership.

35 Daniel Kasper, *Deregulation and Globalization: Liberalizing International Trade in Air Services* (Ballinger: Cambridge, 1988), 45–58. My thanks to Kasper for his extended comments on this comparison.

36 The notion of a globally integrated carrier suggests a single owner of global communications facilities to provide service throughout the world for any individual customer. A reading of the history of industrial organization suggests globally integrated operations replace corporate alliances whenever the costs of establishing close contractual ties become prohibitive. Highly demanding global customers may lead some firms to decide that alliances do not work as the primary mode for organizing for the global market.

37 Cable and Wireless has adopted a strategy of leading major new ventures in cables around the world. It is the second international carrier for the U.K. and controls the telephone company of Hong Kong. It will feature prominently in the new international carrier for Japan. Thus it is preparing to be a global phone company in a radical new sense.

38 For example, AT&T has a number of traffic management programs that are based on patented breakthroughs in advanced mathematics. Given the right regulatory incentives, AT&T would be a very impressive competitor as a global carrier. In my judgement it would do far better than any other national entry if it had the right to operate as a general carrier rather than as a specialized provider of enhanced services plus a partner in basic services.

39 Hitoshi Watanabe, "Trade in Telecom Services," *Transnational Data and Communications Reports* (August/September 1988): 15–17.

40 A French company owns 14.9 percent of FTCC, and Cable and Wireless owns 20 percent of Pacific Telecom. *Telecommunications Reports* (15 February 1988): 23, and *Telecommunicaitons Reports* (8 August 1988): 26–28.

41 Based on author's interviews and *Telecommunications Reports* (11 August 1988): 25.

42 Based on author's personal interview with a senior United States trade official in July 1988.

43 Keith Hayward, *International Collaboration on Civil Aerospace* (New York: St. Martins, 1986).

44 The OECD Secretariat recently suggested that relations between common carriers be subject to a set of ITU rules designed to be more compatible with competition while the GATT would govern all other service providers. This formulation is a shade too ambiguous, but it is on the right track. *Trade in Telecommunications Network Services*, 20.

45 The idea is inspired by the practices of the Bank of International Settlements. For this and a fuller agenda for the GATT talks, see Jonathan David Aronson and Peter F. Cowhey, *When Countries Talk—International Trade in Telecommunications Services* (Cambridge: Ballinger, 1988).

46 The United States pressed Brazil to "clean up" its controversial informatics law by defining a clear set of products that would be reserved for Brazilian manufacturers. This is a minimum reserve policy. The other products would then be subject to trade review rather than continuing a vague ad hoc penumbra of administrative discretion on what products would be protected in order to promote the Brazilian informatics industry.

The Third World and U.S. Telecommunications Policy

1 See Independent Commission for Worldwide Telecommunications Development, *The Missing Link* (Geneva: International Telecommunications Union, 1985); Bjorn Wellenius, "Beginnings of Sector Reform in the Developing World," paper presented at *Seminar on Telecommunications Sector Restructuring and Management*, Commonwealth Telecommunications Organization, Kuala Lumpur, 17–19 November 1987; Michael Agi, "Communications and Third World Development," *Transnational Data and Communications Report* (Springfield, Va.: June 1987) for examples of social costs and returns to investment in rural telecommunications.

 For the studies on Kenya, the Philippines, and Costa Rica, see Communications Studies and Planning International, *The Impact of Telecommunications on the Performance of a Sample of Business Enterprises in Kenya*, a Research Report of the International Telecommunication Union, January 1983, and Charles Jonscher, "Telecommunications Investments: Quantifying the Economic Benefits" in *Telecommunications for Development: Exploring New Strategies*, conference proceedings (available from the International Telecommunication Union), October 1986.

2 Sustained technical advance and falling real costs of equipment stimulated rapid market growth throughout the 1970s and 1980s, despite recession in the international economy. The total world telecommunications equipment market stood at an estimated $109 billion in 1986 and is forecast to reach approximately $240 billion by 1994. The telecommunications equipment sector is one of the largest international industries comparable in size with the automobile and aerospace sectors. Market size data cited in *Financial Times*, "Survey of the Telecommunications Sector," London (19 October 1987).

3 In the United States in the late 1970s government funding for civilian R&D in communications was primarily funneled through the space and energy programs; by 1983, when U.S. government contracts with an R&D component for high technology products and services were running at $55 billion annually, the Department of Defense had taken over as the prime source of government funding for private sector R&D. See Linda Cohen's essay in this volume for a general discussion.

For data, see also M. Savage, C. Catoe, and P. Caughran, "Manned Space Station Relevance to Commercial Telecommunications Satellites: A Prospectus to the Year 2000," paper presented at the AIAA/NASA Symposium, Arlington, Va., July 1983; OECD Secretariat, "Space Products Industry: A Sectoral Study," OECD Department of Science, Technology and Industry, DSTI/SPR/83.104, 9 May 1984, Paris.

4 As is well known and widely reported, the United States has taken the lead here, but similar steps have also been taken in the United Kingdom, Japan, France, Italy, and Germany. For a comprehensive and comparative review of the experiences of the developed countries, see R. Bruce, "The Experiences in Industrialized Countries: An Overview of Options and Developments in the Telecommunications Sector," *Seminar on Telecommunications*, Commonwealth Telecommunications Organization. For a discussion of Japanese and U.S. efforts to deregulate, see *The Economist*, London, 17 October 1987; for the U.K., Kevin Morgan, "Breaching the Monopoly: Telecommunications and the State in Britain," mimeo, Science Policy Research Unit, University of Sussex, January 1987; for Europe, see G. F. Caty and H. Ungerer, "Telecommunications: The New European Frontier," *Futures*, April 1986.

5 This is so even if, for various political reasons in countries such as the United States, such support cannot be provided in an overly direct manner, while the support that is given is felt to be inadequate and even misdirected. See the Cohen essay in this volume for a discussion.

6 Estimates for telecommunications spending by developing countries are from *Financial Times*, 19 October 1987; *Telephone Engineer & Management*, 3 January 1988, and interviews carried out by Michael G. Hobday with Thai and Colombian PTTs in 1987.

7 See *The Missing Link* and D. R. Mahajan, "Telecommunications for Development: A View from India," *Telecommunications* (February 1988): 33–36 for the arguments.

8 For the classic discussion of different aspects of the U.S. case, see Nathan Rosenberg, *Perspectives in Technology* (Cambridge: Cambridge University Press, 1976). For a discussion of the role of capital goods in industrial development in developing and developed countries, see Daniel Chudbnovsky et al., *Capital Goods Production in the Third World* (London: Francis Pinter, 1983). Michael G. Hobday, "Telecommunications—A Leading Edge in the Accumulation of Digital Technology: Evidence from the Case of Brazil," *Vierteljahresberichte*, no. 103, March 1986, contains a discussion of whether telecommunications development could in fact play the role of leading-edge technology in the development of wider, digital information technology capabilities.

9 For a full elaboration of this approach and empirical support, see Michael G. Hobday, *Telecommunications and Information Technology in Latin America: Prospects and Possibilities for Managing the Technology Gap*, UNIDO Technology Division, Vienna, April 1985.

10 See *The Missing Link*, 1985; Mahajan, "Telecommunications," and

"Survey: Development Telecoms," *Communications International* (September 1986): 36, for discussions on these problems.

11 See Hobday, *Telecommunications*, for data on export performance. To lay the groundwork South Korea, which like Taiwan embarked on export-led industrialization in the 1970s, invested $6 billion between 1982 and 1986 in the telecommunications industry within the context of protected markets for mainly public but also some private sector domestic producers. Over this period the number of subscribers increased from 240,000 to over 5 million using an automatic switching network connecting twenty-two major cities, and the R&D and technological framework was laid for the introduction of domestically designed and produced optical fiber cable systems, the development of a Korean digital switching system with a capacity of 10,000 lines, the domestic development of videotex and teletex terminals, and the early introduction of ISDN. See "Fruits of Investment; South Korea," *Communications International*, October 1986.

12 Much of the R&D work that has advanced the technological level of countries such as India, Brazil, China, and Venezuela has been carried out in public sector telecommunications development centers that also have technology development projects that involve computing, informatics, software development, and semiconductor development.

13 See Michael G. Hobday, *Telecommunications and the Developing Countries: The Challenge from Brazil* (London: Harcourt Publishers, 1988) for a review of the empirical literature.

14 This concept and its importance is now a central precept in mainstream thinking about industrialization. See C. J. Dahlman, B. Ross-Larson, and L. Westphal, "Managing Technological Development: Lessons from the Newly Industrializing Countries," *World Development* 15, no. 6 (June 1987); and R. M. N. Bell, B. Ross-Larson, B. and L. Westphal, "Assessing the Performance of Infant Industries," *Journal of Development Economics* 16 (1984): 101–128.

15 See the contrasting positions taken on the Indian case in D. R. Mahajan, "Telecommunications for Development: A View from India," *Telecommunications*, London, February 1988, for the positive viewpoint, and T. H. Chowdary, "Indian Telephone: Troubled by Underinvestment," *Telematics and Informatics* 3, no. 1 (1986) for the negative position.

16 *Communications Systems Worldwide*, London, May 1987 and September 1987.

17 The centralized nature of most telecommunications investment and purchasing is unique within the complex of other information technology industries, where purchasing is usually carried out by a wide range of public and private sector users. Conversely, the large bulk of equipment is normally purchased by a government-owned or government-controlled agency. This monopsony power has, in many cases, proved critical in the bargaining between PTTs and foreign suppliers for favorable technology transfer agreements and developing country PTTs are very unlikely to relinquish it under any circumstances.

18 See Hobday, *Telecommunications.*
19 For a discussion of French tactics in Latin America and the Mexican collaboration with ITT, see Armand Mattelart and Hector Schmuccler, *Communication and Information Technologies: Freedom of Choice for Latin America?*, trans. David Buxton (Norwood, N.J.: Ablex Publishing, 1985).
20 Ericsson of Sweden was particularly quick to recognize that cooperation with developing country industrialization strategies could provide them with competitive advantage over other competitors, especially in the large market countries. In response to government request in Brazil, Mexico, Venezuela, Ecuador, and Colombia, Ericsson has transferred technology and, where appropriate, adapted its systems to suit local needs and introduced local training schemes for indigenous personnel. For details on the Siemens and Taiwan deal, see "News," *Communications SouthEast Asia*, August 1985. For other examples of technology transfer arrangements and home country government support with developing countries, see "Survey: Development Telecoms," *Communications International*, September 1986.
21 NEC now ranks as the third major supplier of public switching equipment to the Third World, after ITT/Alcatel and Ericsson. For details of corporate market share by region in developing countries, see *Communications Systems Worldwide* (May 1987): 36–38.
22 See Wellenius, "Beginnings of Sector Reform," and Robert J. Saunders, "Information Policy in the Developing World: The Infrastructural Constraint," *Telematics and Informatics* 1, no. 4 (1985), for balanced discussions of causes and consequences of telecommunications infrastructural problems in developing countries and the challenges posed by the new telecommunications technologies.
23 Ibid.
24 See examples given in Wellenius, "Beginnings"; the review of Malaysia's privatization policy in "Survey: Development Telecoms"; and E. Siquerira, "Will Brazil Liberalize?" *Communications International*, London, April 1988, for a discussion of the debate on liberalization in Brazil. See Willy Moenandir, "Indonesian Telecommunications Development: An Overview," *Telematics and Informatics* 2, no. 1 (1985), for a description of a highly successful state-run telecommunications sector in Indonesia that has no intention—or necessity—to shift to the private sector.
25 T. Nulty, "Regulatory Policy for Telecommunications in LDCs," paper presented at *Seminar on Telecommunications*, Commonwealth Telecommunications Organization, 1987.
26 See Mahinda Naraine, "European Telecommunications Policy: The Standards Issue," mimeo, Department of Politics, University of Lancaster, October 1985, for an excellent discussion of how European PTTs have successfully resisted liberalization pressures.
27 See Peter Cowhey's essay in this volume.
28 See Constantine V. Vaitsos, "The New International Economics of Major Technological Changes," paper prepared for UNCTAD Secretariat, Geneva,

1987, for extensive discussion of how developed countries use nontariff barriers to maintain closed markets in key information technology sectors to foreign competitors to such an extent that they make the protectionist policies of developing countries seem mild in comparison!

29 Geza Feketekuty and K. Hauser, "A Trade Perspective of International Telecommunications Issues," *Telematics and Informatics* 1, no. 4 (1984): 359–369.

30 A recently published consumer survey stated that in five categories of public service British Telecoms was providing poorer service in 1988 than it did in 1983, the year before privatization. However, some groups have done well from the breakup of the state monopoly into a private duopoly of dubious competitiveness. The stock underwriters who guaranteed the BT stock offering made commission of approximately $650 million, while the loss to the public that resulted from undervaluation of the initial share offer was estimated by the U.K. Institute of Fiscal Studies to be nearly $7 billion!

Unfortunately though, the great British public who were supposed to be the direct beneficiaries of privatization because of the opportunity given them to buy shares in BT did not take up the offer. By 1985 the proportion of BT shares held by private investors had declined to 13 percent. See "BT—Still Out of Order?" in *Which?* published by the Consumers Association, London, June 1988, and *House of Commons, Public Accounts Committee*, "Sale of Government Holding in British Telecommunications," London, HMSO, HC 35, 1985.

A more comprehensive review of the impact of BT privatization on business users and equipment suppliers summed up the now widespread feeling in the U.K. that this exercise has failed to achieve most of its major economic and technological objective.

"The balance sheet reveals some mixed results [which have to] be set against costs . . . some of these costs are to be found in a deteriorating trade deficit, growing dependence on foreign-designed technology, and an indigenous industry which is exposed to liberalization at home, without having gained entry to closed markets abroad. Without heroic optimism, it is difficult to see the UK telecom industry regenerating itself in these circumstances." Morgan, "Breaching the Monopoly," p. 40.

31 Wellenius, "Beginnings." See Mattelart and Schmuccler, "Communication and Information Technologies," for a discussion of the Latin American experience.

32 T. H. Chowdary, "Indian Telephones."

33 Auliana Poon, "The Future of Caribbean Tourism—A Matter of Innovation," mimeo, Science Policy Research Unit, University of Sussex, September 1987.

34 Details taken from Annie Posthuma, "The Internationalization of Clerical Work: A Study of Offshore Office Services in the Caribbean," SPRU Occasional Paper Series no. 24, Science Policy Research Unit, University of Sussex, February 1987.

35 For an extensive discussion of this issues, see Kurt Hoffman, *Managing Technological Change: The Impact and Policy Implications of Microelectronics* (London: Commonwealth Secretariat, 1985).

36 See the discussion in Vaitsos, "The New International Economics," and Nicholas deB. Katzenbach, "The International Protection of Technology: A Challenge for International Law Making," *Technology in Society* 9 (1987). Also see Paul Goldstein's essay in this volume.

37 Vaitsos, "The New International Economics."

38 Ibid., 44.

39 The world market for all telecommunications services is currently growing at 12 percent per annum. Within this, 5 percent is accounted for by telephony and telex (traditional services), compared with 20 percent per annum for new information technology services. *Telecommunications International*, London, October 1987.

40 See Jean-Luc Renaud, "The ITU and Development Assistance," *Telecommunications Policy* (June 1987): 179–192, for a discussion of the ITU's gradual move toward Third World issues and the tensions this has created within the organization and its committees.

41 See G. Finnie, "A Brisk Start for the Development Center," *Communications Systems Worldwide*, October 1987 which describes the problems that the CTD is having in attracting funding from developed countries who are reluctant to contribute on political grounds.

42 With the CCITT and the CCIR there are various study groups which deal with defined area such as transmission and switching and the writing of operating handbooks for developing countries. One very significant recent achievement by the CCITT was an agreement to specify one international broadband telecommunications transport standard for the 1990s. This agreement is a major step forward in the gradual move toward integrated digital networks worldwide.

43 There are problems at the North-South divide, particularly in the committees. For instance, developing countries are unhappy that private sector firms from developing countries (who are allowed to be represented on working groups) represent a majority on all eighteen study groups of the CCITT. Other problems arise from poor attendance by developing country members, inadequate technical preparation and competence on their part, and antagonism over their perception that the committees are not working on issues that have much relevance to their problems. See Renaud, "The ITU and Development Assistance," June 1987, for an extensive discussion.

44 These arguments are put forward succinctly in *Communications Systems Worldwide*, London, November 1987.

45 It is clear from the statements of INTUG, the EEC, U.S., and U.K. delegates, and other interest groups that, if the "arch-regulatory" stance of the ITU would be adopted, it would be rejected in practice.

46 Quoted in *Communications Systems Worldwide*, London, November 1987.

47 For a succinct and excellent review of the main issues in the general area

of services and the developing countries, see Jonathan D. Aronson, "The Service Industries: Growth, Trade and Development Prospects," in *Growth, Exports and Jobs in a Changing World Economy*, ed. John W. Sewell and Stuart K. Tucker (Washington, D.C.: Overseas Development Council, 1988). The issues raised by TBDF concerns, though a subset of service-related problems, are many and complex and cannot be dealt with in any detail here. See Meheroo Jussawalla and Chee-Wah Chea, *The Calculus of International Communications: A Study in the Political Economy of Transborder Data Flows* (Littleton, Colo.: Libraries Unlimited, 1987). See also the Special Secretariat of Information, *Transborder Data Flows and Brazil: The Role of Transnational Corporations and the Effects of National Policies*, SSI, Brasilia, 1982, for the classic statement of the developing countries concerns and policy position.

On U.S. privatization of international data flow and its effect on the Third World, see David Baker, "Remote Future for Third World Satellite Data," *New Scientist*, 22 October 1987, which shows how the privatization of the previously U.S. publicly owned Landsat series of satellites (which provide remote-sensing information) has led to a rapid increase in the price of data needed to plan for rural development projects in countries such as Brazil, Thailand, India, and Indonesia. See also essays by Peter Cowhey and Peter Zimmerman in this volume.

48 See Jussawalla and Chea, *The Calculus*.

49 For a discussion of the outcome of WARC-MOB 87, see FCC *Week*, Alexandria, Virginia, 26 October 1987. R. Savio, "Why the World Needs a New Information Order," *Media Asia* 7, no. 3 (1980), and S.C. Lee, "Some Aspects of the New World Information Order," *Media Asia* 8, no. 2 (1981), discuss the now somewhat discredited concept of a new world information order.

50 For details, see *Telecommunications* (North American edition), Norwood, Massachusetts, August 1987.

51 See FCC *Week*, Alexandria, Virginia, 28 March 1988, for elaboration of the various viewpoints. Here we have one example of the international parallel of the pressures for national regulatory reform that the United States is bringing to bear. A second example is the position of the United States in GATT on TBDF which is extensively discussed in Vaitsos, "The New International Economics." For an exuberant statement of the United States efforts to pursue its privatization mission at the international level, see Mark Fowler, "U.S. Global Telecommunications: The Popcorn Principle," *Telematics and Informatics* 2, no. 1 (1985), and Douglas Goldschmidt, "Leveling the Playing Field in International Satellite Communications," *Telematics and Informatics* 4, no. 2 (1987): 121–132.

52 See Renaud, "The ITU," and Aronson, "The Service Industries."

53 Aronson, "The Service Industries."

54 Given that there are over 1000 U.S. firms currently involved in the design and production of small-scale private sector exchange equipment, most of whom have no interest in overseas markets, it seems that there is great

scope for a profitable expansion of their business.

55 See the discussion and examples given in Heather Hudson, "Toward Greater Developing Country Access to Telecommunications," and R. Hoen, "Financing Development and Telecommunications in Africa," in *Telecommunications for Development*, 1986.

56 See Harry J. Levin, "Emergent Markets for Orbit Spectrum Assignments: An Idea Whose Time Has Come" in *Telecommunications Policy*, March 1988, for a very excellent and useful discussion of these ideas.

57 See Aronson, "The Service Industries."

New Communications Technologies, Banking, and Finance

1 E. Gerald Corrigan, "Financial Market Structure: A Longer View," Federal Reserve Bank of New York (January 1987); Paul A. Volcker, "Statement Before the Committee on Banking, Housing and Urban Affairs," United States Senate, 13 September 1983.

2 Karl Brunner and Allan Meltzer, "The Uses of Money: Money in a Theory of An Exchange Economy," *American Economic Review* (December 1971): 781–805; Eugene Fama, "Banking in the Theory of Finance," *Journal of Monetary Economics* (January 1980): 39–57.

3 In addition to the two funds transfer systems there is also a message based computer and communications system linking over 2000 banks throughout the world (over fifty countries). This message system is called SWIFT (Society for Worldwide Interbank Financial Telecommunications) and operates over leased telephone lines. In 1986 the network handled over 192 million messages which was 22.1 percent more than in the previous year.

4 *American Banker*, 22 December 1986.

5 Deborah G. Black, *Success and Failure of Futures Contracts: Theory and Empirical Evidence*, Monograph Series in Finance and Economics GBA-NYU, 1986, no. 1.

6 It should be noted that CHIPS also breeds the potential for international "contagion effects," that is, the international transmission of a bank-crises from one country to another. Indeed in 1974 when CHIPS was run on a "next day settlement basis" the failure of Bankhaus Herstatt in Germany lead to considerable settlement problems among U.S. banks on the following day. This was one reason why CHIPS moved to *same* day settlement (in October 1981) so as to reduce the risk of interday overdrafts. However, same day settlement still exposes banks to "daylight overdraft" or "intraday" risk problems as discussed above.

7 David B. Humphrey, "Payments Finality and Risk of Settlement Failure" in *Technology and Regulation of Financial Markets*, eds. Anthony Saunders and Lawrence J. White (Lexington: Lexington Books and D.C. Heath, 1986), 97–120.

8 David B. Humphrey, "Future Directions in Payment Risk Reduction," *Journal of Cash Management*, forthcoming 1988.

9 Salomon Brothers, "Technology in Banking: A Path to Competitive Ad-

vantage," in *Research Report*, 1984.

10 Anthony Saunders and Ingo Walter, "'Bank Uniqueness' and the Securities Activities of Commercial Banks," in *Investment Banking Handbook*, ed. J. Peter Williamson (New York: John Wiley & Sons, 1988), 433–442.

11 Anthony Saunders, "Conflicts of Interest: An Economic View," in *Deregulating Wall Street*, ed. Ingo Walter (New York: John Wiley & Sons, 1985), 207–230.

12 Corrigan, "Financial Market Structure"; Volcker, "Statement before the Committee on Banking, Housing and Urban Affairs."

13 *Competitive Equality Banking Act*, Public Law 100-86 (1987). For a discussion of these issues, see Anthony Saunders, "Bank Holding Companies: Structure, Performance and Reform," paper prepared for AEI Conference on Restructuring the Financial Services Industry, Washington, D.C., 16–17 November 1987; Mark J. Flannery, "Payments System Risk and Public Policy," paper prepared for AEI Conference, 16–17 November 1987.

14 Robert Eisenbeis, "Comments on Bank Holding Companies: Structure Performance and Reform," (paper presented at the AEI Conference, 16–17 November 1987).

15 Sherrill Shaffer and David Edmond, "Economies of Super-Scale and Interstate Expansion," *Federal Reserve Bank of New York Research Paper No. 8612*, (1986).

16 Another issue here is that there is also some debate as to whether the Federal Reserve should get into the business of providing POS switching services or whether the development of POS networks should be left to the private sector. It could be argued that unless significant "market failure" is evident the Fed should keep out of this area of retail payments services.

17 David C. Cates, "Commitments and Contingencies: The Invisible Bank," *Proceedings of a Conference of Bank Structure and Competition* (Chicago, May 1985), 528–533.

18 Janice M. Moulton, "New Guidelines for Bank Capital: An Attempt to Reflect Risk," *Business Review*, Federal Reserve Bank of Philadelphia (July/August 1987): 19–33.

19 Salomon Brothers, "Bank Capital Adequacy Guidelines: The Implications of the Federal Reserve Board's New Proposals," in *Research Report*, February 1988.

20 Humphrey, "Payments Finality."

21 In this case many of the more risky loans made by Penn Square (partly to cover the costs of brokered deposits) were sold to Continental Illinois. When the true quality of these loans was revealed, Continental Illinois suffered major losses culminating in its "nationalization" in 1984.

22 United States, Congress Office of Technology Assessment, *International Competition in Services*, OTA-ITE-328 (Washington, D.C.: GPO, July 1987).

23 Jarl G. Kallberg and Anthony Saunders, *Direct Sources of Competitiveness in Banking Services* (report given to the OTA—United States Congress, March 1986); OECD, *The Internationalization of Banking: The Policy Issues*, (Paris: OECD, 1983); Office of Technology Assessment, *International*

Competition in Services.

24 Kallberg and Saunders, *Direct Sources of Competitiveness in Banking Services.*

25 Interestingly a large payment wire system does exist in the United Kingdom (called CHAPS [Clearing House Automated Payment System]). This has resulted in the development of an active interbank market in sterling in which United States banks, such as Citicorp, participate.

26 For example, Citibank's credit card operations were moved from New York to South Dakota because of New York's restrictive usury ceilings.

Index

|||||||||||||||||||||||||||||||||||||||||||||||||||||||||||||||||||||||||||||||||||||||||||||||||||||||||||||||||||||||||||||||||||||||||||||||||||||||||||||||||||||||||||||||||||||

Contributors

Walter S. Baer Director of Advanced Technology, Times Mirror Corporation. Former Director of Energy Policy Program, Rand Corporation. Author, *Cable Television: A Handbook for Decisionmaking*.

Jerry J. Berman Chief Legislative Counsel and Director, Project on Information Technology and Civil Liberties, American Civil Liberties Union.

Linda R. Cohen Assistant Professor of Economics, University of California at Irvine. Member OTA, NAS, and DOE advisory panels.

Peter F. Cowhey Associate Professor of Political Science, University of California at San Diego. Author, *The Problems of Plenty, Profit and the Pursuit of Energy*, coauthor, *When Countries Talk*.

Paul Goldstein Lillick Professor of Law, Stanford University. Chairman, US-OTA Advisory Panel on Intellectual Property Rights in an Age of Electronics and Information.

Michael G. Hobday Research Fellow, Science Policy Research Unit, University of Sussex.

H. Kurt Hoffman Director, Sussex Research Associates. Former Senior Fellow, Science Policy Research Unit, University of Sussex. Consultant to World Bank, United Nations, International Development Research Centre.

Thomas G. Krattenmaker Associate Dean and Professor, Georgetown University Law Center. Former codirector, Network Inquiry Special Staff, Federal Communications Commission. Coauthor, *Misregulating Television: Network Dominance and the FCC*.

Paula R. Newberg Director, Communications Policy Project, Markle Foundation.

James B. Rule Professor of Sociology, State University of New York at Stony

Brook. Author, *Private Lives and Public Surveillance, The Politics of Privacy*.

Anthony Saunders Professor, New York University School of Business Administration. Consultant, Federal Reserve Bank of Philadelphia. Former consultant, IMF, Department of the Treasury, OTA.

Peter D. Zimmerman Senior Associate, Carnegie Endowment for International Peace. Director of Project on SDI Technology and Policy. Former advisor, U.S. START delegation (ACDA).